Cleopatra

Oklahoma Series in Classical Culture

OKLAHOMA SERIES IN CLASSICAL CULTURE

Cleopatra

A SOURCEBOOK

Prudence J. Jones

University of Oklahoma Press : Norman

Cleopatra: A Sourcebook is Volume 31 in the Oklahoma Series in Classical Culture.

Library of Congress Cataloging-in-Publication Data

Jones, Prudence J., 1971–
    Cleopatra: a sourcebook / Prudence J. Jones.
       p.   cm. — (Oklahoma series in classical culture; v. 31
    Includes bibliographical references and index.
    ISBN 978-0-8061-4121-3 (paper)
      1. Cleopatra, Queen of Egypt, d. 30 B.C. 2. Egypt—History—
332–30 B.C.—Sources. I. Title. II. Series.

DT92.7.J66 2006
932'.021'092—dc22

                                           2005053834

The paper in this book meets the guidelines for permanence and durability of the Committee on Production Guidelines for Book Longevity of the Council on Library Resources, Inc. ∞

For my teachers

Contents

Illustrations

Preface

THIS BOOK GREW OUT of a course Julia Gaisser and I developed at Bryn Mawr College on Cleopatra and the reception of her image. When I was teaching the course at Rutgers University, John Drayton of the University of Oklahoma Press offered me the opportunity to write a sourcebook on Cleopatra. This book is the resource I imagined having while teaching those courses.

The book does not claim to be an exhaustive collection of sources on Cleopatra (such a work would fill many volumes); rather, it aims to present, in its first part, the historical Cleopatra through selected ancient sources, and, in its second part, some examples of Cleopatra as she has been reimagined in various periods and cultures. The brief introductions to the passages aim to place the sources in context, both the context in which the texts were written and the context of Cleopatra's story. Translations are my own, except where noted.

Cleopatra's story contains many characters. The glossary contains names that appear in several passages. I have used the familiar forms of names wherever possible (i.e., Mark Antony rather than Marcus Antonius). I refer to Augustus as Octavian, because that is the name appropriate to the period of his life covered in this book. There are, however, some instances in which the ancient sources refer to him as Caesar or as Augustus.

In addition to John Drayton and Julia Gaisser, I would like to thank Julia Dyson, Alla Gaydukova, Camilo Gomez-Rivas, Thomas

Jenkins, Mary Lefkowitz, Debra Nousek, Mark Schiefsky, Richard Thomas, and the students of Classics 201 (spring 2001) at Bryn Mawr College and Classics 318 (spring 2003) at Rutgers University.

Introduction

WHO WAS CLEOPATRA? Who is Cleopatra? Portrayed as both goddess and monster in her own lifetime, through the ages she has become both saint and sinner, heroine and victim, femme fatale and star-crossed lover, politician and voluptuary, black and white. A protean figure, Cleopatra defies categorization. This sourcebook holds up not only a mirror to Cleopatra but also a prism, to detail what we know of the historical Cleopatra and, in addition, to show the diversity of representations that emerge as various cultures and periods receive and recreate her image.

Part one searches for Cleopatra VII, the last of the Ptolemaic queens, in primary sources from the ancient world. These texts, written by people from Cleopatra's world (and, in some cases, by people who knew her), provide the evidence from which we must reconstruct Cleopatra. And yet we must be wary of these witnesses. All have biases; some are overtly hostile. Cleopatra was an enemy of Rome, after all, and many of those who wrote about her lived in an empire founded on her defeat.

In the barest outline of her life, Cleopatra VII was born in 69 B.C. to Ptolemy XII Auletes and (most probably) his sister-wife Cleopatra V Tryphaena. They were members of the Ptolemaic dynasty of Macedonian Greeks, who ruled Egypt after the death of its conqueror, Alexander the Great. Following the custom of the Egyptian pharaohs, the Ptolemies practiced brother-sister marriage; thus,

Cleopatra was married to and ruled with her brother, Ptolemy XIII. A power struggle between the two of them resulted in Cleopatra's exile to Syria. She returned to Alexandria and gained the support of Julius Caesar, who had arrived there in 48 B.C. after defeating Pompey to become the most powerful man in Rome. Caesar restored the balance of power between Cleopatra and Ptolemy XIII, but Cleopatra succeeded in engineering the murder of her brother-husband. Cleopatra then was married to and ruled with her other brother, Ptolemy XIV, though in fact, as Caesar's ally and mistress, she was the dominant partner. In 47 B.C. she gave birth to a son, Ptolemy XV, whom she called Caesarion in order to let it be known that he was Caesar's son. Cleopatra accompanied Caesar to Rome in 46 B.C. After Caesar's assassination in 44 B.C., Cleopatra returned to Alexandria. Upon her arrival there, she saw to it that her brother-husband Ptolemy XIV was killed.

In 41 B.C. Mark Antony, in need of resources for his military campaigns in the East and for his conflict with Caesar's heir, Octavian, arranged a meeting with Cleopatra. The two became allies and lovers. They had three children—twins, Alexander Helios and Cleopatra Selene, and a son, Ptolemy Philadelphus. Octavian waged a propaganda war against Antony and Cleopatra, stressing Cleopatra's status as a woman and a foreigner who wished to share in Roman power. The conflict between Antony and Octavian came to a head in the Battle of Actium in 31 B.C., in which Cleopatra's fleet was defeated. Antony and Cleopatra escaped to Alexandria, where the fighting continued. In 30 B.C. both committed suicide: Antony stabbed himself upon hearing an inaccurate report that Cleopatra was dead, and Cleopatra preferred to inflict the bite of a poisonous snake upon herself rather than to become Octavian's captive.[1]

Part two investigates the literary and cultural afterlife of Cleopatra. Through studying the reception of her image in a variety of time periods, we learn as much about the cultures that created those portraits as we do about Cleopatra herself. By examining sources from the fourteenth to the twentieth century, from the Romantics to the Afrocentrists, from Middle English to modern Arabic, we see successive reinventions of Cleopatra as each culture makes her its

---

1. Fuller accounts of Cleopatra's life are available in Grant 1972 and Chauveau 2002.

own. Cleopatra becomes a metaphor, a conveyer of meaning, a canvas onto which are painted ambivalence toward female power, fascination with the exotic East, and romantic notions of perfect love. As we shall see, Cleopatra captivates two of the most powerful men in Rome, becomes the sole ruler of Egypt, gains legendary status for her lavish banquets, and chooses to die rather than endure disgrace as Octavian's prisoner. This dramatic narrative provides a backdrop against which disparate characterizations of the Egyptian queen unfold their stories. Cleopatra may be pure of heart or cold and calculating as she woos Antony; she may die for love or pride; her legacy may be one of heroism or deceit.

Who was Cleopatra? Who is Cleopatra? This sourcebook addresses both of these questions. Various types of evidence—literary, historiographical, and documentary—all contribute to an understanding of Cleopatra in her own time and ever since. The ancient sources, with the vagaries of preservation and the inevitability of bias, often raise as many questions as they resolve. This tantalizing evidence, however, has motivated centuries of rewriting Cleopatra. The readings in this book introduce a multitude of Cleopatras, each a unique persona but all heirs to a common legacy.

PART ONE

Ancient Sources

1

The Ptolemies

THE DESCENDANTS OF PTOLEMY I, a general in Alexander the Great's army, officially ruled Egypt from 305 to 30 B.C. Cleopatra VII was the last Ptolemaic ruler. The Ptolemies adopted the titles, iconography, and traditions of the Egyptian pharaohs, including the custom of marriage between brothers and sisters. The official language of the dynasty, however, was Greek.

THE DIVISION OF ALEXANDER'S EMPIRE

When Alexander the Great died without naming a successor in 323 B.C., his kingdom, which had extended the boundaries of the known world as far as India and Egypt, was broken into parts, each controlled by one of his generals. Egypt came under the control of Ptolemy I, the ancestor of Cleopatra.

1.1. Diodorus Siculus, *The Library of History* 18.1.1–5 (60–30 B.C., Greek, prose)

Diodorus Siculus wrote a history of the world extending from the realm of myth to 60 B.C. Despite his claim to write a universal history, Diodorus focuses primarily on Greece, Sicily, and Rome. His knowledge of Egypt, however, was likely firsthand, as he is thought to have done research for his history there between 60 and 56 B.C.

Pythagoras of Samos, along with some other ancient thinkers, demonstrated that human souls are created immortal and that, following this doctrine, a soul knows the future at the moment of death when it separates from the body. The poet Homer seems to have agreed with them, as he presents Hector, who, at the moment of his death, predicts to Achilles the death that will soon follow for him also. So too in recent times it is said that the phenomenon described above has happened to many at the end of their lives and, in particular, to Alexander of Macedon when he died. For when he was ending his life in Babylon and, as he was breathing his last, his companions asked to whom he bequeathed his kingdom, he replied, "To the best man, for I see my funeral games as a great contest among my friends."[1] And the prediction came true: for the most illustrious of Alexander's companions, in their competition for supremacy, engaged in many great contests after his death.

1.2. Pausanias, *Description of Greece* 1.6.2–4, 1.6.8–1.7.1 (ca. A.D. 150, Greek, prose)

The Description of Greece *is a travel guide in which Pausanias demonstrates considerable interest in and knowledge of the topography of Greece and its monuments. Greek speakers who resided outside Greece, often in Asia Minor, constituted a significant part of his audience. During the Roman Empire, there was considerable interest in the Greek past; thus, Pausanias includes some historical information along with his topographical observations. In the passages that follow, Pausanias recounts the events that followed the death of Alexander the Great—in particular, how Ptolemy I, one of Alexander's generals, established his dynasty in Egypt.*

6. The Macedonians think that Ptolemy was the son of Philip, son of Amyntas, although he is called the son of Lagus, for Ptolemy's mother was already pregnant with him when Philip gave her in marriage to Lagus. They say that Ptolemy accomplished many notable deeds in Asia, especially when he, more so than any of Alexander's other companions, protected him when he was in a dangerous situation with the Oxydracae. After Alexander died, Ptolemy opposed those who

---

1. The death of a great man might be memorialized by athletic competitions held in his honor.

wanted to hand over the whole empire to Arrhidaeus,[2] the son of Philip, and, thus, he was responsible for the peoples being divided into kingdoms. After crossing into Egypt, Ptolemy killed Cleomenes, whom Alexander had appointed to govern Egypt, because he was an associate of Perdiccas[3] and therefore not loyal to Ptolemy. He also persuaded the Macedonians appointed to convey Alexander's body to Aegae[4] to surrender it to him. He buried it in Memphis with a Macedonian ceremony but, since he knew that Perdiccas would initiate hostilities, he kept Egypt under guard. Perdiccas joined himself to Arrhidaeus, the son of Philip, and Alexander, the son of Alexander the Great and Roxane,[5] daughter of Oxyartes, to make his conquest look legitimate, but in fact he planned to usurp Ptolemy's Egyptian kingdom. Perdiccas, however, driven out of Egypt, no longer admired for his military skill, and fallen from favor with the Macedonians, died at the hands of his bodyguards. Ptolemy's prospects improved immediately as a result of Perdiccas's death: he conquered the Syrians and Phoenicians, he received the exile Seleucus,[6] son of Antiochus, who had been driven out by Antigonus,[7] and himself prepared to retaliate against Antigonus. He persuaded Cassander, son of Antipater,[8] and Lysimachus, ruler of Thrace, to ally with him on the grounds that Seleucus was an exile and that Antigonus was a growing threat to all of them.

When Antigonus died, Ptolemy again overpowered the Syrians and Cyprus and reinstated Pyrrhus to Thesprotia. When there was a rebellion in Cyrene, Magas, the son of Berenice, Ptolemy's wife at the time, conquered Cyrene in the fifth year after the revolt. If Ptolemy was in fact the son of Philip, son of Amyntas, he seems to have acquired from his father a passion for women: although he was married to Eurydice, the daughter of Antipater, and had children with her, he fell in love with Berenice, whom Antipater had sent to accompany Eurydice to Egypt. After falling in love with Berenice,

---

2. Half brother of Alexander the Great.
3. Another of Alexander's generals.
4. The Macedonian capital.
5. The wife of Alexander the Great.
6. Another of Alexander's generals.
7. Another of Alexander's generals.
8. The general Alexander left in charge of Macedonia when he went on campaign.

Ptolemy had children with her and, when he reached the end of his life, he left the kingdom of Egypt to the Ptolemy who shares his name with an Athenian tribe. This was the Ptolemy born from Berenice and not from Antipater's daughter.

7. This Ptolemy fell in love with and married his full sister Arsinoe, an act that in no way followed Macedonian customs, but rather those of the Egyptians he ruled. Secondly, he executed his brother Angaeus, who was accused of plotting against him. He also brought Alexander's body back from Memphis. He killed another of his brothers as well, this one the son of Eurydice, when it was discovered he was fomenting revolt among the Cyprians. When Magas, Ptolemy's half-brother, was made governor of Cyrene by his mother, Berenice (his father was Philip, a Macedonian of low birth), he organized a revolt against Ptolemy in Cyrene and launched an attack on Egypt.

ALEXANDRIA

Alexandria, Egypt, one of many Alexandrias founded by Alexander the Great during his campaigns, had a particularly strategic location: as a coastal city it boasted access to commerce and communication. It was also protected, however, by the harbor formed by the island Pharos (see map 1). Its position at the mouth of the Nile also provided easy access to inland locations. This topography contributed to Alexandria's rise to prominence in the Hellenistic world.

1.3. Plutarch, *Life of Alexander* 26.3–6 (A.D. 110–15, Greek, prose)

For more on Plutarch, see selection 2.1. Here, Plutarch describes a dream Alexander the Great had that led to the founding of Alexandria.

Then at night, as he slept, an amazing sight came to him: a stately, gray-haired man seemed to be standing beside him and saying these words:

> "An island lies in the swell-filled sea,
> in front of Egypt; they call it Pharos."[9]

9. Homer, *Odyssey* 4.354–55.

Instantly, he stood up and went to Pharos, which was then still an island a little above the mouth of the Nile at Canopus, but now is attached to the mainland by a causeway. When he saw the place was perfectly shaped (for the island is fairly similar in width to an isthmus and lies between the lagoon and the open sea, which itself ends in a large harbor), he said that Homer was not only wonderful in other respects, but also was the wisest of all builders and he decreed that they draw up plans for the city suited to the site. They had no chalk, so they took barley and drew a curved line on the dark ground. Straight lines extended from its inner edge to form the shape of a cloak, just like the lines that extend from the hem of a cloak when the top is gathered, narrowing its area symmetrically. As the king was appreciating the plan, suddenly a vast multitude of birds of every size and variety from the river and the lagoon alighted upon the place like clouds and left no trace of the barley, an omen that worried even Alexander. Nevertheless, the prophets advised him to take courage, saying that the city he founded would be extremely productive and would nurture all sorts of men.

1.4. Strabo, *Geography* 17.1.7–9 (A.D. 18–23, Greek, prose)

Strabo researched his Geography *largely during the Augustan period, intending it to be of use to rulers and generals. He visited Egypt after the death of Cleopatra and thus had firsthand knowledge of the topography. Here he is concerned with the merits of Alexandria's location and its characteristics as a city.*

7. The site has many advantageous features. The region is bordered by two seas: the so-called Egyptian Sea to the north and to the south the Mareian Lake, which is also called Mareotis and into which many canals from the Nile empty from above and from both sides; these canals can accommodate larger import ships than the canals leading to the sea and, as a result, the harbor of the lake surpasses that of the sea in wealth; the place also has more exports from Alexandria than it has imports; one can determine in Alexandria and in Dichaearchia,[10] when one sees the merchant ships as they arrive

10. Puteoli.

and as they depart, how much heavier and how much lighter they sail to and from there. In addition to the wealth generated by commerce from both directions for the lake harbor and the sea harbor, the air quality is worth mentioning. Indeed, this too is thanks to water on both sides and the well-timed risings of the Nile. Other cities located on lakes have heavy and stifling air during the heat of summer, because the edges of the lakes grow marshy from evaporation caused by the sun. This moisture draws up noxious substances and the air is unhealthy for breathing and causes contagious diseases. In Alexandria, however, when summer begins, the Nile is full and it fills the lake and thus does not allow any marsh to produce harmful exhalations. Then, too, the Etesian winds blow from the north and from the entire sea and, as a result, the Alexandrians have pleasant summer weather.

8. The city is shaped like a cloak: its long sides are along the two coasts; it is approximately thirty stades[11] at its longest and its short sides are the isthmuses, which are each seven or eight stades long and bordered on one side by the sea and on the other by the lake. Streets good for horseback riding and chariot driving cut through the whole city; two of the streets are particularly broad, as they are more than one hundred feet wide, and they intersect one another at right angles. The city has exceedingly beautiful public parks and palaces covering a quarter or a third of its area, since each of the kings, just as he contributed some enhancement to the public monuments, so too he added to the existing buildings a private residence, so that now, as the poet says,

They are one on top of the other.[12]

They are all connected to one another, however, and with the harbor, even those located outside the harbor. One part of the palaces is the Museum, which has a path for walking, an exedra,[13] and a large house in which is the common dining room of the learned men who are members of the Museum. These members not only own common property, but also have a priest devoted to the Museum, at one time an official appointed by the kings, but now appointed by Augustus.

11. A stade is approximately six hundred feet.
12. Homer, *Odyssey* 17.266, describing the palace of Odysseus.
13. An exedra is a hall furnished with seats, used for lecturing and conversing.

The Monument, as they call it, also is part of the palaces. It is an enclosure in which are the burials of the kings and of Alexander. Ptolemy, the son of Lagus, preempted Perdiccas[14] by robbing him of Alexander's body, as he brought it from Babylon and was passing near Egypt, so strong was Ptolemy's greed and desire for control of Egypt. Indeed, Perdiccas died, killed by his soldiers when Ptolemy attacked and blockaded him on a deserted island. Thus, Perdiccas died, run through by the javelins of his men as they attacked him. With him were kings, Arrhidaeus and Alexander's children, along with Roxane, the wife of Alexander;[15] they all went to Macedonia, but Ptolemy took Alexander's body and buried it in Alexandria, where it remains to this day, though not in the same sarcophagus. The current one is glass, whereas Ptolemy placed him in one made of gold. The Ptolemy known as Cocces and Pareisactus[16] despoiled it. He had come from Syria, but was killed right away, so he never saw any profit from his plundering.

9. On the right-hand side of the great harbor near the entrance are the island and tower known as Pharos; on the other side are reefs and the headland called Lochias, on which a palace is located. On the left as one sails into the harbor are the inner palaces, which are adjacent to those on Lochias and have many multicolored dwellings and groves. Beneath these is the man-made harbor, hidden from view and for the private use of the kings; there is also Antirrhodos, an island located just outside the man-made harbor, that has a palace and small harbor. It is called Antirrhodos because it rivals Rhodes.[17] Above lies the theater; then comes the Poseidion, an elbow-shaped outcropping near the so-called Emporium that has on it a temple of Poseidon. To this promontory, Antony added a causeway, extending it even further into the middle of the harbor, and, at its end, he constructed a royal residence that he named the Timonium.[18] This

14. Perdiccas was a close associate of Alexander the Great. After Alexander's death, his successors vied for possession of his remains, which served as a powerful representation of one's status and connection to Alexander. Perdiccas was responsible for bringing Alexander's body back to Macedonia, but Ptolemy hijacked the coffin and brought it to Egypt.

15. Alexander's will granted Perdiccas custody of Philip Arrhidaeus, Alexander's half brother; his children; and his wife Roxane.

16. Cocces, "Scarlet"; Pareisactus, "Usurper" or "Illegitimate"; identified as Ptolemy XI.

17. The island of Rhodes was known for its five harbors, which made it well suited to commerce; it was also a cultural center that attracted philosophers, artists, and writers.

18. Timon was an Athenian whose friends deserted him when he lost his money; when he became rich again, they returned, but he drove them away.

was his final project: after being abandoned by his friends when he returned to Alexandria following the defeat at Actium, he chose to live out his days like Timon, spending his time alone, apart from that type of friends. Next comes the Caesarium, the Emporium, and the storehouses. After these come the shipyards, which go all the way to the Heptastadium. These are the things around the great harbor.

PTOLEMY I IN THE AFTERLIFE

In the Hellenistic period, Alexandria began to surpass Athens as the intellectual center of the Mediterranean world. Some of the finest literature of the period was written at Alexandria by poets such as Theocritus and Callimachus. These poets, who were scholars as well, oversaw the collection of the greatest works of Greek literature in the Library of Alexandria. The Ptolemies, as monarchs, took on the role of patrons.

1.5. Theocritus, *Idyll* 17 (278–270 B.C., Greek, verse)

Originally from Syracuse, Sicily, Theocritus became a court poet in Alexandria. He founded the literary genre of bucolic poetry, which takes as its theme shepherds, their songs, and their loves. Theocritus was a contemporary of Callimachus and, like Callimachus, valued highly refined, polished poems. In the selection that follows, Theocritus crafts an encomium of the Ptolemies as he asks Ptolemy II Philadelphus for his patronage.

Let us begin from Zeus and let us end with him also, Muses.	1
Of the immortals, Zeus is best, but whenever we sing	
of men let Ptolemy be mentioned first, last,	
and in the middle, for he is the most outstanding of men.	
The ancient heroes were born from demigods	5
and after accomplishing noble deeds, found wise poets	
to memorialize them, but since I know how to praise,	
let me sing of Ptolemy:[19] poems are a prize of the gods too.	
The woodcutter who comes to densely forested Mt. Ida	
peers about, surrounded by abundance, to see where to begin	10
the task. What shall I mention first? The gods have honored	

19. Ptolemy I Soter, "Savior."

the best of kings with gifts too numerous to recount.
It was evident from his ancestry that Ptolemy, son of Lagus,
was the sort of man to accomplish a great deed, when he
had a plan in mind such as no other man could have imagined.   15

The father honored him equally with the blessed
immortals, and a golden throne is set up for him in the house
of Zeus; next to him sits his friend Alexander,
hated by the Persians, a god whose crown gleams.
Across from these sits the chair of centaur slaying   20
Heracles, which is made of unyielding adamant.
There, he feasts with the other gods as he
rejoices exceedingly in his sons' sons,
because the son of Cronus removed age from their limbs
and that his offspring are called immortal.   25
Heracles' mighty son was the ancestor of Ptolemy
    and Alexander
and they both count Heracles as their most distant ancestor.[20]
Therefore, after drinking all the fragrant nectar
he desires, Heracles, departing for his wife's quarters,
gives one of them his bow and the quiver he carries under
    his arm,   30
and to the other his iron hard club rough with knots,
as they lead Zeus's bearded son with his weapons
to the ambrosial bedroom of white-ankled Hebe.
How conspicuous was legendary Berenice
among wise women, and what a boon to her parents.   35
To her perfumed bosom the august queen of Cyprus,
daughter of Dione,[21] pressed tender hands; and so
it is said that no man loved his wife
as much as Ptolemy loved his Berenice.
But she loved him much more. Thus, a man   40
having confidence in his children, might turn over to them
his whole estate, since he went to bed with his loving wife.
But if a woman is heartless, she is always thinking of another,

---

20. In the ancient world the Macedonian royal family's genealogy was traced to Caranus,
a descendant of Heracles.
21. In Homer, Aphrodite was the daughter of Zeus and Dione.

they give birth carelessly, and the children do not look like
    their father.
Aphrodite, revered goddess, surpassingly beautiful,   45
Berenice was your care; because of you, graceful
Berenice did not cross pitiable Acheron,
but you snatched her up before she approached the dark
ship and the gloomy ferryman of the dead,
you took her away to your temple, giving her some of your
    honors.   50
She is kind to all mortals and she inspires them with soft
loves, and makes cares light for those who yearn.
Dark-browed woman of Argos,[22] you bore savage Diomedes
by your union with Tydeus, a Calydonian man;
deep-bosomed Thetis bore spear-throwing Achilles   55
to Peleus, son of Aeacus; and you, spearman Ptolemy,[23]
illustrious Berenice bore to Ptolemy the spearman.
Cos[24] raised you, having received you as a newborn
from your mother, when first you looked upon the light.
There, the daughter of Antigone,[25] heavy with labor,   60
called upon girdle-loosening Eleithuia;[26] and she
propitiously stood beside her and soothed the pain
in all her limbs. The beloved child was born
and he resembled his father. Seeing this, Cos rejoiced
and, holding the child in kindly arms, said,   65
"May you be fortunate, child, and may you honor me
as much as Phoebus Apollo honored Delos of the dark
    blue coast;
and with equal honor inaugurate the Triopian hill,[27]
and apportion equal respect to the Dorians who are nearby;
king Apollo loved Rhenaea as much as Delos."[28]   70
So the island spoke. From above, a great eagle cried out
three times from the clouds, a bird of prophecy.

22. Deipyle was the daughter of the king of Argos and the wife of Tydeus.
23. Ptolemy II Philadelphus.
24. An island in the southeastern Aegean Sea.
25. Berenice was the daughter of Antigone.
26. The goddess of childbirth.
27. There was a temple to Triopian Apollo on a promontory in southwest Asia Minor.
28. Rhenaea: an island near Delos.

This was a sign from Zeus: revered kings are the care of
Zeus, son of Cronus. But preeminent is he whom Zeus loves
from the moment of his birth; great good fortune will be his and   75
he will rule many lands and many seas.
Many continents and many races of men
grow their crops, aided by Zeus's rain,
but no land flourishes as much as Egypt's floodplains,
when the Nile flood softens the clods,   80
and no land has so many cities of men skilled in their crafts.
Egypt has three hundred cities,
plus three thousand, plus three times ten thousand,
plus two times three, plus three times nine,
and king Ptolemy rules them all.   85
He also has a share of Phoenicia, of Arabia,
of Syria, of Libya, and of the dark Ethiopians;
he has command of all the Pamphylians, the Cilician
    spear-throwers,
the Lycians, the bellicose Carians,
and the islands of the Cyclades, as he possesses the best ships   90
to sail the sea. Every sea, every land,
all the rushing rivers are subject to Ptolemy;
many horsemen, many shield-bearers
equipped with gleaming bronze, gather around him.
He could outweigh all kings in wealth,   95
so much comes daily to his rich palace
from everywhere. The people attend to their work with security,
for no inland enemy crosses the Nile, abundant in fish,
and sounds the battle cry in the towns of others,
no one leaps from a swift ship onto the beach   100
and, hostile, takes up arms against Egypt's cattle.
Such a man holds sway over these wide plains,
fair-haired Ptolemy, skilled in casting the spear,
to whom it is a care to guard his inheritance,
as is fitting for a good king, and he also wishes to add to it.   105
But the gold does not collect uselessly in that rich house,
like the wealth of the ceaselessly toiling ants:[29]

---

29. Herodotus tells of "ants" (probably marmots) that turn up gold while digging
their burrows (3.102–5). See Peissel 1984.

the famous temples of the gods receive much,
since Ptolemy always dedicates the first fruits and adds
    other offerings;
he has given much to powerful kings,   110
much to cities, and much to his noble companions.
No man skilled in singing a clear-toned song comes
to the sacred contests of Dionysus
without receiving a prize commensurate with his talent.
Those who speak for the Muses celebrate Ptolemy in song   115
for these benefactions. After all, what is more noble
for a wealthy man than to have a good reputation among men?
Fame is all that remains for the sons of Atreus:[30] all the
    treasure
they acquired when they captured Priam's great palace
is now hidden in that gloom from which there is no return.   120
This man alone of those who lived long ago and those whose
footprints are still warm in the dust they trod beneath their
    feet,
has established incense-filled temples to his mother and father;
in them, he has placed beautiful statues of them, made of
gold and ivory, as saviors of all mortals.   125
There too, he burns many rich thighs of cattle
on the glowing altars, as the months pass,
along with his stately wife, than whom no wife better
holds her husband in her arms in his home,
for she cherishes from the heart her brother and husband.   130
So too was the sacred union of the immortals
whom Queen Rhea bore to rule Olympus:[31]
Iris, still a virgin, after purifying her hands with perfume,
made up a single bed for Zeus and Hera to sleep in.
Farewell, King Ptolemy, and I will sing of you and the other   135
demigods equally and I will speak words that will not, I think,
    be lost
to those who come after. But for the glory itself, you must
    ask Zeus.

30. Agamemnon and Menelaus.
31. I.e., Zeus and Hera.

THE LOCK OF BERENICE

The lock in question belonged to Berenice II (b. ca. 273 B.C.), wife and cousin of Ptolemy III. The occasion of these poems was a dedication by Berenice of a lock of her hair at the temple of Arsinoe Aphrodite at Zephyrium. The offering fulfilled a vow to dedicate a lock of hair upon her husband's safe return from the Third Syrian War (247–246 B.C.). The lock mysteriously disappeared from the temple, and Conon, the court astronomer, identified it with a group of stars, the constellation Coma Berenices.[32]

1.6. Callimachus, *Aetia* frag. 110, edited by Pfeiffer[33] (246–245 B.C., Greek, verse)

Callimachus, a poet active in Alexandria during the reigns of Ptolemy II (282–246 B.C.) and Ptolemy III (246–221 B.C.), exemplifies the poetic sensibilities of the Hellenistic period. His highly polished verses constitute a polemic against epic bombast. As Callimachus himself said, epic is a broad, muddy river, while his poetry is a pure spring (Hymn *2.108–12*).[34]

"The Lock of Berenice" comes from Callimachus's partially preserved poem, the *Aetia*, an episodic exploration of the origins of various religious cults, festivals, and places. This fragment is a good example of Callimachus's penchant for nonepic subject matter: his topic is not the queen, but a lock of her hair. In this passage, the lock speaks.

Having looked over the whole charted sky and where
   [the stars] go   1

Conon saw me too in the air, the lock   7
of Berenice, which she dedicated to all the gods

And I swore by your[35] head and your life   40

The shining descendant of Theia[36] is carried over the spit   44

---

32. The constellation is still known as the Coma Berenices and is located north of Virgo, between Boötes and Leo. See Ferguson 1980, 50.
33. Pfeiffer 1965.
34. On Callimachus's views on water and poetry, see Cameron 1995, 363–66.
35. Berenice's.
36. "The descendant of Theia" probably refers to the sun.

of your mother Arsinoe,[37] and the deadly ships of the Persians
went through the middle of Athos.[38]
What are we locks of hair to do, when such mountains yield
    to iron?
Would that the race of the Chalybes[39] might perish,
since they brought it forth from the earth like an evil plant,
they who first revealed it and devised the workmanship of
    hammers.   50
Just now my sister-locks were lamenting me, newly-shorn as
    I was,
and at once the brother of Ethiopian Memnon,
delicate wind beating his dappled wings,
horse of violet-girdled Locrian Arsinoe,
snatched and seized me with his breath, and bearing me
    through the moist air   55
placed me in the lap of Cypris.[40]
Aphrodite Zephyritis[41] herself inhabiting the Canopic coast
[chose] him to fill that need.
And so that not only the . . . of the Minoan bride[42]
[may shine] on men, but I too,   60
the beautiful lock of Berenice may be counted
among the many stars,
Cypris placed me, bathed in the waters[43] and
rising near the immortals, as a new star among the ancient ones

we go forth . . . late autumn to the Ocean   67

These things do not bring me as much joy   75
as I feel grief over no longer touching the head
from which, when she was still a maiden, I drank in many
    simple perfumes,
but I did not partake of womanly myrrh.

    37. "The spit" may refer to an obelisk, which would be an object shaped like a spit
used for roasting meat; could also refer to Mt. Athos. "Your mother Arsinoe": Arsinoe II.
    38. The Persian general Xerxes made a canal through the Chalcidian promontory
where Mt. Athos is located, 483–481 B.C..
    39. A Scythian people credited with inventing ironwork.
    40. Aphrodite.
    41. The deified Arsinoe.
    42. Ariadne; see note 56.
    43. I.e., setting in the ocean.

1.7. Catullus, *Poem* 66 (59–58 B.C., Latin)

Poem 66 *is Catullus's translation of Callimachus's "The Lock of Berenice" (see selection 1.6). Catullus was one of a number of writers in the Roman Republic known as* poetae novi *(new poets), who preferred to write short poems on personal themes rather than epics. In writing poems of this type, Catullus embraces the Alexandrian poetic ideals also evident in Callimachus's poetry. Catullus's translation appears quite faithful to Callimachus's rendition as far as we can tell, given the fragmentary nature of the original.*[44] *The final ten lines, however, may well be Catullus's own creation.*[45]

Poem 66 seems to be the translation that Catullus mentions in *Poem* 65, which takes the form of a letter to his friend Hortalus. In that poem Catullus says that although he is still mourning the death of his brother, he is enclosing the translation Hortalus had asked for:

> But nevertheless, amid such sorrows, Hortalus, I am sending you
> these translated verses of Callimachus
> (lest you think that your words, entrusted to the wandering winds,
> by chance slipped away from my mind) . . .
>
> Catullus, *Poem* 65.15–18

The fact that Catullus's brother died abroad may resonate with the subject matter of "The Lock of Berenice" and thus may not be a purely incidental detail.

He who observed all the lights of the great universe,   1
who ascertained the risings and settings of stars and
how the fiery glow of the white-hot sun is eclipsed,
how planets withdraw at prescribed times,
how the sweet love that stealthily banished Trivia[46] to Latmian
    caves[47]   5
calls her away from her celestial course:
that same man, Conon, saw me,
a lock from Berenice's head,

---

44. Quinn 1985, 355.
45. Hutchinson 1990, 323.
46. The moon goddess; a reference to the myth of Selene and Endymion.
47. Latmus: a mountain in Caria.

shining brightly on heaven's threshold. Berenice,
stretching out her smooth arms, had promised me to many
    of the goddesses,   10
in the season when the king, newly married to my mistress,
had gone to plunder the Assyrian territories,[48]
taking with him the sweet traces of a nighttime scuffle
waged over maidenly spoils.
Is Venus hateful to new brides? Or are happy parents   15
deceived by insincere tears
that flow copiously in the bedroom?
Those tears are false, I swear.
My queen taught me this through her many laments,
when her new husband went off to war.   20
But you, Berenice, abandoned, say you mourned not your
    bereft bed,
but rather the lamentable absence of your dear brother?
I say a profound grief has eaten away your melancholy heart!
Why, you were out of your mind with worry then,
when you swooned with fear! But I at least   25
recognized your courage even when you were a child.
Or have you forgotten the noble crime (one a stronger man
did not dare commit), by which you won a royal marriage?[49]
But what sad words you spoke, the day you bid your husband
    farewell!
By Jupiter, how often you wiped your eyes with your hand!   30
What god had the power to change your mind? Or is it that
    lovers
wish not to be far from a lover's touch?
And then you offered me, not without a bull's blood,
in exchange for your husband's return.[50]
In short order, he had added   35

48. In 247–246 B.C. Ptolemy III, husband and cousin of Berenice II, waged the Third Syrian War to avenge the murder of his sister (Quinn *ad* 66.12).

49. Berenice had been instrumental in the assassination of her former husband, Demetrius, who had been her mother's lover. Berenice's subsequent marriage to Ptolemy III made her queen of Egypt (Quinn *ad* 66.26–28).

50. A prayer to a god for the safe return of a loved one might be accompanied by a vow to dedicate some gift (here, a lock of hair) to that god upon fulfillment of the prayer. In this instance the sacrifice of a bull also accompanied the prayer.

a captive Asia to Egyptian borders.
I, in exchange for a prayer fulfilled, was handed over to the
    celestial assembly,
an innovative offering to fulfill a classic vow.
Unwilling, my queen, I left your head,
unwilling: I swear by you and your head   40
(may anyone who swears by it in vain get what he deserves).
But who could claim to be equal to a steel blade?
That mountain, the largest one that Thia's bright son[51]
travels over, also was overthrown,
when the Persians spawned a new sea, and when the barbarian   45
youth and his fleet sailed through the middle of Athos.[52]
What can hair do, when such things yield to steel?
Jupiter, would that the whole race of the Chalybes[53] might
    perish
as well as the man who first decided to seek
veins of metal under the ground and to cast iron!   50
The sisters of the recently shorn lock were lamenting
my fate, when the twin brother of Ethiopian Memnon,
beating the air with his undulating wings, presented himself
as the winged horse of Locrian Arsinoe[54] and, carrying me,
flew off through the celestial shadows   55
and placed me in the chaste lap of Venus:[55]
Zephyritis herself, the Greek inhabitant of
Canopic shores, had sent her servant there.
Then Venus, lest Ariadne's golden crown[56]

51. Helios, the sun.
52. In his attack on Greece, the Persian king Xerxes (486–465 B.C.) dug a canal through the peninsula in northern Greece where Mt. Athos is located.
53. The Chalybes lived in the region of the Black Sea and were famous for mining and metalwork.
54. Memnon's twin brother is Zephyr, the West Wind. Catullus imagines the Wind taking the form of a winged horse. Quinn notes that attributing to Zephyr the transport of the lock to heaven is a pun on Aphrodite Zephyritis, with whom Arsinoe was identified after her death. The title Zephyritis means "having power over Zephyrium" (the location of a temple dedicated to her), but Catullus "pretends it means 'having power over Zephyrus,' i.e., able to send the West Wind on errands" (Quinn *ad* 66.52–58).
55. Venus also refers to Aphrodite Zephyritis.
56. Ariadne's crown became the constellation Corona, or the Northern Crown. The crown had been a gift from Dionysus when he found Ariadne abandoned by Theseus. After Ariadne's death Dionysus threw the crown into the sky, where it remained as a constellation.

sit alone on the variegated threshold of the sky,   60
set me there, still moist, so that I, too, might shine
as the dedicated spoils of a golden head.
I have come from the waves to the precincts of the gods,
as a new star among the ancient ones.
Touching the lights of Virgo and fierce Leo,   65
next to Callisto, daughter of Lycaon,
I face west, a leader before slow Boötes,
who, late coming, scarcely is dipped in deep Ocean;
but although the footprints of the gods press upon me at night,
the light returns me to white-haired Tethys.[57]   70
By your leave, Ramnusian maiden,[58] I would speak here,
for I will not veil the truth because of any fear—
not if the stars tear me apart for my threatening words—
as a matter of fact I will disclose hidden truths of my heart:
I do not so much rejoice in this turn of events   75
as much as I am distressed that I will always be absent,
absent from the head of my mistress. Once, while my mistress
    was a girl,
I was deprived of all perfumes; since then, I have drunk
    many thousands with her.
You, women, now bound by the marriage torch,
do not cast aside your clothing, bare your breasts   80
and hand over your bodies to kindred-spirited husbands
until you have poured me pleasant libations from an
    onyx jar[59]—
your jar; you obey the laws of marriage and keep a virtuous bed.
(But anyone who has given herself to impure adultery,
may her evil gifts—ah!—be nullified and dissolve into the earth: 85
for I seek no offerings from the unworthy.
Rather, brides, may harmony and
constant love always inhabit your dwellings.)
You, truly, my queen who watches over the stars,
when you please divine Venus on holy days,   90
do not allow me, since I am yours, to be deprived of perfume,

---

57. I.e., the constellation sets into the ocean. Tethys is the wife of Oceanus.
58. Nemesis, a goddess of vengeance.
59. A liquid offering is to be poured to the lock, as to a god.

but rather give me abundant gifts,
so that the stars repeat, "would that I might become royal hair!
Let Aquarius's neighbor Orion shine!"[60]

A DECREE OF PTOLEMY V

The Ptolemies, as a Macedonian dynasty ruling in Egypt, faced the challenge of communicating their authority to subjects who did not necessarily speak Greek. They accomplished much through iconography: we see Ptolemaic rulers depicted as pharaohs in consciously Egyptianizing style (e.g., Cleopatra and Caesarion in fig. 1). We also find bilingual inscriptions. One of these, the Rosetta Stone, proved invaluable to the deciphering of hieroglyphics.

1.8. The Rosetta Stone (March 25, 196 B.C., Egyptian and Greek, prose)

The Rosetta Stone (see fig. 2) was the key to unlocking the mystery of Egyptian hieroglyphics, a writing system that was only deciphered in 1822 by Thomas Young and Jean-François Champollion. The stone, named for the Egyptian town (now called Rashid) where Napoleon's troops discovered it in 1799, contains the inscribed text of a decree of Ptolemy V written in two languages (Eygptian and Greek) and three scripts (hieroglyphics, demotic, and Greek). The different languages and scripts reflect the need for the decree to be read by various groups of people. Hieroglyphics were the Egyptian characters used for religious documents and were read by priests, demotic was the common script for the Egyptian language, and Greek was the language of the Ptolemies.

The inscription records a decree written by a group of Egyptian priests honoring the current Pharaoh, Ptolemy V. In it, they list Ptolemy's various achievements and benefactions and detail the honors he is due.

(1)[61] In the reign of the young man who has received his father's kingdom, the master of kingdoms, great in reputation, restorer of Egypt, (2) pious toward the gods, mightier than his rivals, improver

---

60. I.e., the other stars would rather be the Coma Berenices than Orion, however bright the latter constellation may be.
61. Numbers in parenthesis are line numbers of the inscription.

Fig. 1. Relief from the Temple of Hathor at Dendera, before 30 B.C. Adkins Archaeology.

of men's lives, master of the thirty-year cycles,[62] (3) a king, like the great Hephaestus,[63] like the great king Helios,[64] of both upper and lower lands,[65] descendant of the gods named Philopator;[66] Hephaestus approved of him; Helios gave him victory; he was created in Jupiter's own image, the son of Helios, (4) Ptolemy, immortal, cherished by Ptah, in the ninth year, when Aetos son of Aetos is the priest of Alexander[67] and of the gods named Soter[68] and of the gods named Adelphos[69] and the gods named Euergetes,[70] and the gods named Philopator[71] and the god Epiphanes Eucharistos;[72] (5) when Pyrrha, daughter of Philinus, is the prize-bearer of Berenice Euergetis; when Areia, daughter of Diogenes, is the basket-bearer of Arsinoe Philadelphos; when Eirere, daughter of Ptolemy, (6) is priestess of Arsinoe Philopator, on the fourth day the month Xandikos and the eighteenth day of the Egyptian month Mecheir,[73] a Decree:

The high priests and prophets and those who come to the sanctuary (7) to enrobe the gods and the fan-bearers and holy scribes and all other priests who have come from temples throughout the land to Memphis to meet the king, the immortal, beloved of Ptah, the god Epiphanes Eucharistos, (8) for the festival of the transfer of the Ptolemaic kingdom, which he received from his father, all of these being assembled at the temple in Memphis on this day proclaimed:

(9) Whereas King Ptolemy, the immortal, beloved of Ptah, the god Epiphanes Eucharistos, son of King Ptolemy and Queen Arsinoe, the gods named Philopator, has in many ways benefited the temples (10) and those in them and all those subject to his rule, since he is a god born from a god and a goddess, like Horus, the son of Isis and Osiris, the avenger of his father Osiris (11)

---

62. Rites to renew a king's power were held every thirty years during his reign.
63. Hephaestus was the Greek god of the forge. He was associated with Ptah, the Egyptian god who created the world and was the patron god of craftsmen and artisans.
64. Helios was the Greek sun god, equated with the Egyptian sun god Ra.
65. I.e., Upper and Lower Egypt.
66. Ptolemy IV Philopator and Arsinoe III.
67. Alexander the Great.
68. Ptolemy I Soter and Berenice I.
69. Ptolemy II Philadelphos and Arsinoe II.
70. Ptolemy III Euergetes and Berenice II.
71. Ptolemy IV Philopator and Arsinoe III.
72. Ptolemy V Epiphanes; Eucharistos, "Most Gracious."
73. March 25.

Fig. 2. The Rosetta Stone, 196 B.C. © Copyright The British Museum.

and he has been favorable toward the affairs of the gods and has donated to temples revenues of silver and grain

and has incurred many expenses for the sake of leading Egypt to prosperity (12) and of restoring the temples

and he has humanely exercised all his own powers and of the taxes and tributes existing in Egypt, some he has completely repealed and others he has lightened (13) so that the people and all others might live in happiness during his reign

and he has forgiven the majority of royal debts owed by those in Egypt and in the rest of his kingdom and he has freed from their charges those in prison (14) and those living under accusations for a long time,

and he ordered that tributes paid to the temples (15) and gifts to them of grain and silver continue on a yearly basis,

and likewise that the customary portions allotted to the gods from the vineyards and gardens (16) and the other places over which the gods preside during his father's reign would continue throughout the region;

and he decreed that the priests would contribute no more toward (17) the quota for their first year than what his father set;

he freed those of the priestly class from the annual journey by boat to Alexandria;

he proclaimed that the draft for the navy (18) would be suspended and he gave back two shares of the linen cloth made in the temples for royal use and he restored all things neglected in the past to their customary state, making sure that the rituals were performed for the gods (19) according to tradition,

and he apportioned justice to all equally, like the great, great Hermes;

he ordered also that those who return from banishment for armed revolt (20) or plotting rebellion in times of disorder, if they return, should remain on their property;

he also considered how he might deploy mounted and foot troops and ships (21) against those invading Egypt by sea and by land and how he might support the great expenses in silver and grain so that the temples and citizens of Egypt might be safe;

(22) arriving at Lycopolis in Busirite, which had been captured and reinforced for a siege and provided with a great supply of weapons and other resources, as if (23) estrangement had been long established for those evil ones gathered in it who were plotting many ruinous things for the temples and for those dwelling in Egypt and, (24) establishing themselves, had surrounded it with ditches and impressive walls;

and when the Nile made its great rise in the eighth year and, as usual, flooded the plains, (25) he held it off from many places by damming the mouths of the channels, spending no small amount of money on the project and stationing cavalry and foot soldiers as a garrison, (26) he soon took the city by force and destroyed the godless men in it, just as Hermes and Horus, son of Isis and Osiris, conquered their foes (27) previously in the same location, and those who led the rebels in his father's day and destroyed the land and dishonored the temples, he punished them all (28) appropriately according to the occasion when he arrived in Memphis to avenge his father and his kingdom and to participate in the rites prescribed for assuming the rule;

he remitted (29) the things in the temples owed to the palace up to the eighth year—no small amount of grain and silver; likewise also the value of the linen cloths not made for royal use (30) and the profits from those made as samples during the same time;

he freed the temples from the tax of a measure of grain per acre of sacred land and likewise (31) a clay vessel per acre of vineyard;

he gave many things to Apis and Mneuis and to all the other sacred animals of Egypt, much more than the kings before him, as he cared for the things pertaining to them (32) in all respects and he gave fitting things for their burials generously and nobly, and the things required for their individual temples when there were sacrifices and assemblies and other traditions,

(33) and he preserved the honors of the temples and of Egypt throughout the land following the laws,

and he decked the temple of Apis with expensive works, spending no small amount of gold and silver (34) and precious stones on it;

and he erected temples and shrines and altars, and authorized the things needed for their decoration, inspired by the divine intellect of the god Euergetes in these matters;

(35) after making an inquiry, he restored the most honored temples throughout his realm, as was appropriate, and in return the gods gave him health, victory, strength, and all the other good things (36) of a kingdom remaining to him and his children for the rest of time with good fortune;

It seemed right to the priests of all the temples throughout the land to continue the honors that have been established (37) for the immortal king Ptolemy, beloved of Ptah, the god Epiphanes Eucharistos, and likewise to increase greatly the honors of his parents, the gods named Philopator, and those of his grandparents, the gods named Euergetes, and those (38) of the gods named Adelphos, and those of the gods named Soter, and to erect a statue of the immortal king Ptolemy, the god Epiphanes Eucharistos, in each temple in the most manifest place,[74] (39) and it will be called the statue of Ptolemy the defender of Egypt, and next to it will be the most powerful god of the temple, handing him the triumphant weapon, and these things will be prepared in the Egyptian way, (40) and the priests will serve the statues three times daily and adorn them with holy decoration and complete the other rites as they do for the other gods in festivals throughout the land; (41) and to dedicate for King Ptolemy, the god Epiphanes Eucharistos, son of King Ptolemy and Queen Arsinoe, the gods named Philopator, a carved wooden statue and a shrine of gold in each of the (42) temples and to situate them in the sanctuaries with the other shrines and during the great festivals, in which the shrines are brought forth, the shrine of the god Epiphanes Eucharistos will be brought forth as well; (43) and so that it may be auspicious both now and in the future, the king's ten gold crowns will be placed on the shrine and an asp placed on top, just like the asp-shaped crowns (44) on all the other shrines; and there will be in the middle of them the crown called Pschent,[75] which he was wearing when he went to the temple in Memphis to perform (45) the customary rites for assuming the kingship; and on the square around the crowns near the crown already mentioned will be placed ten golden amulets on which it will be written (46) that it is the shrine of the king who makes the upper land and the lower land manifest;

And on the thirtieth day of Mesore, on which the birthday of the king is observed, and likewise on the seventeenth day of Mecheir, (47) on which he assumed the kingdom from his father, he is celebrated by name in the temples, and these days are the source of all good things for everyone, and during these days they should hold a feast and festival (48) monthly in temples throughout Egypt, and they should perform sacrifices and libations on these days and observe other customs just as in other festivals . . .[76] (49) held in the temples; and a

---

74. This is a pun on his name, Epiphanes, which means "Made Manifest."
75. The double crown of Upper and Lower Egypt.
76. There is a gap in the text.

feast and festival should be held in honor of the immortal King Ptolemy, beloved of Ptah, the god Epiphanes Eucharistos, every year in the temples throughout (50) the land, from the new moon of Thouth for five days, on which they will wear crowns while performing sacrifices and libations and other rituals, and they will call the priests of the other gods (51) the priests of Ptolemy in addition to the other names of the gods whom they serve, and they will place on all the transactions and other . . .[77] (52) his priesthood; and it will be permitted for other private citizens to observe the feast and to set up the aforementioned shrine and to hold amongst themselves the customary rites in feasts held monthly (53) or yearly, so that it may be understood why the Egyptians celebrate and honor the god Epiphanes Eucharistos the king, as is lawful for them to do;

This decree will be written on a stele (54) of hard stone in the sacred and native and Greek scripts and it will be erected in each of the first, second, and third rank temples next to the statue of the immortal king.

PTOLEMY XII AND THE END OF THE DYNASTY

Ptolemy XII, a descendant of Ptolemy I and the father of Cleopatra VII, was officially known as Ptolemy XII Theos Philopator Philadelphus Neos Dionysus (the god, lover of his father, sister-lover, the new Dionysus). He also had two nicknames that betray more personal attributes: Nothos (Bastard)[78] and Auletes (Flute Player). Ptolemy XII had six children: Cleopatra VI Tryphaena, Cleopatra VII (the subject of this sourcebook), Berenice IV, Arsinoe IV, Ptolemy XIII, and Ptolemy XIV, the last two each ruling briefly with Cleopatra VII. The identity of Cleopatra VII's mother is not certain.[79]

1.9. Strabo, *Geography* 17.1.11 (A.D. 18–23, Greek, prose)

For more on Strabo, see selection 1.4. In the following passage, Strabo summarizes the reign of the Ptolemies, with an emphasis on the ancestry of

---

77. There is a gap in the text.
78. He was the son of Ptolemy IX by a concubine, and thus the identity of Cleopatra VII's grandmother is not known.
79. Grant 1972 considers it most likely that Cleopatra V, Ptolemy XII's wife, was Cleopatra VII's mother. Cleopatra V was dead by early 68 B.C., but Cleopatra VII was born

Cleopatra VII.

Ptolemy,[80] son of Lagus succeeded Alexander; Philadelphus[81] succeeded him; then came Euergetes;[82] then Philopator,[83] son of Agathocleia; then Epiphanes;[84] then Philometor,[85] the son always succeeding the father. Philometor, however, was succeeded by his brother, the second Euergetes,[86] also known as Physcon; then came the Ptolemy referred to as Lathyrus;[87] then came Auletes,[88] our contemporary, who was the father of Cleopatra. All the Ptolemies after the third, led astray by luxury, ruled rather poorly, but the worst were the fourth, the seventh, and the last, Auletes. In addition to his other extravagances, he was trained to accompany choruses with the flute and he took such pride in this activity that he did not hesitate to hold competitions in the palace, where he would enter himself to compete against the other competitors. The Alexandrians exiled him, but since there were three daughters, the oldest of whom was legitimate, they appointed her queen.[89] His two infant sons were completely left out of these affairs. Once she had been placed on the throne, they sent her a husband from Syria named Cybiosactes, who had passed himself off as an heir to the Syrian throne. Within a few days, he was dead by strangulation, on the queen's orders: she could not stand his vulgar and slavish nature. His replacement was a man who pretended to be the son of Mithradates Eupator. He was Archelaus, son of the Archelaus who fought against Sulla, was honored afterwards by the Romans, was the grandfather of the last king of the Cappadocians in our time, and was a priest of the Comanae in Pontus. He had, at that time, been spending time with Gabinius, in order to fight with him against the Parthians, but, in secret from Gabinius, some men escorted him to the queen and appointed him king. At the same

---

in 69 B.C. Grant argues that if there had been any rumor that Cleopatra was illegitimate, Octavian would have used it against her in his propaganda (1972, 3–4).

80. Ptolemy I Soter, "Savior."
81. Ptolemy II Philadelphus, "Sister-Lover."
82. Ptolemy III Euergetes, "Benefactor."
83. Ptolemy IV Philopator, "Father-Lover."
84. Ptolemy V Epiphanes, "Made Manifest."
85. Ptolemy VI Philometor, "Mother-Lover."
86. Ptolemy VIII Euergetes II; Physcon, "Potbelly."
87. Ptolemy IX Soter II; Lathyrus, "Chickpea."
88. Ptolemy XII Auletes, "Flute-Player."
89. Berenice IV (Cassius Dio 39.13).

time, Auletes had arrived at Rome and was welcomed by Pompey the Great, who presented him to the Senate and negotiated reinstatement for him and ruin for most of the one hundred ambassadors who had undertaken the embassy against him.[90] The head ambassador among these was Dion, the Academic.[91] After being restored to power by Gabinius, Ptolemy executed both his daughter and Archelaus. His reign did not last much longer, however, as he died from a disease, leaving two sons and two daughters, the eldest of whom was Cleopatra. The Alexandrians appointed the elder of the sons and Cleopatra to rule, but the boy's partisans formed a faction and exiled Cleopatra, who fled to Syria with her sister. At the same time, Pompey the Great had arrived, fleeing from Palaepharsalus to Pelusium and Mt. Casius.[92] The king's followers treacherously killed Pompey, but Caesar, when he arrived, killed the young king, recalled Cleopatra from exile, put her on the Egyptian throne, and appointed her remaining brother to rule with her, despite his tender age. After Caesar's death and the Battle of Philippi,[93] Antony crossed into Asia and bestowed upon Cleopatra the honor of choosing her as his wife and having children with her. He fought at her side in the Battle of Actium and fled with her too. Then, Augustus Caesar, after pursuing them, brought about both their deaths and ended the drunken abuse of Egypt.

90. The embassy was sent by Ptolemy XII's enemies at Alexandria. Ptolemy XII plotted to have many of the ambassadors murdered; a number of Romans, including Pompey, were implicated as well (Grant 1972, 16). Cf. Cassius Dio 39.13.

91. "Academic" refers to followers of Plato's philosophy; Plato taught at a gymnasium near Athens known as the Academy.

92. Pompey was fleeing from Julius Caesar after being defeated in the Battle of Pharsalus during the civil war. Pompey hoped to form an alliance with the Egyptians, but they considered Caesar more likely to emerge victorious and felt they could not afford to back the loser.

93. The Battle of Philippi was fought between Octavian and Mark Antony in 42 B.C.

2

Cleopatra's Early Career

IN 51 B.C. EIGHTEEN-YEAR-OLD Cleopatra VII and her ten-year-old brother, Ptolemy XIII, became rulers of Egypt upon the death of their father, Ptolemy XII Auletes. Because of Ptolemy XIII's youth, Cleopatra was the dominant partner. She inherited in Alexandria a thriving and diverse city, and she soon showed her interest in increasing relations with the native people of Egypt.

A PORTRAIT OF CLEOPATRA

It is difficult to ascertain exactly what Cleopatra looked like. Plutarch refers to her as beautiful (*Life of Antony* 25.4–5) and Cassius Dio comments on her seductiveness (*Roman History* 42.34.4), but many portraits of her present a woman we might not see as beautiful, at least in the conventional sense. Figures 1, 3, and 4 show several ancient portraits. Stylistic differences contribute to the many faces of Cleopatra that we have from the ancient world. She might appear as an Egyptian pharaoh in a portrait intended for an audience of native Egyptians, or in the style of the classical period in a Hellenizing portrait bust, or looking very much like Mark Antony in a coin portrait.[1]

---

1. Goudchaux disputes the perception, based on some of these portraits, that Cleopatra was ugly (2001, 210–14).

2.1. Plutarch, *Life of Antony* 27.2–4 (A.D. 110–15, Greek, prose)

Plutarch, a Greek living in the Roman Empire, spent most of his life in Athens, although he visited Egypt and taught in Rome. He was active in public life during the reigns of Trajan and Hadrian and authored a number of works, including a number of comparative biographies, the Parallel Lives. *Each pair of lives juxtaposes a Greek and a Roman whose careers had something in common.*

Following the extension of the Roman Empire into many Greek-speaking areas, a demand arose for books on Roman subjects written in Greek. Works such as Plutarch's Lives, *Cassius Dio's* Roman History, *and Dionysius of Halicarnassus's* Roman Antiquities *provided Greek speakers with information regarding a culture of which they suddenly found themselves members.*

In his writings Plutarch advocates a partnership between Greece, the intellectual power, and Rome, the political power. In some ways Plutarch's point of view coincides with the vision Antony and Cleopatra had for an empire, had they emerged victorious over Octavian. Perhaps, under Antony and Cleopatra, the world would have seen the Greek and Roman parts of the empire as relatively equal partners rather than Rome as the undisputed ruler of the Mediterranean.[2] Nevertheless, in his Life of Antony *Plutarch conveys the negative assessment of Antony that was prevalent in the wake of Octavian's victory. Plutarch pairs Antony with Demetrius I of Macedonia, who attempted to reunite the empire of Alexander the Great against the will of the Macedonians. In the final reckoning, Plutarch finds them both lacking the morals essential to a great man.[3]*

Plutarch does not wholly demonize Antony, however, and some indications of the pro-Antonian viewpoint can be found in the Life of Antony. *Likewise, while Plutarch ultimately considers Cleopatra a danger to Rome, he does not fail to point out her positive qualities as he considers the reasons for her irresistibility in this, the closest we have to a detailed description of Cleopatra's appearance.*

For indeed her own beauty, as they say, was not, in and of itself, completely incomparable, nor was it the sort that would astound those who saw her; but interaction with her was captivating, and her

2. Grant 1972, 235–38.
3. One of Plutarch's goals in the *Lives* was the moral edification of his audience.

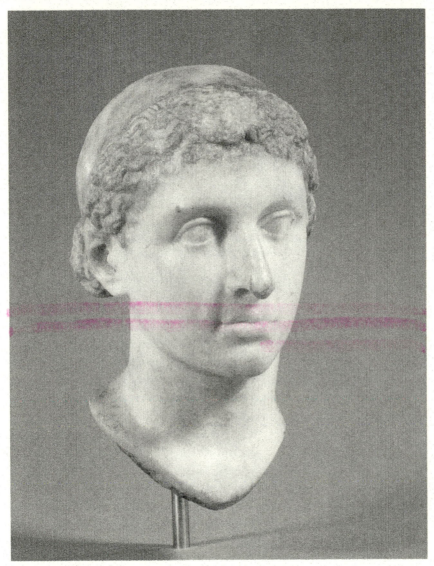

Fig. 3. Cleopatra VII, marble bust, before 31 B.C. Photo: Johannes Laurentius. Bildarchiv Preussischer Kulturbesitz / Art Resource, NY.

appearance, along with her persuasiveness in discussion and her character that accompanied every interchange, was stimulating. Pleasure also came with the tone of her voice; and her tongue was like a many-stringed instrument: she could turn it easily to whichever

Fig. 4. Silver denarius of Cleopatra VII and Mark Antony, obverse (left) and reverse (right), 32 B.C. © Copyright The British Museum.

language she wished and she conversed with few barbarians entirely through an interpreter, and she gave her decisions herself to most of them, including Ethiopians, Troglodytes, Hebrews, Arabians, Syrians, Medes, and Parthians.[4] She is said to have learned the languages of many others also, although the kings before her did not undertake to learn the Egyptian language, even though some of them had abandoned the Macedonian dialect.

A Visit to Hermonthis

Buchis bulls were sacred to the city of Hermonthis, near Thebes in Upper Egypt, and were seen as a living representation of the war god Mentu and as a manifestation of the gods Re and Osiris. There was only one Buchis bull at a time, chosen based on its markings. When the bull died, it was given a formal burial and replaced with a new bull. In 51 B.C. a new bull was consecrated. This was the year in which

4. Plutarch is our only ancient source for Cleopatra's knowledge of these languages. Note that Latin is not included in the list. It is possible that Latin was one of the many other languages with which Plutarch credits Cleopatra, but Julius Caesar and Mark Antony spoke Greek, so communication would not have been a problem. See Grant 1972, 42 n.42, 63 n.9, and Chauveau 2002, 10.

Cleopatra became pharaoh, and—as the inscription indicates—she was part of the bull's escort on its boat trip up the Nile to its sanctuary. The trip was probably the first opportunity her Egyptian subjects had to see their new ruler; thus, it afforded Cleopatra an important opportunity to present herself to the people of Egypt.

2.2. The Buchis Stela[5] (51 B.C., Egyptian, prose), translated by H. W. Fairman[6]

The consecration of a new Buchis bull was commemorated with an inscribed stela. The translation that follows is of the stela in honor of the bull consecrated in 51 B.C.. The relief on the stela shows the pharaoh offering the fields. The Buchis bull is depicted with the headdress typical of the god Apis (see fig. 5).

Utterance by the Osiris Buchis, living Ba of Re,[7] manifestation of Re, who was born of the great cow.

(1) Year 1, Pharmuthi 21 of Caesar,[8] the mighty one (?), beloved of the Osiris Buchis, Great God, Lord of the House of Atum.[9] On this day, the second *Ms-pr*,[10] the majesty of (2) this noble god went up to heaven as Re the Old.[11] Mayest thou be united with the Disk, and may the rays of Re be beautiful in thy body. Mayest thou settle down on thy image,[12] (3) and may it make excellent thy condition. May Amun[13] breathe forth sweet breath into thy nostrils, may thy nostrils inhale the goodly north wind, without ever being separated from thee. Mayest thou be glorious; mayest thou be powerful; (4) may thy Ba[14] be stable; mayest thou grow young like the moon. Mayest thou pass through the (holy) cities, mayest thou traverse the

---

5. Inscription 13 in Mond and Myers 1934.
6. Mond and Myers 1934, vol. 2, 11–13.
7. Ba: the soul after death, also the animal form of a god; Re: the sun god.
8. It makes most sense to take Caesar here as referring to Augustus. Thus, the dates in the inscription indicate that the bull was born in 53 B.C., was installed in 51 B.C., and died in 29 B.C. (Mond and Myers 1934, vol. 2, 32).
9. Atum was an Egyptian god associated with the sun and creation.
10. The sixteenth day of the lunar month.
11. I.e., the previous Buchis bull.
12. I.e., the stela.
13. Amun was another Egyptian god associated with the creative force.
14. The soul after death.

Fig. 5. Buchis Stela, 51 B.C. New Carlsberg Glyptotek, Copenhagen.

temples of the gods in their festivals. The Ba of Re causes thy Ba to live, the Ba of Shu[15] (5) endues thy nostrils. Thy mother is Nut,[16] she places thee within her, and is not devoid of thee for ever. Mayest thou see Re when he shines forth by day, and *Dt* when he enters by night. The house of (6) Atum, mayest thou live therein, and not perish within it for ever. In the year 28, phamenoth 12, "The Night of the Favourite of the Osiris Buchis", in the time of the majesty of the King of Upper and Lower Egypt, Lord of the Two Lands ( );[17] (7) son of Re, Lord of Diadems ( ), there appeared Buchis, the living Ba of Re, the manifestation of Re, who was born of the Great Cow, Tenen[18] united with the Eight Gods.[19] He is Amun who goes on his four feet, (8) the image of Mentu,[20] Lord of Thebes, Father of the Fathers, the Mother of the Mothers, who formed the Ennead,[21] who renews the life of every one of the gods. He is the image of Onnophris,[22] the justified, the sacred image of the Ba of Re, the bik n nb (9) in . . . . He came to Hermonthis in the goodly festival of the twentieth day of Pakhons, the festival of Mentu, Lord of Hermonthis, his seat of eternity. He reached Thebes, his place of installation, (10) which came into existence aforetime, beside his father, Nun the Old.[23] He was installed by the King himself in year 1, Phamenoth 19. The Queen, the Lady of the Two Lands ( ), the goddess who loves her father, (11) rowed him in the barque of Amun, together with the boats of the king, all the inhabitants of Thebes and Hermonthis and priests being with him.[24] He reached Hermonthis, his (12) dwelling-place, on Mechir 22.[25] The length of his life was 24 years, 1 month, and 8 days. His Ba went up to heaven as Re. He was buried therein in one day. Ceremonies were performed

---

15. Shu: Egyptian god of the air.
16. Nut: the Egyptian sky goddess.
17. The cartouches are left blank in this inscription.
18. Tenen: Egyptian god who personified the fertile silt of the Nile.
19. A group of primordial gods worshipped at Hermopolis.
20. Mentu: Egyptian war and sun god.
21. The nine most important gods of the Egyptian pantheon.
22. An epithet meaning "he who is continuously happy," given to Osiris after his resurrection.
23. Nun: Egyptian god personifying swampy water chaos.
24. This sentence refers to Cleopatra; calling her "the goddess who loves her father" refers to her adoption of the title Thea Philopator upon taking the throne.
25. As Fairman notes, this date may be in error; it is more likely that the bull arrived on Phamenoth 22, four days after his departure (Mond and Myers 1934, vol. 2, 13).

(13) for his Ka[26] at every good festival, by his true servant, his delight, his true libationer, who makes his libations, the baron and count, priest of Mentu, Lord of Hermonthis, Re-Horakhte,[27] and his Ennead, priest of the Osiris (14) Buchis, Lord of the House of Atum, Kalasiris,[28] son of Pa-Amen-Pwny (?), born of Ta-senty, that he might be granted life for ever in life, stability, and well-being.

AID FOR POMPEY

After the First Triumvirate broke up, Pompey and Caesar engaged in a civil war. In 48 B.C. one of Pompey's naval bases, Dyrrachium, came under attack by Caesar's forces, but Pompey successfully repelled them.

2.3. Appian, *Civil War* 2.71 (early 2nd c. A.D., Greek, prose)

Appian, like Plutarch, wrote on Roman topics for a Greek-speaking audience, his writings covering all of Roman history. Born in Alexandria in the late first century A.D., in the early second century Appian moved to Rome and became a Roman citizen. He has a favorable view of the Roman character, although he sees the breakdown of that character as a cause of the civil wars. Because of his Alexandrian background, events concerning Egypt receive particular emphasis.

In addition to the Greeks, almost all of the peoples of the eastern Mediterranean aided Pompey, including the Thracians, the Hellespontines, the Bithynians, the Phrygians, the Ionians, the Lydians, the Pamphylians, the Pisidians, the Paphlygonians, Cilicia, Syria, Phoenicia, the Hebrew people, the Arabs who live next to them, the Cyprians, the Rhodians, the Cretan slingers, and all the other islanders. Kings and dynasts were present, each with his own army: Deiotarus, the tetrarch of the eastern Galatians, and Ariarathes, the king of the Cappadocians. Taxiles the general led the Armenians from this side of the Euphrates; Megabates, the lieutenant for King Artapates led the Armenians from beyond the Euphrates; other minor dynasts shared in the campaign. Sixty ships are said to have

---

26. Ka: the protective divine spirit of a person.
27. A combination of the god Re with the god Horus, the falcon god who was also associated with light.
28. A priest of Buchis.

been furnished to him by the Egyptian rulers, Cleopatra and her brother, though the latter was still a child. These ships did not participate in the battle, however, nor did any other navy. Rather, they sat idly in Corcyra. In this respect, it seems that Pompey acted very foolishly by ignoring the ships, with which he was so capable that he could have deprived the enemy of supplies from every side, and by engaging in a land battle with men celebrating their recent achievements and being savagely eager for battle. He had withstood them at Dyrrachium, but now a curse from the gods seemed to afflict him, which proved to be the most opportune event for Caesar, for, because of it, Pompey's troops set out foolishly and, taking the command into their own hands, went at their task as if they had no experience in war.

SIBLING RIVALRY

It soon became clear that Cleopatra desired sole power, as she came into conflict with the advisors of her brother and coruler, Ptolemy XIII. These tensions finally resulted in her flight from Egypt and her need for Caesar's intervention.

2.4. Appian, *Civil War* 2.84–86 (early 2nd c. A.D., Greek, prose)

For more on Appian, see selection 2.3. After being defeated by Caesar's forces at Pharsalus in northern Greece, Pompey fled to Egypt, hoping to receive resources and troops from the Ptolemies in order to continue fighting. The Ptolemies, however, could not afford to ally themselves with the losing side, as they needed the protection Rome could provide. Judging that Caesar was more likely to emerge successful from the civil war, they wished to make their support for him evident.

84. For these reasons, Pompey sailed to Egypt.[29] Recently, Cleopatra had been exiled from Egypt, where previously she had ruled with her brother; now she was gathering an army in Syria. Her brother Ptolemy was in Egypt, lying in wait in Cassium for Cleopatra's attack. By some chance, the wind brought Pompey to Casium. When Pompey saw a great army on the shore, he stopped his ship and inferred, as

---

29. Egypt was a rich country, and Pompey needed resources; also, he had been a friend of Ptolemy XII, Cleopatra's father.

was in fact the case, that the king was there. He sent a messenger to announce his arrival and mention his friendship with Ptolemy's father. The king was around thirteen years old; Achillas managed his army and Pothinus the eunuch his treasury. The two of them discussed what to do about Pompey. Also present was Theodotus, a rhetorician from Samos, who was Ptolemy's tutor; he suggested the nefarious deed, that they ambush Pompey and kill him to gratify Caesar. They adopted this proposal and sent an inexpensive boat for him, allegedly because the sea was shallow and not fit for large ships. Some of the king's rowers came on the boat, along with Sempronius, a Roman who was at the time enlisted in the king's army, but who had previously served under Pompey. He offered his right hand, extending greetings from the king to Pompey and suggested he sail to the young man as if going to meet a friend. As these events unfolded, the whole army was stationed on the shore, as if in Pompey's honor, and the king was in the middle, conspicuous in a purple robe.

85. Pompey was suspicious of everything: the array of soldiers, the cheapness of the boat, and the failure of the king to meet him in person or send any of his officers. But he got on the boat, repeating to himself some verses of Sophocles, "Whoever has dealings with a tyrant is his slave, even if he goes as a free man."[30] He grew even more suspicious when all were silent as they rowed. When he either recognized Sempronius as a Roman and former soldier of his or guessed it because he was the only one standing (following military protocol, one does not sit in the presence of a commander), Pompey turned to him and said, "Do I know you, my fellow soldier?" Sempronius nodded and, turning away, at once stabbed Pompey and the others followed suit. Pompey's wife and friends saw these things from a distance and cried out and raised their hands to the gods who protect truces. Then they quickly sailed away from those who were clearly enemies.

86. Pothinus's servants cut off Pompey's head and kept it for Caesar, in hopes of a great reward (in fact, he punished them as their crime deserved). Someone buried the rest of Pompey's body on the shore and erected an unimpressive grave marker. Someone else added an inscription: "How poor a tomb stands for one so rich in temples."

---

30. Sophocles, fragment 873, Pearson.

In time, the whole tomb was hidden by sand and the bronze statues, which his relatives later set up in his honor near Mt. Casius, were all dishonored and moved to the innermost room of the temple. In my time, the Roman emperor Hadrian looked for them and found them when he traveled there. He restored the tomb to be again recognizable and displayed Pompey's statues there.

This was the end of Pompey's life. He had carried out the greatest wars and greatly increased the size of Rome's empire, because of which he received the epithet Great. He was never defeated before his final conflict,[31] but had been undefeated and very fortunate from his youth. From the time he was twenty-three until he was fifty-eight, he was continuously in power and had as much power as a king, but, in comparison with Caesar, he appeared democratic in the way he exercised it.

2.5. Cassius Dio, *Roman History* 42.3–5.6 (A.D. 202, Greek, prose)

Born in Bithynia, between A.D. 194 and 229 Cassius Dio held a number of political offices at Rome and was a member of the Senate. He wrote a history of Rome in eighty books, covering events from the founding of the city to A.D. 229. Cassius Dio was a proponent of the Roman Empire, believing that only an emperor could effectively rule the Roman world. In his account of Pompey's death, he emphasizes the roles played by chance and by supernatural forces.

3. Pompey hastened away to Egypt, for the reasons given above,[32] and, having followed the coast to Cilicia, from there he crossed open water to Pelusium, where Ptolemy was camped while fighting his sister Cleopatra. Pompey anchored his ships offshore and sent some men to remind Ptolemy of the ancestral relationship between them and to request a landing on certain firm conditions, for he did not dare leave his ship before receiving some promise of safety. Ptolemy made no reply (he was still utterly a child), but some of the Egyptians, along with Lucius Septimius, a Roman who had at one time served in

31. Appian is incorrect; Sertorius defeated Pompey in Spain.
32. Pompey had been a friend of Ptolemy XII. Although Pompey had thought of asking the Parthians for help, they were at that time particularly hostile to the Romans; therefore, the Egyptians represented a better choice.

Pompey's army and who, after attaching himself to Gabinius, was left behind by him with some troops to guard Ptolemy, approached, appearing friendly. They were, however, wickedly plotting against Pompey and, as a result, they brought a curse upon themselves and all of Egypt: they themselves died not long afterward and the Egyptians first were enslaved to Cleopatra, which they did not want, and then were declared subject to Rome.

4. At this time, Septimius and Achillas, the army commander, along with others who were with them, said that they would happily receive Pompey so that he might easily be entrapped and caught. They sent his representatives back first, telling them to have confidence, and then they embarked on small boats and sailed out to him. After they offered many greetings, they invited Pompey to come aboard their boat, claiming that his ship was not able, because of its size and the shallow water, to approach the shore and that Ptolemy was very eager to see him quickly. And so, although all of those on Pompey's boat tried to dissuade him, he trusted them, saying merely:

> Whoever has dealings with a tyrant,
> is his slave, even if he goes as a free man.[33]

They, as they approached the shore, were afraid that he might encounter Ptolemy and be saved either by the king himself or by the Romans who were with him or by the Egyptians (for they had great affection for him), and so they killed him on board the boat. Pompey said nothing and did not even cry out: as soon as he perceived the plot and realized that he could not defend himself against them or escape, he covered his face.

5. Such was the death of Pompey the Great; it was an event that demonstrated the weakness and strangeness of the human race. Although Pompey was not lacking in foresight, but had always been very secure against any harmful force, he was tricked. Although he had won many unexpected victories in Africa, Asia, and Europe on land and on the sea ever since he was a young man, he was inexplicably beaten at age fifty-eight. Although he had tamed the whole sea of the Romans, he was ruined on that same body of water. Although, as the story goes, he commanded a thousand ships, he was destroyed in a

---

33. Sophocles, fragment 873, Pearson.

small boat near Egypt and in some way by Ptolemy, whose father he had restored to that place and to his throne. Although Roman soldiers were guarding Ptolemy—they were left there by Gabinius as a favor to Pompey because of the Egyptians' hatred of Ptolemy's father— Ptolemy seemed to have killed him and to have employed both Egyptians and Romans in carrying out the deed. Indeed, Pompey, previously thought to be the most powerful of the Romans (he was even called Agamemnon), was slaughtered like some lowly Egyptian, not only near Mt. Casius, but on the anniversary of the day he had led a triumph over Mithradates and the pirates. Thus, even in this there was a reversal, for on that day previously he had attained the greatest success, but subsequently he suffered the most terrible fate; based on an oracle, he had suspected all citizens named Cassius, and he died and was buried near a mountain of the same name.

PROPHECIES

In the ancient world, prophecies were often consulted in times of crisis. Predictions might be obtained by visiting an oracle and posing a question or by consulting a collection of written predictions. All types of prophecies tend to be cryptic and open to interpretation; thus, the analysis can be as important as the content of the prediction.

2.6. Sibylline Oracles 3.350–80, 3.75–92 (ca. 31 B.C., Greek, verse)

The Sibylline Oracles *are a collection of prophetic texts compiled over a long period of time. The Romans turned to these prophecies for guidance in times of need, believing that the predictions had been made by Sibyls, semimythical prophetesses. Book 3 of the* Sibylline Oracles, *from which these selections come, was written in Egypt.*[34] *The first of the two selections, written shortly before the Battle of Actium, details the vengeance a lady from Asia will take on Rome. It is likely that the lady referred to is Cleopatra.*[35] *The second selection dates from the period immediately following the Battle of Actium and again refers to Cleopatra. In this passage, however, she has not conquered the world but has brought it to ruin.*

34. Charlesworth 1983, vol. 1, 355.
35. Ibid.

3.350–80

As much as Rome took in from tribute-paying Asia,   350
Asia will get back three times as much
from Rome, and will repay her for her destructive pride.
However many from Asia were enslaved to an Italian house,
Twenty times as many will be slaves in Asia:
Italians, who, living in poverty, will pay their debt many
    times over.   355
Delicate, golden child of Latium, Rome,
maiden, often drunk with marriages to many
suitors, you will marry as a slave, indecently,
and often the mistress[36] cuts your soft hair
and, in pursuit of justice, will hurl you from the sky   360
down to earth, and then raise you from the earth back
up to the sky, for mortals are ensnared in a trivial and
    unjust life.
Samos will be sand; Delos will become indistinct;
Rome will be a mere road: the predictions will come true.
Once Smyrna has disappeared, no record will remain. An
    avenger   365
will arise, but for ill-intentioned plots and corruption of leaders
. . . .[37]
Tranquil peace will come to the Asian land;
then Europe will prosper; the pure air will stimulate the
    pastureland
for years to come and will be vigorous: no storms or hail;
it will bear everything: both birds and animals that crawl
    on the ground.   370
Blessed is the man who lives until that time,
or indeed the woman; they will be deemed blessed by the
    rustics,
for all kindness and righteousness will come to men
from starry heaven, and with it sensible
harmony, which for mortals surpasses everything,   375
and affection, trust, and even the bond between strangers.

36. The "mistress" is generally identified as Cleopatra.
37. There is a gap in the text.

Ill-will, censure, envy, rage, recklessness, and
want will be absent from men, as will compulsion
murder, ruinous discord, miserable disputes,
nocturnal larceny, and every evil of those times. 380

3.75–92

Then the world will be ruled by a woman's 75
hands and will obey her in all matters.
And when a widow is queen of the whole world
and tosses gold and silver into the mighty sea,
and bronze as well, and casts iron of mortal men
into the ocean, then indeed all the elements 80
of the cosmos will be widowed, when the god
dwelling in the heavens rolls up the sky like a book
and the whole vault with all its diversity falls on the
great earth and sea; a relentless rush of raging
fire will flow, burning earth and sea and 85
melting the vault of the sky, the days, and the whole
universe into one substance and then dissolving them
into thin air. No longer will there be lights dancing in the sky,
no night, no dawn, no care-filled days,
no spring, no summer, no winter, no fall. 90
Then indeed the great god will bring his judgment to bear
on the great epoch, when all these things come to pass.

3

Caesar

JULIUS CAESAR ARRIVED IN EGYPT in 48 B.C., pursuing Pompey. At age fifty-two, he was thirty-one years Cleopatra's senior. If we believe Suetonius, however, Caesar had a weakness when it came to women, a trait Cleopatra exploited. With Pompey's defeat, Caesar emerged as the most powerful man in Rome. When it came to Egypt, however, he proceeded with caution, refraining from making it into a Roman province. He could have conquered the country, given the internal strife between Ptolemy XIII and Cleopatra, and Rome could have benefited from Egypt's wealth. But that wealth represented a danger: there was a potential for anyone appointed governor of Egypt to use the resources of Egypt to rival the Roman government.

PORTRAITS OF CAESAR

Julius Caesar ambitiously sought power and demonstrated considerable success in attaining it. In the end, however, this ambition proved fatal. We see in biographical sketches of Caesar some of the qualities that contributed to his success and also aroused the ire of some Romans.

3.1. Suetonius, *The Divine Julius Caesar* 45–51, 72–76 (A.D. 119–21, Latin, prose)

Suetonius wrote his famous biographies of the "twelve Caesars," Roman leaders from Julius Caesar to Domitian, during the reign of the emperor Hadrian. As a biographer, Suetonius makes it a priority to convey the character of his subjects. He frequently employs anecdotes to illustrate his general statements. Suetonius's biographies do not follow their subjects chronologically through their lives but rather have a thematic organization. The following selections describe Julius Caesar's personality with reference to incidents from various periods of his life.

45–51

45. He is said to have been tall in stature and fair in complexion, to have had shapely limbs, a somewhat large mouth, dark and lively eyes, and good health, except that, toward the end of his life, he tended to suffer from fainting and nightmares. Twice, while working, he had epileptic seizures. He was somewhat fastidious about the care of his body: he not only diligently clipped and shaved, but also plucked, certain sources say.[1] He did not endure the flaw of baldness with equanimity, but often suffered the indignity of jests from his detractors. For this reason, he combed over what hair he had left and, of all the honors the senate and people decreed for him, none was more willingly received or adopted than the right of always wearing a laurel crown.

They also say he was notable for his style of dress: he wore his purple-striped tunic with fringed long sleeves and always with a loose belt over it, a custom that gave rise to Sulla's oft-repeated warning to the aristocrats, "beware the boy whose belt is loose."[2]

46. He first lived in the Subura in a modest house. After he became Pontifex Maximus, he lived on the Sacred Way in a public house.[3] Many sources attest to his neatness, elegance, and diligence: after building a new villa in Nemi[4] and completing construction at great expense, he tore the whole thing down because it did not completely suit him, although at the time he was not well off and was in

1. The plucking of unwanted hair was considered a sign of effeminacy.
2. Wearing one's belt loose was a sign of effeminacy. A belt, normally worn with an ordinary tunic, was not usually worn with the tunic having two purple stripes from its neck.
3. The Subura was a noisy and squalid district of Rome home to manufacturing and prostitution. The Pontifex Maximus, the chief priest of Rome, lived in an official residence.
4. Lake Nemi was a fashionable and popular spot for country houses.

debt. People say he brought on his campaigns mosaics and flooring of cut marble.

47. They say he invaded Britain for its pearls, which he would weigh in his hand to measure their value. He also enthusiastically collected gems, embossed metalwork, statues, and antique paintings. He bought attractive and well-trained slaves at such high prices that even he was embarrassed and forbid the amounts to be entered in the accounts.

Romanticizing Ceaser

48. As he traveled through the provinces, he banqueted constantly and had two dining rooms, one for soldiers and Greeks and one for Romans and the more distinguished provincials. He oversaw domestic affairs both great and small with such attentiveness and seriousness that he had a baker arrested who gave him bread different from that served to his guests. He had a favorite freedman executed for committing adultery with the wife of a Roman knight, even though no one brought a charge.

49. Nothing damaged his reputation for modesty except his intimacy with Nicomedes, a serious and enduring reproach and one held up to public reviling. I don't need to mention the well-known verses by Calvus Licinius:

> whatever Bithynia
> and the buggerer of Caesar ever had.

Nor will I bring up what Dolabella and the Elder Curio did: Dolabella called him "the king's mistress, most intimate companion of the royal bed," and Curio said he was "a Bithynian brothel for Nicomedes." Then there was the decree of Bibulus that described Caesar as "his colleague the Bithynian queen, who previously wanted to be a king's lover and now wants to be a king." At that time, as Marcus Brutus relates, Octavius, who tended to blurt out the first thing that came to mind, when he had addressed Pompey as "king" in a great assembly, then addressed Caesar as "queen." But Gaius Memmius charged that he had been Nicomedes' cupbearer, along with the other good-for-nothings, at a banquet attended by some city businessmen he names. Cicero was not satisfied to have written in some letters that Caesar had been led by attendants to the king's bedroom and that he reclined on a golden bed with purple coverlets and, thus, a descendant of Venus lost his virginity in Bithynia. Indeed, Cicero even said to

Caesar as he defended Nicomedes' daughter Nysa in the senate and recounted the favors the king had done him, "Put those things aside, please, since it is well known both what he gave you and what you gave him." Finally, at his Gallic triumph, his soldiers shouted out the following vulgar chant among the other songs customarily sung in jest by those following the general's chariot:

> Caesar dominated the Gauls, Nicomedes Caesar:
> look, a triumph for Caesar who dominated the Gauls,
> no triumph for Nicomedes who dominated Caesar.

50. It is common knowledge that he engaged in affairs readily and lavishly and that he seduced many famous women, including Postumia, wife of Servius Sulpicius, Lollia, wife of Aulus Gabinius, Tertulla, wife of Marcus Crassus, and Mucia, wife of Pompey. To be sure, both the Elder and the Younger Curio, along with many others, reproached Pompey for marrying Caesar's daughter out of a desire for power, when it was Caesar's fault Pompey had divorced his wife, Mucia, who had borne him three children, and it was Caesar whom Pompey, in despair, had called "Aegisthus."[5] But Caesar loved Servilia, the mother of Marcus Brutus, above all others and during his first consulship he bought her a pearl costing sixty thousand sesterces. In addition to other loot from the civil war, he knocked down auctions for her. When people marveled at the deals she got, Cicero found a clever turn of phrase: "The price was even better than you think, since there was a tertiary discount." You see, Servilia was believed to have prostituted her daughter Tertia to Caesar.

51. He had affairs in the provinces as well, as another couplet sung by the soldiers at the Gallic triumph, indicates:

> Romans, hide your wives: here comes the bald adulterer.
> He took out loans, then blew it all on Gallic whores.

Double standard w/t Cleopatra

72–76

72. He always treated his friends such great affection and generosity that when Gaius Oppius, who was accompanying him on a

---

5. Pompey married Caesar's daughter Julia in 59 B.C. Aegisthus was the lover of Clytemnestra. The pair plotted death for Agamemnon, Clytemnestra's husband, upon his return from the Trojan War.

journey through the forest, took sick, Caesar gave him the only lodging available and himself slept on the ground under the stars. When he became powerful, he elevated certain men of humble birth to lofty positions and, when he was accused of doing just that, openly professed, "if I had employed the assistance of loafers and murderers in protecting my reputation, I would offer them equal gratitude."

73. But he never took feuds so seriously that he was not willing, should the occasion present itself, to put them aside. He was a supporter of Gaius Memmius in the latter's bid for the consulship, even though he had replied in kind to Memmius's speeches attacking him. He wrote to Gaius Calvus, who had insulted him in well-known epigrams, when Calvus made overtures of reconciliation through friends. He invited Valerius Catullus to dinner on the very day the poet apologized, although Caesar had never concealed the fact that the poems about Mamurra had forever blemished his reputation.[6] He also continued to accept the hospitality of Catullus's father, as he had been accustomed.

74. He was by nature lenient in exacting revenge. When he crucified the pirates by whom he had been captured, only because he had sworn beforehand that he would, he ordered their throats cut first, then that they be crucified. He never got around to punishing Cornelius Phagita. Caesar, sick and in hiding lest he be brought before Sulla, scarcely had escaped Phagita's nocturnal traps by paying a bribe. He did not punish Philemon, his slave and assistant, who had promised Caesar's enemies that he would poison his master, cruelly or unusually, but simply put him to death. Against Publius Clodius, who allegedly committed adultery with Caesar's wife, Pompeia, and polluted sacred rites, Caesar, when summoned as a witness, refused to testify, although both his mother Aurelia and his sister Julia had reported everything truthfully to those same judges. When asked why, then, he had divorced his wife, Caesar said, "because my family must be as innocent of suspicion of wrongdoing as of wrongdoing itself."

75. Truly, he demonstrated admirable restraint and clemency not only in governing but also in his victory in the civil war. While Pompey was denouncing as an enemy of the state all who did not support the Republic, Caesar announced that those who were neutral and not

6. Catullus, *Poems* 29 and 57.

opposed to him would be numbered among his supporters. To all those whom he had promoted to centurion on the advice of Pompey, he gave the option of transferring to Pompey's side. When the conditions of surrender were being discussed at Ilerda, and when, with both sides fraternizing, Afranius and Petreius, after a sudden change of heart, had killed the soldiers of Caesar they had caught inside their camp, Caesar could not stand to emulate the treachery perpetrated against him. At the Battle of Pharsalus, he proclaimed that he would spare the citizens and then granted to each of his own men to save one, whomever he wished, of the opposing army. No one is said to have perished at Pharsalus, other than in the combat itself, with the exception of Afranius, Faustus, and young Lucius Caesar.[7] And they think that not even these were killed by Caesar's will, although the first two had attacked again after pardon was obtained and Lucius Caesar had callously killed his freedmen and slaves with iron and fire and slashed the throats of the animals procured for a public display. Finally, late in his career, Caesar allowed all those whom he had not yet pardoned to return to Italy and assume magistracies and commands. He also replaced statues of Lucius Sulla and Pompey that the people had torn down; and if after that anything was seriously thought or said against him, he preferred to discourage it rather than exact revenge. And so he did not prosecute conspiracies or nocturnal meetings when he found out about them, but rather put out a decree that he knew of them and he considered it enough to give notice before the assembly to slanderers to stop what they were doing: he endured with equanimity the damage done to his reputation by the slanderous writings of Aulus Caecina and the insulting poems of Pitholaus.

76. Nevertheless, other words and deeds of his tilt the balance against him and suggest that he abused his power and was justly assassinated. For not only did he accept too many honors: an endless consulship, a dictatorship without end, and the oversight of morals and customs, the title Imperator preceding his name, the designation "Father of his Country," his statue placed among those of the kings, box seats at the theater; but he also allowed honors to be decreed for him greater than are appropriate to mortals: a gold chair in the senate house and in front of the speaker's platform, a chariot and litter for

7. Lucius Caesar was distantly related to Julius Caesar but fought on Pompey's side.

his statue in the parade at the circus, temples, altars, statues of him next to images of the gods, a ceremonial couch, priests for his cult, a month named after him.[8] There were hardly any honors he did not allow himself to enjoy. He took his third and fourth consulships in name only, as the power he derived from the dictatorship conferred at the same time was sufficient. During both of those consulships, he substituted new consuls for himself in the final three months of the term, so that in the meantime the assembly elected only tribunes and aediles of the plebs and he appointed prefects instead of praetors to govern the city in his absence. When a consul died suddenly on the last day of December, he gave the last few hours of that office to a man who requested the nominal position. Disregarding ancestral custom, he showed similar license in appointing magistrates years in advance, in granting consular insignia to ten men who had held only the praetorship, and in accepting into the senate foreigners who had received Roman citizenship, including semibarbarous Gauls. Moreover, he appointed his private slaves to oversee the public revenues of the mint. He assigned the care and command of the three legions, which he left in Alexandria, to Rufio, the son of one of his freedmen.

3.2. Catullus, *Poems* 57 and 93 (61–58 B.C., Latin, verse)

For background on Catullus, see selection 1.7. In the following poems Catullus abuses Julius Caesar. To insult such a powerful man was not as dangerous as it might seem in the Roman Republic. Freedom of speech was a valued right, and Roman citizens expected to be able to criticize their politicians. As Suetonius relates (see selection 3.1), Caesar forgave Catullus for his harsh words.

Poem 57

It's all well and good for the wicked buggers,   1
Mamurra[9] and Caesar—they suck.
No wonder: they both have the same defect,
one got in Rome and the other in Formiae.

---

8. July, which had been called Quintilis.
9. Mamurra was an associate of Julius Caesar. Originally from Formiae, a fashionable resort town south of Rome, he accumulated great wealth on campaign with Caesar in Spain and Gaul.

Content to be blemished, they will never come clean: 5
each the equally diseased twin of the other,
two pseudo-intellectuals in one bed.
The one no more voracious an adulterer than the other,
they have a friendly rivalry over girls.
It's all well and good for the wicked buggers.   10

Poem 93

I'm not too eager, Caesar, for you to like me,   1
nor to know whether you are a white man or black.[10]

CAESAR ARRIVES IN ALEXANDRIA

After defeating Pompey at the Battle of Pharsalus, Caesar pursued him to Egypt. The Ptolemies were unwilling to risk offending Caesar by harboring Pompey, as Caesar appeared to have become the most powerful man in Rome. At the time Ptolemy XIII ruled Egypt alone, since he had expelled his co-ruler, Cleopatra. Because of his youth, however, he was under the control of his advisors, Achillas, Pothinus, and Theodotus.

3.3. Cassius Dio, *Roman History* 42.7–9.1 (A.D. 202, Greek, prose)

For more on Cassius Dio, see selection 2.5. Here he describes Caesar's arrival in Egypt and his discovery that Pompey has been murdered.

7. At this time, Caesar learned that Pompey was sailing to Egypt and, fearing that if Pompey occupied Egypt first, he would again grow strong, he hastened there with all speed. Caesar found that Pompey was no longer alive and so he sailed on to Alexandria with just a few men, arriving before Ptolemy came from Pelusium. Since he found the Alexandrians greatly disturbed over Pompey's death, he did not dare to go ashore right away, but retreated from the harbor and held back until he saw Pompey's head and ring, which Ptolemy sent to him. Then he landed his ship with confidence, but, since the crowd disapproved of his litter, he was glad to escape to the palace.

---

10. "To know whether you are a white man or black" was probably proverbial, meaning something like "to know anything about you." White and black may have the connotations of good and evil as well.

Of his soldiers, some had their weapons confiscated and, because of that, the rest put out to sea again, until all the ships could land.

8. When Caesar saw Pompey's head, he wept and lamented, calling Pompey his fellow-citizen and son-in-law and recounting all the things they had done for one another. Regarding Pompey's murderers, Caesar, rather than saying he owed them a favor, denounced them and ordered the head to be adorned, prepared, and buried. For this act he won praise, but for his disingenuousness he brought ridicule upon himself. From the beginning, he had been terribly eager for power; he had hated Pompey as an adversary and rival; he had done many things against Pompey, but in particular he had declared war on him for no other reason besides bringing about Pompey's destruction and his own success. He had come to Egypt for no other reason than to defeat Pompey, if he found him alive, but he pretended to miss Pompey and to be angry over his murder.

9. Since Caesar thought that, with Pompey removed, no hostility remained toward him, he spent his time in Egypt imposing taxes and mediating the disputes between Ptolemy and Cleopatra.

3.4. Suetonius, *The Divine Julius Caesar* 35 (A.D. 119–21, Latin, prose)

For more on Suetonius, see selection 3.1. Here Suetonius attributes mixed feelings to Caesar upon his learning that Ptolemy has killed Pompey as a show of support.

After returning to Rome, Caesar crossed into Macedonia and, after besieging Pompey for almost four months, defeated him in the Battle of Pharsalus and pursued him as he fled to Alexandria. When he found Pompey dead, he waged a very difficult war on King Ptolemy, whom he perceived plotting treachery against him. Both time and place were inconvenient: it was winter and the enemy was skillful and well supplied within the city walls. Caesar lacked supplies and preparation. Victorious, Caesar allowed Cleopatra and her younger brother Ptolemy to rule Egypt, since he feared that if he made it a province, in the future it might be a means of political insurrection for a rather impetuous governor. From Alexandria, he passed into Syria and from there to Pontus, on the urgent reports that Pharnaces, the son of Mithradates the Great, had opportunistically started a war and was having considerable success. Within five days of arriving and within four hours of spotting Pharnaces, Caesar prevailed in a single battle and often commented that Pompey was lucky that he had made his reputation as a general fighting so docile an enemy. From here he conquered Scipio and Juba, who were marshalling the remnants of Pompey's army in Africa. He also defeated Pompey's sons in Spain.

3.5. Plutarch, *Life of Caesar* 48.1–2 (A.D. 110–15, Greek, prose)

For more on Plutarch, see selection 2.1. Plutarch's Life of Caesar *was the Roman counterpart to his* Life of Alexander. *In this passage Caesar follows Pompey to Egypt after defeating him at the Battle of Pharsalus in Greece. In Egypt a rift had occurred between co-rulers Cleopatra and her younger brother, Ptolemy XIII. Ptolemy, influenced by his advisors, had driven Cleopatra out of Egypt.*

Caesar, in honor of his victory, liberated the Thessalian people. He then pursued Pompey. Arriving in Asia, Caesar freed the Cnidians, as a favor to Theopompus the story collector, and, for all those living in Asia, forgave a third of their tribute. Reaching Alexandria right after Pompey died, he turned away from Theodotus,[11] who was offering him Pompey's head, but he accepted Pompey's seal ring and wept. All of Pompey's friends and supporters, who had been captured by the king as they wandered through the country, Caesar treated generously and brought over to his side. He wrote to his friends in Rome that he enjoyed this part of his victory most of all: saving some of the citizens who had fought against him.

CLEOPATRA AND CAESAR IN ALEXANDRIA

While he was in Alexandria, Caesar attempted to resolve the dispute between Cleopatra and her brother-husband Ptolemy XIII. Hostilities became open, and Caesar took Cleopatra's side in the Alexandrian War, which they won when Ptolemy drowned accidentally. Although historians often frame the dispute as being between Cleopatra and Ptolemy, in fact the young king was very much at the mercy of his advisors, Achillas, Pothinus, and Theodotus. In the end, however, they proved no match for Caesar and Cleopatra.

---

11. One of the advisors to the young King Ptolemy XIII.

5. Cassius Dio, *Roman History* 42.34.3–35 (A.D. 202, Greek, prose)

For more on Cassius Dio, see selection 2.5. Here, Cassius Dio elaborates on Caesar's role in mediating the dispute between Cleopatra and her brother Ptolemy.

34. It seems that Cleopatra was pleading her case against her brother with Caesar through intermediaries, but as soon as she learned of his nature (for he had a propensity for affairs and had been with many other women every time the opportunity presented itself), she sent word to him, saying that her friends were betraying her and requesting that he let her speak for herself. She was a particularly beautiful woman and, at the time, being in her prime, she was conspicuously lovely. She also had an elegant voice and she knew how to use her charms to be attractive to everyone. Since she was beautiful to look at and to listen to, she was able to captivate everyone, even a man tired of love and past his prime. Thus, she thought it appropriate for her to meet with Caesar and she rested all her hopes of a successful outcome on her beauty. Therefore, she requested permission to go before Caesar and, when she received it, she put on all her finery so as to appear to him stately and pitiable at the same time. Once she had devised the perfect look, she entered the city (for she had been outside it) and approached the palace at night, keeping her arrival a secret from Ptolemy.

35. When Caesar saw her and heard her speak, he was immediately so captivated that he sent for Ptolemy on the spot, even though it was before dawn, and attempted to reconcile them. He found himself an advocate for the woman for whom previously he had been a judge. Therefore, the young Ptolemy, because of Caesar's actions and because he was surprised to see his sister inside the palace, was filled with anger and, rushing outside, shouted to the crowd that he had been betrayed. Tearing the crown from his head, he threw it down. In the resulting confusion, Caesar's soldiers seized Ptolemy and the Egyptians remained agitated. They might have taken the palace without resistance, as they attacked simultaneously by land and sea (for the Romans were not prepared for battle, since they thought the people were friendly), but Caesar, who was alarmed, came before them and, standing in safety, assured them that he would do anything

they wanted. After this, he attended their assembly and brought with him Ptolemy and Cleopatra. He read their father's will, in which it was written that they were to live together, following Egyptian custom, that they were to rule together, and the Roman people were to have guardianship of them. After doing this, he added that he, as dictator and as the most powerful of the people, would have control of the children and would carry out their father's wishes. He then granted the kingdom to both of them and to Arsinoe and the younger Ptolemy, their siblings, he granted Cyprus. Indeed, such fear seized him that he not only took nothing of Egypt's territories, but gave them some of his own.

3.7. Plutarch, *Life of Caesar* 49 (A.D. 110–15, Greek, prose)

For more on Plutarch, see selection 2.1. In this passage Plutarch describes the strategy by which Cleopatra secured a meeting with Caesar in order to gain his support against her brother.

Cleopatra, taking with her only Apollodorus the Sicilian out of all her entourage, traveling in a small boat, approached the palace as dusk was already falling; having no other means of escaping notice, she cloaked herself in a bedding sack and lay down flat. Apollodorus tied the bedding sack with a leather strap and carried it inside to Caesar. It is said that Caesar was taken with Cleopatra because of this first artifice, since she seemed intrepid and alluring, and, being no match for her charm and the pleasure of associating with her, he reconciled her with her brother, stipulating that she would have equal power. Later, when all were feasting in celebration of the treaty, one of Caesar's slaves who served as his barber, because of an unparalleled insecurity that caused him to scrutinize everything, listened closely and meddled and detected a plot against Caesar masterminded by Achillas the general and Pothinus the eunuch.[12] When Caesar was warned of the plot, he placed a guard in the banquet hall and executed Pothinus; Achillas, after fleeing to the army encampment, initiated against Caesar a serious war that was hard to win for someone facing a great city and army with a small force. In the conflict, Caesar first

---

12. Achillas and Pothinus were advisors of Ptolemy XIII.

was in danger of having no water supply; for the enemy had cut off the channels; second, the enemy blockaded his fleet and he had to drive them back with fire, which spread from the harbor and destroyed the great library; third, when fighting erupted around Pharos, he leapt from the causeway into a boat and brought help to the combatants, but, when the Egyptians came from all sides and surrounded him in their ships, he hurled himself into the water and swam away, only narrowly escaping. It is said that he was, at the time, carrying many documents that he would not let go, although he was the target of enemy missiles and was trying to stay afloat. Holding the documents above the water, he swam with his other hand, as his boat had long since sunk. Finally, when the king had retreated to the enemy, Caesar attacked, joined battle with him, and won; many men were killed and the king himself was nowhere to be found. Leaving Egypt to be ruled by Cleopatra, who shortly thereafter bore him a son called Caesarion by the Alexandrians, he hastened to Syria.

3.8. Caesar, *Civil War* 3.111–12 (46 B.C., Latin, prose)

Caesar provides one of the only firsthand accounts of this period, describing Cleopatra in the context of the civil war he fought against Pompey and writing about himself in the third person. His work takes the form of a commentarius, *purporting to be a collection of notes from which a history might be written. Throughout his works, Caesar emphasizes the exemplary qualities of his troops. In this passage he stresses the strategic importance of Pharos and the crucial role it played in his victory.*

111. Achillas, confident in his troops and contemptuous of Caesar's small army, occupied Alexandria, except for that part of the town Caesar and his forces were holding, and attempted to break into his house with the first assault. But Caesar withstood his attack, thanks to cohorts deployed throughout the streets. At the same time, there was fighting at the harbor, and this brought the greatest struggle by far. Simultaneously, scattered troops were fighting in many streets, and in a great throng the enemy was trying to occupy the long ships, of which there were fifty that had been sent to help Pompey and had returned home after the fighting in Thessaly ended. They were all *quadriremes* and *quinqueremes,* fitted out and equipped with everything needed for sailing; except for these twenty-two, which were

intended to be for guarding Alexandria, all were covered.[13] If they had taken these, they would take Caesar's fleet and hold the harbor and the whole sea in their power and cut off Caesar's supply line along with his hope of aid. And so, the battle was fought with as much intensity as it deserved, since the one side saw in it swift victory, and the other saw that their safety depended on it. Caesar gained the victory and burned all the ships, including those left in the dock-yards, because he was not able to keep watch so widely with so small an army, and at once he ferried soldiers to Pharos.

112. Pharos is a tower of great height on an island; its construc-tion is amazing and it took its name from the island. This facing island created the harbor of Alexandria; but under the earlier kings it was joined to the city by a bridge and a mole extended in its narrow course eight hundred paces into the sea. On it is housing for the Egyptians and a settlement the size of a town; and whenever ships deviate slightly from their course due to bad judgment or bad weather, the residents are in the habit of robbing them as pirates do. More-over, if those who hold Pharos are unwilling, it is not possible for ships to enter the harbor because the passage is so narrow. Caesar had been afraid of this and, thus, while the enemy was occupied with a battle, after stationing soldiers there, he took Pharos and placed a garrison there. By this strategy, he brought it about that food and reinforcements could safely be delivered to him in ships. Indeed, he sent word around to all the nearby provinces and summoned help from them. The fighting in the remaining parts of the city was such that the battle ended in a draw and neither side was routed—the narrowness of the place caused that—and when a few on each side had been killed, Caesar, encircling the most essential locations, fortified them by night. In this section of the city was a small section of the palace, which he first of all took as his own quarters, along with the theater attached to the dwelling, because it had a lookout place and access to the harbor and to the royal navy. In the following days, he increased the fortifications so that he had defenses in front of the wall and would not be forced into a battle. Meanwhile, the younger daughter of King Ptolemy, believing that the throne was vacant, left the palace, went over to Achillas, and began to direct the

---

13. A *quadrireme* had four banks of oars, while a *quinquereme* had five.

war herself. But soon disputes over leadership arose between them, and this increased the corruption among the soldiers; for each was winning over the troops' minds at great expense. While these things were going on among the enemy, Pothinus sent messengers to Achillas and urged him not to give up his attempts and to be of good courage. The messengers, however, were betrayed and apprehended and Caesar put Pothinus to death. These were the beginnings of the Alexandrian War.

3.9. [Caesar], *Alexandrian War* 31–33 (46–43 B.C., Latin, prose)

The Alexandrian War *circulated under Caesar's name but was most likely written by Aulus Hirtius, one of his officers. It continues the narrative of Caesar's* Civil War *and describes Caesar's capture of the city of Alexandria. Here, the author focuses on the end of Caesar's time in Alexandria.*

31. Caesar saw that his soldiers could not fight any more fiercely and that nothing much was being gained due to the difficulty of the terrain; he also noticed that the Alexandrians had left the highest part of their camp, not only because it was well fortified on its own, but also because they had run down to the battlefield out of enthusiasm, some for fighting and some for watching. Therefore, he ordered cohorts to go around the camp and attack the summit. He put Carfulenus in command, a man outstanding in character and in knowledge of military matters. When they arrived there, a few were defending the fort and, against them, our soldiers fought fiercely. The Alexandrians, terrified by the shouts from both sides and the battle, began to rush to every part of the camp. The spirits of our troops were so goaded by their disorder that they entered the camp at almost precisely the same time from all sides, although they took the highest point first. From there they then rushed down and killed a great multitude of the enemy in the camp. Most of the Alexandrians, as they fled this danger, threw themselves all at once from the rampart into the area next to the river. The first ones were crushed by the great fall into the trench of the fortification, but the rest had an easier escape. It is agreed that the king himself fled the camp, was taken aboard a ship, and perished when the whole number of those who were swimming to the nearest ships were drowned when the ship sank.

32. This matter was so fortunately and successfully carried out that Caesar, along with his cavalry, headed for Alexandria by the nearest overland route, confident of a great victory. He entered the city as a victor from the part of town occupied by the enemy garrison. Nor was he deceived in his conjecture that the enemy would cease to think of war once they learned of that battle. When he arrived, he reaped the well-deserved fruits of courage and generosity: for the whole multitude of Alexandrians threw down their arms, left their fort, donned the clothing with which suppliants were accustomed to beg victors for mercy, and brought out all the sacred objects that had the sanctity with which they were used to softening the bitter and angry hearts of kings. And so when Caesar arrived, they went to meet him and surrendered themselves to him. Caesar consoled them after placing them under his protection. After passing through the enemy fort, he came into the part of town he occupied as his men congratulated him. They were happy not only about the outcome of the war and the conflict, but also that his arrival was so auspicious.

33. Caesar, in control of Egypt and Alexandria, installed as kings those whom Ptolemy had designated in his will, and he implored the Roman people not to make any changes. Since the elder of the two boys, the king, had died, Caesar handed over the kingdom to the younger boy and to the elder of the two daughters, Cleopatra, who continued to enjoy his loyalty and protection. But he decided to remove Arsinoe, the younger daughter, from the kingdom, since, as we have shown, Ganymede[14] had been ruling recklessly in her name for a long time. This move was designed to prevent new frictions from arising among mutinous men, before time could reinforce the power of the kings. Caesar took with him the veteran sixth legion, but he left the others to strengthen the authority of the rulers, who could have neither the love of their people, since they had remained faithful friends of Caesar, nor could they have the authority that comes with experience, since they had ruled only a few days. Caesar also considered it appropriate to the dignity of our empire and to public welfare that, if the kings remained loyal, they should be safe through the protection of our troops; but, if they were ungrateful,

14. Ganymede was a eunuch who was an advisor to Arsinoe IV.

that they could be restrained by those same troops. Once he had completed and settled all this business, he departed into Syria.

3.10. Florus, *Epitome of Roman History* 2.13.53–60 (2nd c. A.D., Latin, prose)

Lucius Annaeus Florus wrote an abridged version of Roman history that focused on the wars predating Augustus's principate. Florus takes a pro-Roman point of view and, through his choice of content, implies that Augustus was responsible for bringing peace. Florus's work became a school text for Roman history and was used as such into the seventeenth century. In the following passage, Florus summarizes the events following Pompey's death.

Who would not believe that the war ended along with Pompey's life? But the ashes of the Thessalian inferno reignited much more fiercely and violently. Indeed, in Egypt there was a war against Caesar unrelated to party politics. Since Ptolemy, the king of Alexandria, had committed the greatest crime of the civil war and made a pact of friendship with Caesar and sealed it with Pompey's head, a reason was not lacking for Fortune to seek revenge for the shade of such a famous man. Cleopatra, the king's sister, falling at Caesar's knees in supplication, asked for part of the kingdom to be returned to her. Her beauty was obvious and was increased by the following conditions: because she seemed to have suffered an affront and because he so hated the king, who had accomplished Pompey's murder for the future of his party, not for Caesar, against whom he doubtless would have dared to commit the same crime, if he had the chance. When Caesar commanded that Cleopatra return to her kingdom, he was at once held hostage in the palace by the same men who had killed Pompey. He resisted with admirable bravery the force of a huge army, although he had only a few troops. First he held off the enemy weapons by burning nearby buildings and ships; next he escaped to the peninsula of Pharos; from there he was forced into the sea and swam with amazing good fortune to the nearest ships, his cloak left in the water either by fate or by plan, so that it was made a target for weapons and stones launched by the attacking enemy. Then, once on board by his men, at once he assailed the enemy on all sides and brought the cowardly and faithless people to justice for the murder of his son-in-law. Indeed, Theodotus, the director and originator of the whole war, along with Pothinus and Ganymede (inhuman demons that they were), were overtaken by death as they fled through various lands and seas. The king's body was found buried in a marsh still wearing his gold breastplate.

3.11. Lucan, *On the Civil War* 10.1–192, 332–546 (A.D. 60–65, Latin, verse)

Lucan was born in A.D. 39 in Spain but was educated in Rome, where he received training in the philosophy of the Stoics. He joined the inner circle of the emperor Nero but fell out of favor, perhaps because On the Civil War *betrayed a preference for the republican over the imperial system in its emphasis on the horrors of war and the loss of liberty experienced by the Roman people.*[15] *Lucan joined a conspiracy against Nero; when it was discovered in A.D. 65, he was forced to commit suicide. The republicanism of his poem may have been inspired by disillusionment with the empire as a result of Nero's excesses. In book ten Lucan describes, in colorful detail, the wonders Caesar experienced in Alexandria.*

1–192

As soon as Caesar, in pursuit of Pompey's head,   1
made landfall and stepped onto the fatal sands,
the leader's fortune challenged the fate of guilty
Egypt, to see whether the kingdom of Lagus[16] would be taken
by Roman arms, or the blade of Memphis would snatch from   5
the world the heads of both victor and vanquished. Your
        shade was useful,
Pompey, your soul snatched your father-in-law from death,
and prevented the Roman people from loving the Nile after
        you were gone.
Then Caesar confidently entered the African city,
which had pledged its allegiance with so violent a crime.   10

---

15. Conte 1999, 440.
16. Lagus: the father of Ptolemy I, the general of Alexander the Great who founded the Ptolemaic dynasty in Egypt. Memphis: a city in Egypt, here standing for Egypt as a whole.

But he gathered from the din of the crowd, as they lamented
that the fasces[17] and Roman laws were imposed upon their own,
that their hearts were at odds and their minds ambivalent;
    that Pompey
was not killed for him. Then, his face concealing his fear,
he calmly toured the shrines of the gods and the temples
    of ancient   15
powers, testaments to the ancient Macedonian strength,
and betrayed no interest in the beauty of the artifacts:
neither the gold and the ornaments of the gods, nor the city
    walls
attracted him as he descended eagerly into the hollow of a
    tomb.
There lies the insane issue of Pellaean Philip,   20
the lucky bandit, seized by a death that was the world's
avenger:[18] in a sacred shrine lay his limbs, limbs that should
    have been
scattered throughout the world; fortune spared
his soul, and it was destined for his rule to last to the end.
For he had been preserved as an object of ridicule, in case
    freedom   25
ever handed the world back to itself, born as an example for
    the world
of what not to do: that so many lands should not be ruled
by one man. He left behind the borders of Macedonia and the
    haunts
of his own people and he passed over Athens, the city made
    subject to
his father. Through the peoples of Asia he hastened, driven by   30
pressing fate, and accompanied by human carnage; he
    penetrated
every territory with his sword. He polluted newly discovered
    rivers,
the Euphrates with Persian blood and the Ganges with Indian.
He was a fatal blow to the lands, a thunderbolt that

17. The fasces were bundles of rods and axes that were the emblem of the office of
consul.
18. Alexander the Great.

blasted all peoples equally, a star of disaster 35
for the races. He was planning to sail his fleet to the outer sea
of Ocean. Neither fire nor flood
nor the Libyan desert nor Syrtean Ammon stood in his way.
He would have gone to the West, following the curve of the
    world,
and he would have circled the earth via the poles and drunk
    from the 40
Nile's source: but the final day came, and only nature
could put an end to this mad king.
Jealously, he took with him the power by which he had
conquered the world and, leaving no heir
to all his fortune, offered up the cities to bloody division.[19] 45
He died in Babylon, which was his. He was still feared by
    the Parthians.
For shame! The Eastern peoples feared more the sarisas[20]
than now they fear Roman javelins. Although we rule
as far as the North Pole and the realms of the West Wind
    and we
control the lands from which the burning South Wind comes,
    we will 50
yield the East to the master of the Parthians.[21] Parthia,
    ill-fated for the Crassi,
was a hassle-free province for a little town called Pella.[22]
Now the young king, coming from the Pelusian mouth
of the Nile, had put to rest the anger of the peaceable citizens:
with him as a hostage to insure peace, Caesar was safe in 55
Pellaean halls, when young Cleopatra, after bribing the guard
to undo the chains that closed the harbor of Pharos,
had her small ship rowed to the Macedonian royal residence
without Caesar knowing, Cleopatra the dishonor of Egypt,
the savage Fury of Latium, the unchaste downfall of Rome.
    As much as 60

19. For more on the division of Alexander the Great's empire, see selections 1.1 and 1.2.
20. The sarisa was a Macedonian spear.
21. Alexander the Great, who conquered Persia.
22. Crassus, a member of the First Triumvirate along with Caesar and Pompey, campaigned against the Parthians in 53 B.C. The mission was a failure, as Crassus was killed in battle and the Parthians captured the standards of the Roman army.

that Spartan woman routed Argos and Troy with her baneful
    beauty,
to the same degree, Cleopatra contributed to the furor in Italy.
She terrified the Capitoline (how can that be?) with her
    sistrum[23]
And she went after Roman standards with unwarlike Canopus,
about to lead Pharian triumphs featuring a captive Caesar;   65
and the outcome was in doubt on the Leucadian swells,[24]
whether a woman, and a non-Roman at that, would rule
    the world.
This scheme of hers owes its inception to that night on which
    the unchaste
daughter of the Ptolemies first lay with a Roman general.
Who would not grant indulgence to you, Antony, for your
    insane   70
love, when even the stalwart heart of Caesar burned for her?
In the middle of the frenzy and in the middle of the madness,
with Pompey's ghost haunting the halls,
Caesar, still wet with the blood of Thessalian slaughter,[25]
an adulterer, he added love to his mental turmoil and mixed
    with war   75
both illicit affairs and bastard children.
For shame! Forgetful of Pompey, he gave you, Julia, brothers
from an indecent mother, and, allowing the ousted party
to regroup in the far reaches of Libya,
he shamefully gave his attention to his Egyptian love affair,   80
since he preferred to give Egypt away rather than conquer
    it himself.
Cleopatra, relying on her looks, came to him looking sad
but not crying, carefully arrayed in pretended grief,
as much as was attractive, with her hair in disarray as if she
    had torn it,
and thus she began: "If nobility is anything to you, o greatest
    Caesar,   85

23. The sistrum was a rattle used in the worship of Isis.
24. Leucadian swells refer to the waters around the island of Leucas, off Actium,
where the Battle of Actium was fought in 31 B.C.
25. The Battle of Pharsalus.

I am the renowned daughter of Pharian Lagus,
an exile, forever deprived of the ancestral scepter,
unless your right hand restores me to my inherited destiny:
as a queen, I entreat you. You have come as a favorable
star to our people. I will not be the first woman   90
to rule the cities along the Nile: gender makes no difference
    in Egypt;
this land knows how to be ruled by a queen. Read my father's
last words, since he granted me equal rights of rule with my
brother, and made me his wife. My brother loves me,
or he would if he were free. But his emotions, like his troops,   95
Pothinus controls. I don't seek any of my father's power
for myself: just release our house from this immorality
and shame, and divest the lackey[26] of his arms
and reinstate the king. What vanity
the servant contemplates! He has beheaded Pompey   100
and now—may the fates avert it—he threatens you.
This one indignity suffices, Caesar, for you and for the world,
that Pompey's death was credited as Pothinus's crime."
She would have assailed Caesar's unyielding ears in vain,
but her expression bolstered her entreaties and her evil beauty   105
pleaded the case for her. She spent a sinful night with the
    corrupted judge.
Once the leader's agreement was acquired and purchased
    with great presents,
banquets followed the delight in such achievements,
and with a great commotion, Cleopatra exhibited her
    extravagance,
which was of a sort not yet part of the Roman tradition.   110
The space was like a temple, though a degenerate age would
    hardly build
such a temple; the paneled ceilings held rich decorations,
and thick gold had hidden the beams.
Nor did the palace shine with only a thin facing
of marble; agate too stood supporting its own weight,   115
and porphyry as well, and onyx was used as flooring

26. Pothinus.

that covered the whole hall. Egyptian ebony was not just
a veneer for the doorposts, but it stood in place of inexpensive
    oak,
a structural support rather than a decoration for the palace.
    Ivory
covered the foyer, and hand-dyed Indian tortoiseshell adorned   120
the doors, its markings punctuated by many emeralds.
The couches shown with precious stones, wares, glowing
yellow with jasper, burdened the tables, which dazzled with
technicolor cloths,[27] most dyed with the Tyrian hue that results
from repeated and lengthy steeping in the dye pots,   125
some bright with woven-in gold, and some afire with scarlet,
as is the custom on Egyptian looms to weave with multiple
    wefts.
Then came legions of slaves.
They varied in skin color and in age;
some had the dark hair of Libya and others had hair so tawny   130
that Caesar denied he had ever seen such red hair
in the lands watered by the Rhine; some were dark-skinned
and had woolly hair that receded from their foreheads;
there were also youths kept soft by the knife
and bereft of their manhood: opposite were older boys   135
who, nevertheless, had scarcely any beard on their faces.
There the monarchs reclined along with Caesar
whose power was greater; and the queen, her dangerous
    beauty enhanced
by cosmetics, not content with her own sovereignty nor her
    brother-husband,
decked out in the spoils of the Red Sea,[28] she wore riches   140
on her head and neck and felt the weight of her jewelry.
Her alabaster breasts shone through diaphanous Sidonian
    cloth,
which had been woven tightly by the Oriental shuttle and
    then loosened
by the Egyptian needle that relaxes the threads in the taut cloth.

27. This phrase was inserted by Housman (1958).
28. Pearls.

Here, they place rounds cut from the woods of Atlas   145
on snow-white tusks, of the sort that had not passed
before Caesar's eyes even when he defeated Juba. How blind,
    how
insane with frenzied ambition they must have been to display
    their wealth
to one fighting a civil war, to set an armed guest's
mind on fire. Even if Caesar were not ready, in his sinful war,   150
to seek wealth at the price of the world, take for instance
the leaders of old and the names from a time of modest means:
the Fabricii and the severe Curii, let him recline here who
was plucked from his humble plowing in Etruria to be consul.
Even he will desire a magnificent triumph for his country.   155
They laid out a banquet on golden service: whatever the land,
    the air,
the sea, and the Nile had to offer, whatever extravagance raving
with mad ostentation sought out anywhere on earth (though not
motivated by hunger). They served up many birds and animals
    that the
Egyptians consider divine, a crystal pitcher offers   160
Nile water for their hands, and goblets of precious stone
hold wine (but not wine from Egyptian grapes: rather it was
esteemed Falernian which, in a few years, Meroe[29] ages
by inducing the untamed vintage to ferment.
They don crowns of flowering spikenard   165
and roses that bloom all year round, they scent
their perfume-drenched hair with cinnamon,
which has not yet diminished its fragrance in foreign
air but still carries the scent of its native land,
and also with cardamom, freshly and locally harvested.   170
Caesar takes a lesson in wasting wealth plundered from the
    world,
and it embarrasses him that he fought a war against a pauper
like Pompey, and he wishes there were a cause to declare war
    on Egypt.
When pleasant satiety curbed his hunger for food

---

29. Meroe: the capital of Ethiopia.

and wine, Caesar began to fill the nights with   175
long discussions. He addressed friendly words to
linen-clad Acoreus, who reclined at the head of the table:
"Aged sir, student of sacred matters, whom the gods protect
(as your age demonstrates), relate the origins of the Egyptian
people and the lay of their lands and the customs of the
    population   180
and the nature of your gods and their worship; teach me what
    is inscribed on your ancient temples and show me the gods
who wish to be understood. If your ancestors instructed
Athenian Plato in their rituals, what guest was ever more worthy
of hearing this lecture or more capable of mastering its content?   185
Indeed, what I heard about Pompey brought me to the
    Pharian cities,
but your reputation brought me here as well; even in the
    midst of battles
I always had time for the stars, the zones of the sky, and the
    heavenly bodies,
nor will the Julian year be second to Eudoxus's calendar.
But, although such excellence resides in me,   190
and such love of truth, there is nothing I would prefer to learn
than the secrets that river has concealed for so many centuries
and its unknown source: if I had certain hope of seeing
the springs of the Nile, I would give up civil war."[30]

*There follows Acoreus's description of the Nile. After the excursus, Lucan
returns to the banquet scene.*

332–546

And so they spent the middle part of the night
as if in safe and secure peace. But the insane mind of Pothinus,
once marred by cursed murder, was never free from
thoughts of crime: Pompey's killer now considers   335
nothing forbidden. Ghosts haunt his heart, and the
vengeful goddesses transform his frenzy into new demons.
He thinks his lowly hands worthy of that blood as well,

---

30. Lake Victoria was discovered to be the ultimate source of the Nile in the nineteenth century.

the blood which Fortune intends to pour over the defeated
    senators,
that penalty for civil war, the avenging of the senate, 340
was almost granted to a slave. Banish this crime far off,
Fates, lest Caesar's head roll without Brutus present.
Otherwise, the Roman tyrant's punishment merely adds guilt
    to Egypt,
and the lesson goes unlearned. Rash Pothinus constructs
his doomed plot and, rather than planning to commit murder
    in secret, 345
he openly declares war on the undefeated general.
His life of crime has given him such audacity that he orders
Caesar's head cut off and put next to yours, Pompey;
and he commanded his faithful slaves to deliver a message
to Achillas, his co-conspirator in Pompey's assassination. 350
The peace-loving young Ptolemy had put Achillas in charge
of the military and had given himself no authority in that area:
Achillas had the power of life and death over all, even the king.
    Pothinus said,
"Do you think it wise at this time to rest on your soft couches
    and enjoy
sweet sleep? Cleopatra has taken over the palace; Pharos[31] is
    not just 355
betrayed but it is made a gift for the enemy. Do you alone
    hesitate to
rush to our mistress's chambers? That evil sister married her
    brother,
and now is led as the bride of Latium: rushing between
husbands, she is Egypt's master but Rome's whore.
Cleopatra must have conquered aged Caesar with drugs. 360
As for the boy, you'd be a fool to trust him, whom just one night
of incestuous embraces and unlawful lust
hidden under the name of loving devotion
would cause to sell both your head and mine perhaps for
    the price

---

31. The island (and eponymous lighthouse) at the entrance to the harbor of Alexandria. Here used by extension to signify all of Egypt.

of just one kiss. We will pay on the cross or at the stake   365
if he finds his sister attractive. There is no help for us
now: on this side is the royal husband, on that the adulterer
     Caesar.
And we are, I confess, guilty in the eyes of so harsh a judge:
whom of us does Cleopatra not believe guilty?
Only he (if there is such a man) who has not had his way
     with her.   370
I charge you to step forward by the crime we committed all
     together,
by the sin we committed in vain, by the pact struck on
     Pompey's blood:
incite war with a sudden disturbance, let us disrupt the   _
     wedding night with
bloodshed and let us slaughter our unkind mistress in her
     own bed
along with whoever shares that bed. We should not shy
     away from our daring   375
because of the good fortune that has elevated the Roman
     leader
and made him master of the world: the glory belongs to us
     as well;
our success, too, comes from Pompey's death. Look upon
     the shore:
it gives hope to our plot; see what power the sea, stained
     with a consul's blood,
gives us; look how Pompey's tomb, made from   380
a little dust, does not cover his whole body.
The man you fear is just like Pompey. We are not of pure
     breeding
(why does that matter?), nor do we command the resources
     and power of nations: but crime is our talent and our
     destiny. Fortune delivers
those men into our hands: look—another, nobler victim   385
approaches. Let us pacify the peoples of Italy
with a second murder: slitting Caesar's throat
will guarantee this for me: that the Roman people
will love those guilty in Pompey's murder. Why do we fear

the great name and army of Caesar, when without them 390
he is just a soldier? Tonight will put an end to civil war
and perform last rites for nations and send to the shades
the head owed to them all along. Go fiercely
for Caesar's throat; let the Egyptian youth furnish this
to their king and let the Romans answer for themselves.
    Make no delay. 395
You will find him satiated with food and wine and ready for
love; take courage, the gods will grant you the prayers
of so many Catos and Brutuses."[32] Not indolently did Achillas
obey the one who urged this evil: he gave his troops the signal
    to go forth
(though without the usual fanfare) and thus did not betray his
    army's 400
position with trumpet blasts. In haste, he seized all the
    implements
of savage war. The greatest part of his forces
was drawn from the common people of Latium; but their minds
were so forgetful and so corrupted by foreign license
that they marched under the command of a slave and a
    follower 405
when they should not have bowed even to a pharaoh.
These mercenaries have no faith, no honor,
their hands were bought: the biggest payday is the greatest cause;
they go for Caesar's throat not for their own reasons, but for
small wages. What justice? Where does our ill-fated 410
society not find civil wars? The forces,
after they left Thessaly, rage on the banks of the Nile
at the state of their country. What more would the Lagid
    dynasty
have dared, if they had taken Pompey in? Every right hand gives
the gods what they are owed, and no Roman can 415
legitimately be idle. It pleases the gods thus to cleave
the Roman state; the people are not truly split between
Pompey and his father-in-law: an underling has stirred up
this civil war and Achillas takes the role of a Roman;

32. Champions of the Republic.

unless the fates keep them from Caesar's blood,   420
they will prevail. Both sides arrived swiftly.
The palace, distracted by the feast, was ripe
for plots and Caesar's blood might have been shed
over royal goblets and his head might have fallen upon
the table. The attackers, however, feared a night assault,   425
lest Ptolemy be killed in the confusion of an
uncontrolled situation. Putting too much faith in their swords,
they failed to seize their opportunity, cocky and contemptuous
of their chance. It did not seem an irreparable loss to those slaves
that they had put off the hour of Caesar's murder.   430
He was spared and would pay his penalty in daylight;
one night was granted to the general and he lived, by the grace
of Pothinus, and to see another sunrise.
The morning star shone from Mount Casius and welcomed
the day to Egypt, which was already scorching at sunrise,   435
when far off from the ramparts a battle line comes into view,
not scattered and ill-prepared troops, but in perfect formation
they advance on the enemy with an even front line: they are
    ready
to fight hand to hand and to bravely charge. Caesar,
    distrusting the city walls,
closed the gates and sequestered himself in the palace,   440
a refuge unworthy of him. He did not even have control of
the whole palace: he had mustered a few troops in
one wing. Anger and fear assailed his mind,
and he was afraid of the attack and angry that he was afraid.
Just as a noble beast rages when confined in a small cage   445
and shatters its mad teeth on the bars as he tries to bite
    through them,
and just as your flames, Vulcan, would seethe in the Sicilian
    caves,
if someone capped the summit of Aetna.
Bold Caesar, who recently under Thessalian Haemus's cliff
was not afraid of all the Roman leaders and the senate's forces   450
and Pompey the general, though his cause did not justify his
    hopes,
convinced himself he would beat the odds.

Now he fears the plots of slaves and is assailed by weapons
as he hides inside a house. Neither the Alanians, nor the
    Scythians,
nor the Moors who mock a guest by stabbing him could have   455
harmed Caesar, but he seeks refuge in a house, though the
    expanse
of the Roman world is not sufficient for him, though he thinks
    India
and Tyrian Gades are too small a kingdom. He is like an
    unarmed boy,
or a woman in an occupied city: all his hopes of survival rest
    on a
closed door, and he traverses the halls with uncertain steps,   460
Nevertheless, he is never far from the king, whom he makes his
constant companion, to punish him and to offer him as an
alternate victim, even ready to toss your head, Ptolemy, against
those slaves, should he lack arrows and flaming projectiles.
Thus Medea is believed to have awaited her father,   465
prepared with her sword and her brother's head,
since she feared his revenge for her usurping and her flight.
Nevertheless, the dire straits compel Caesar to try for peace,
    and a royal
messenger was sent to deliver the absent dictator's reproach to
the fierce slaves and to determine on whose authority they
    initiated hostilities.   470
But neither the law nor the treaties sacred to the peoples
was strong enough to keep the king's spokesman and mediator
from dying by the sword. Though who would consider such
    deeds
worth mentioning among the number of your crimes,[33] Egypt,
guilty of so many monstrous acts? Neither the Thessalian land,
nor the empty kingdom of Juba, nor Pontus and the disloyal
    rebellion   475
of Pharnaces,[34] nor the land the frigid Hiberus[35] demarcates,
    nor the

33. Part of this sentence was composed by Housman (1958) to improve the sense.
34. Pharnaces rebelled against his father, Mithradates.
35. Spain.

barbarian Syrtes[36] has dared as many crimes as rich Egypt
has committed. War presses on all sides: weapons
rain down on the palace and the household gods tremble.
There is no battering ram to breach the walls in one blow   480
and break into the palace, there is no siege engine,
nor do flames do the work for them: rather, the young troops,
without any strategy, split up and surround the palace,
and the battle line never musters its full force.
The fates oppose them and Fortune acts as the city's bulwark.   485
The palace also weathered attacks from ships, where the
rich dwelling thrust its bold profile into the harbor.
But Caesar was its ubiquitous defender and
warded off the incursions with swords and fire:
he had such presence of mind that, although he was besieged,   490
he carried on like an invader. He ordered torches soaked
in pitch launched at the sails of the tightly massed fleet.
The flames were not slow to lick the flaxen ropes and
the decks caulked with wax: at once the
rowing benches and the high rigging were ablaze.   495
Now the almost half-burned fleet sinks into the waves;
now the enemy and their weapons dot the water's surface. Nor
did the flames hit only the ships: houses bordering the shore
caught fire as the heat engulfed them, aided by
the South wind. The flames, whipped up by the wind,   500
leapt from roof to roof with a motion that can only be likened
to a meteor as it cuts a furrow across the heavens,
and burns not with any fuel but by air alone.
The conflagration temporarily distracted the population
from besieging the palace as they set about to save the city.
    Caesar   505
wasted no time in sleep, but took advantage of the distraction to
board a ship in the dark of night: as always, using to his
    advantage
sudden developments in a battle. On this occasion too,
    seizing the
moment, he occupied Pharos, gateway to the harbor. This island

36. Parts of the coast between Carthage and Cyrene that were treacherous for ships.

once stood in the middle of the sea (back in the days of   510
the prophet Proteus), but now it lies adjacent to the city walls.[37]
This island offered Caesar twin benefits in war.
First, thanks to Pharos, Caesar robbed the enemy of an
    escape via
its narrow entrance, and when he saw the gateway to the sea
open, he no longer put off the fate and punishment   515
Pothinus deserved. He did not suffer the cross, the stake,
or the teeth of wild beasts, as would have been appropriate,
but he experienced the death Pompey had. Second, Arsinoe,
smuggled out by the trickery of her slave Ganymede, infiltrated
Caesar's enemies. She controlled their camp, as they lacked
    a king   520
and she was a member of the royal family. With a just sword,
she stabbed Achillas, the vile slave of Ptolemy.
Now another victim has been sacrificed to your ghost, Pompey,
but Fortune still thinks it not enough. Heaven forbid that
this should be the end of your revenge. Not if the king
    himself paid   525
the ultimate price would it be sufficient, not if the whole dynasty
of Lagus did. Only when Roman blades plunge into Caesar
will Pompey be avenged. But the frenzy did not end once
its instigator was removed: for his forces return to arms
under the command of Ganymede and they wage many battles   530
with Mars on their side. With Caesar in such danger, a
    single day
could have become famous and gone down in history.
While his men were closely packed in the narrow mole,
and while he prepared to move the battle onto the ships,
suddenly he is beset by fear of battle: 535
here tightly massed ships protect the shore,
here foot soldiers hem him in from behind. There is no way
    to safety,
no refuge, no courage; there is scarcely even hope of a noble
    death.

37. A causeway had been built to connect the island to Alexandria. Proteus was a sea
god with prophetic powers.

Thus, Caesar would be conquered neither by the flight of his
   troops
nor by piles of fallen men, but rather with no blood at all.   540
A captive of the place he happened to choose, he hesitated:
   he was
uncertain whether to fear death or to hope for it; he looked back
at the crowded ranks and saw Scaeva, already deserving of
   everlasting
fame because he alone, on your plains, Epidamnus, held at bay
Pompey, who surmounted the collapsing walls.[38]   545

CLEOPATRA AND CAESARION IN ROME

Cleopatra accompanied Caesar to Rome, much to the vexation of the
Romans. Cleopatra's presence in Rome—even if she was staying not
in Caesar's own residence but in a house he owned across the Tiber—
was a scandal, as Caesar was married and Cleopatra was a foreigner.

3.12. Cassius Dio, *Roman History* 43.27.3 (A.D. 202, Greek, prose)

*For more on Cassius Dio, see selection 2.5. Here, Dio describes the reaction
Cleopatra received in Rome.*

   Caesar received the most blame from everyone because of his love
for Cleopatra, not his relationship with her in Egypt (for that was
only speculation), but for that which happened in Rome. She came
to the city with her husband[39] and stayed in a house owned by Caesar; as a result, he too was disparaged on account of both of them.
He cared nothing about this, however, and enrolled them as allies of
the Romans.

3.13. Suetonius, *The Divine Julius Caesar* 52 (A.D. 119–21, Latin,
prose)

*For more on Suetonius, see selection 3.1. Here, Suetonius elaborates on
Caesar's womanizing and reports a surprising legal maneuver.*

---

38. The poem ends abruptly; perhaps Lucan's death interrupted its composition.
39. The thirteen-year-old Ptolemy XIV.

Caesar also had affairs with queens, among whom was Eunoe the Moor, wife of Bogudes. Naso tells us Caesar gave many valuable gifts to her and to her husband. But most famously he had an affair with Cleopatra, with whom he often extended banquets until dawn. He would have gone with her in her luxury barge through Egypt almost up to Ethiopia, if his army had not refused to follow. Finally, he called her to Rome and only sent her back to Egypt after granting her the highest honors and awards. He also allowed her to name her son after him.[40] Some Greek writers relate that the boy was like Caesar in both appearance and gait. Mark Antony also asserted in the senate that Caesar had acknowledged the boy as his own and that Gaius Matius, Gaius Oppius, and other friends of Caesar knew it. Oppius, as if the matter clearly required his defense and protection, published a book stating that the boy Cleopatra said was Caesar's son in fact was not. Helvius Cinna, a tribune of the plebs, revealed to many people that he had written and prepared a law, which Caesar had instructed him to get passed in Caesar's absence, stating that it was permitted to take wives, whichever ones and however many were desired, for the purpose of producing children. But lest there be any doubt as to his extremely disgraceful lewdness and adultery, let us recall that the elder Curio in one of his speeches called Caesar every woman's man and every man's woman.

3.14. Appian, *Civil War* 2.102 (early 2nd c. A.D., Greek, prose)

For more on Appian, see selection 2.3. Caesar's triumph in 46 B.C. included a significant tribute to Cleopatra.

They say that the money carried in the triumph amounted to sixty thousand five hundred talents and two thousand eight hundred twenty-two gold crowns, which weighed twenty thousand four hundred fourteen pounds.[41] From this sum, immediately after the triumph Caesar made payments of what he owed and more, with each soldier collecting five thousand Attic drachmas, each centurion double that, and each infantry and cavalry commander four times that. To each

---

40. Caesarion, whose official name was Ptolemy XV Caesar.
41. It is difficult to estimate with any reliability the amount of money this would represent today. During the Roman Republic, a craftsman might earn one denarius (silver coin) per day. At this wage a talent would be approximately seventeen years' pay.

plebeian, he gave one Attic mina.[42] He also sponsored various spectacles with horses, music, a mock infantry battle with a thousand soldiers on each side, a mock cavalry battle with two hundred on each side, a mixed combat of cavalry and infantry together, a battle of elephants with twenty on each side, and a mock naval battle with four thousand rowers and one thousand soldiers on each side. He built a temple to Venus Genetrix,[43] as he had vowed before the Battle of Pharsalus. He also set up a precinct around the temple for a forum for the Romans. It was not for commerce, but a meeting place like the Persians have, where one can seek justice or learn the laws. He set up a beautiful statue of Cleopatra next to the statue of the goddess; it still stands there today. He instituted a census of the people, and it is said that he found half the number there had been before the war, so much had the rivalry between Caesar and Pompey reduced the population.

THE IDES OF MARCH

Caesar was assassinated in a meeting of the Senate on March 15, 44 B.C. A conspiracy had been hatched against him by men who believed he was becoming a king. Marcus Brutus, Cassius, and others felt it was their duty to save the Republic from tyranny.

3.15. Suetonius, *The Divine Julius Caesar* 81–82 (A.D. 119–21, Latin, prose)

For more on Suetonius, see selection 3.1. It was common in the ancient world to claim that a catastrophe had been preceded by bad omens. Many of those listed here are canonical and are mentioned in the context of other disasters as well.

81. Caesar's impending murder was heralded by obvious signs. A few months before, the settlers who colonized Capua under the Julian law were dismantling ancient tombs in order to build houses.[44] Indeed they were particularly eager for the task since they found a hoard of

---

42. A mina was a small amount of money.
43. The epithet Genetrix highlights Venus's role as a mother goddess and the ancestor of the Julian family.
44. Julius Caesar distributed the territory to colonists.

antique vases and, in one tomb, said to be the tomb of Capys, the founder of Capua, a bronze tablet was found with a Greek inscription: "When the bones of Capys are unearthed, it will come to pass that his descendent will die by kindred hands but soon be avenged at Italy's great cost."[45] The source of this story is Cornelius Balbus, a great friend of Caesar, and, thus, no one should think it invented or fictional. In the following days, herds of horses, which Caesar had set free after dedicating them to the Rubicon when he crossed it, completely gave up grazing and began to weep copiously. The haruspex[46] Spurinna warned Caesar as he sacrificed, "beware of danger, which will come no later than the Ides of March."[47] Moreover, on the day before the Ides, a wren, also known as the king bird, flew into the hall of Pompey[48] carrying a sprig of laurel and was pursued and torn apart by a host of various birds that swooped in from a nearby grove. Indeed, on that night, to which the day of his death put an end, Caesar dreamed that he flew through tranquil air above the clouds and that he shook the hand of Jove. His wife Calpurnia dreamed that the apex of the roof fell and that Caesar was in her arms, impaled. Suddenly the bedroom doors flew open on their own. Because of these signs and his infirm health, he hesitated for a long time as to whether he should stay home and put off making his proposal to the Senate. Finally, at Decimus Brutus's urging that he not disappoint those who were assembled and awaiting his arrival, he set out a little before noon and, when a passerby handed him a note detailing the plot to assassinate him, he put it with the other papers he was carrying in his left hand, as if he would read it soon.[49] Then, when a number of victims had been sacrificed, although he was not able to obtain favorable omens, Caesar entered the hall in contempt of the ritual and mocking Spurinna for making false predictions, since the Ides of

---

45. Capys was a companion of Aeneas who founded Capua in Italy.
46. The haruspex was a religious official who interpreted omens by examining the entrails of sacrificed animals.
47. March 15.
48. In the complex of buildings centered on the Theater of Pompey, there was a meeting hall, which was deemed a more secure meeting place for the senate than the senate house in the Roman Forum.
49. Decimus Brutus was a relative and fellow conspirator of Marcus Brutus, one of the principal conspirators against Caesar.

March had arrived without harm to him; Spurinna replied that the
Ides had indeed come but had not yet gone.

82. As Caesar took his seat, the conspirators gathered around him,
as if in deference. Tillius Cimber, who had taken a leading role, came
close as if to ask Caesar something. When Caesar shook his head and
gestured as if to put off the inquiry to another time, Cimber grabbed
his toga by both shoulders. Caesar protested, "This is force!" One of
the Casca brothers stabbed him from behind, just below the throat.
Caesar stabbed at Casca's arm with his stylus and tried to break free
when another blow prevented him. When he realized that he was
surrounded on all sides by drawn daggers, he covered his head with
his toga, at the same time loosening the garment and letting out its
length so that he might fall modestly with the lower part of his body
covered. And so he was stabbed twenty-three times. After groaning
at the first blow, he did not make a sound, although some have
reported that, as Marcus Brutus attacked him, he said, "Even you,
my boy?"[50] As all the senators scattered in shock, Caesar lay dead
until three slave boys placed his body on a litter, one arm hanging
off, and carried him home. Among so many wounds, the physician
Antistius found that only one was lethal: the second one, which he
had taken in the chest. The conspirators agreed that the corpse of
the slain man should be thrown into the Tiber, that his property
should be confiscated, and that his decrees should be overturned,
but out of fear of Mark Antony, the Consul, and Lepidus, the Master
of the Horse, they refrained.

3.16. Plutarch, *Life of Antony* 12–14 (A.D. 110–15, Greek, prose)

For more on Plutarch, see selection 2.1. The Ides of March event was sig-
nificant for Antony as well as Caesar. Plutarch highlights the role Antony
played in the events leading up to and following Caesar's assassination.

---

50. The statement often reported as "Et tu, Brute?" Suetonius and Cassius Dio both
quote Caesar in Greek. Explanations for the Greek phrase, which, literally translated,
means "Even you, my child?" vary. Some consider it a reference to an affair Caesar had
with Brutus's mother, Servilia, while others see it as Caesar's expression of surprise that
Brutus, whom he considered a friend and for whom he had done several favors, would
betray him. James Russell (1980, 123–28) surveys the evidence for these claims and offers
an alternative: that the phrase is an insult idiomatic in Greek, meaning something like "To
hell with you!"

12. Antony unwittingly offered the conspirators the perfect excuse. The Romans had a festival of the Lycaea, which they call Lupercalia,[51] and Caesar, decked out in triumphal attire and sitting on the speakers' platform in the Forum, was observing the runners. Many young men, patricians and politicians, were running back and forth, anointed with oil, playfully chasing everyone they encountered with thongs of shaggy goatskin. Among these runners was Antony, who departed from the traditional ritual and ran up to the speakers' platform and, lifted up by the other runners, he placed a diadem entwined with a laurel wreath on Caesar's head, as if to say it was fitting for him to be a king. When Caesar demurred and turned away, the people noticed and applauded. Antony brought it back and again Caesar brushed it aside. They disputed in this way for some time, as a few of Antony's friends cheered him on when he pressed the crown upon Caesar and the whole crowd shouted their approval when Caesar refused it. The amazing thing was that, although they were already, for all practical purposes, under the rule of a king, they rejected the title, as if it represented the loss of freedom. Then Caesar, annoyed, stood up from the speakers' platform, opened his toga, baring his neck, and shouted that anyone who wished to should cut his throat. The wreath was placed on one of Caesar's statues, but some tribunes of the people removed it. The people followed them, shouting their approval, but Caesar removed them from office.

13. These events encouraged Brutus and Cassius:[52] enlisting those of their friends who were trustworthy in the plot, they inquired about Antony. Everyone was eager to admit him, but Trebonius opposed it: he said that, at the time when many went to meet Caesar as he returned from Spain, he and Antony had traveled together and shared a tent and that he had gently and discreetly inquired about Antony's opinion, but that, while Antony understood him, he did not approve of the plot, but he said nothing to Caesar, instead faithfully keeping the secret. After this, they thought of murdering Antony after they had killed Caesar; Brutus stopped them on the

51. Lupercalia was a fertility ritual in which young men ran through the city attempting to strike young women with leather thongs; being hit by the thongs was thought to insure fertility. The festival was also associated with the purification of the city.
52. Brutus and Cassius led the conspiracy to assassinate Caesar.

grounds that a deed undertaken in the name of the law and justice should be pure and uncorrupted by injustice. Some, afraid of Antony's strength and political reputation, assigned several of the conspirators to watch him, so that when Caesar entered the Senate and the deed was about to be done, they might restrain him by engaging him in some urgent conversation.

14. The plot was carried out as it had been devised and, when Caesar fell in the Senate, Antony immediately went into hiding, dressed as a slave. When he was certain the men were not harming anyone else, but were assembled on the Capitoline, he persuaded them to come down, taking his son as a hostage; he even dined with Cassius, and Lepidus with Brutus.[53] Calling a meeting of the Senate, he recommended amnesty and the assignment of provinces to the supporters of Brutus and Cassius; the Senate ratified these measures and voted that none of the motions brought by Caesar should be changed. Antony left the Senate a most illustrious man: he was credited with averting civil war and demonstrating great discretion and diplomacy in matters that carried unusual difficulties and disturbances. The mood of the public, however, quickly shook Antony from these reasoned considerations and he steadfastly hoped that, with Brutus out of the picture, he might be the most powerful man. It happened that, when Caesar's body was carried out, as was the custom, Antony delivered the eulogy in the Forum. When he noticed that the crowd was incredibly moved and enthralled, he added to his praises pity and outrage at what Caesar had suffered. As he ended his speech, he held aloft the slain man's tunic, bloodied and torn by the blades, and called the men responsible for these things murderers polluted by blood-guilt. The extent of his anger incited the crowd to cremate Caesar's body in the Forum after gathering up benches and tables and then, lighting torches from the pyre, to take them to the homes of the assassins and attack them.

CLEOPATRA LEAVES ROME

After Caesar's assassination, Cleopatra had to make a hasty escape from Rome. She returned to Alexandria, and the Romans were not sorry to see her go.

53. Lepidus, Octavian, and Antony formed the Second Triumvirate.

3.17. Cicero, *Letters to Atticus* 14.8.1, 14.20.2, 15.1.5, 15.4.4, 15.15.2 (44 B.C., Latin, prose)

Cicero is most famous for the speeches he made as he argued law cases, but he also wrote hundreds of letters to his close friend Atticus. These selections come from the year 44 B.C., in the months following the assassination of Julius Caesar. Cicero wrote from various places in central Italy: Sinuessa, Puteoli, Arpinum (his hometown), and Astura. As we can see from the following selections, Cicero's letters often address many topics in quick succession and telegraphic style. Many of his comments on current events are cryptic, and many of the incidents to which he refers are otherwise unknown. While we do not know the specifics of Cicero's involvement with Cleopatra, his opinion of her was no secret.

14.8.1

April 16, 44 B.C., Sinuessa
Cicero to Atticus

You thought, when you wrote, that I was by now at my place on the coast; but I received your letter on April 15 at my cabin near Sinuessa. About Marius: it is for the best, though I feel sorry for Lucius Crassus's grandson. I am glad, however, that our Brutus approves of Antony. About the moderate and kindly letter you say Junia brought, Paulus gave me one sent to him by his brother; at the end it said there was a conspiracy against him and that he knew it on certain authority. This information did not please me and it pleased him much less. The queen's[54] flight doesn't annoy me at all. Please write to me what Clodia has done.

14.20.2

May 11, 44 B.C., Puteoli
Cicero to Atticus

First, thanks for what you have done concerning my affairs, both the payment and the Albianus business. But about your Buthrotum affairs, while I was in Pompeii, Antony came to Misenum. He left there before I heard that he had arrived; from that fact you know

54. Cleopatra.

what you can expect. So we will talk about Buthrotum at Rome. Lucius Antonius's[55] speech for the assembly is terrible, but Dolabella's is outstanding. After that performance, he can keep the money, so long as he pays on the Ides.[56] I was sad to learn of Tertulla's miscarriage. The Cassii have to keep up with the Bruti in numbers.[57] About the queen: I hope that it is true about her and about that Caesar.[58] That answers your first letter; now I come to your second.

15.1.5

May 17, 44 B.C., Puteoli
Cicero to Atticus

About Brutus asking me to meet before the Kalends:[59] he too has written to me and perhaps I will do it. But I don't exactly know what he wants. What counsel can I offer him, when I myself need counsel and when he has more regard for his own legacy than for peace in our own time? The rumor about the queen is abating. I beg you, do something about Flamma if you can.

15.4.4

May 24, 44 B.C., Arpinum
Cicero to Atticus

About Menedemus: I wish it had not been true. About the queen: I hope it is true. Let us discuss other things face to face, most of all what our friends should do, what I should do, if Antony besieges the senate with his army. I was afraid that the courier would open this letter if I gave it to him and so, since you needed a reply, I sent it by special messenger.

15.15.2

June 13 (?), 44 B.C., Astura
Cicero to Atticus

55. The brother of Mark Antony, who, along with Fulvia, Mark Antony's wife, supported the Perusians in their rebellion against Octavian.
56. The middle of the month.
57. Tertia (Tertulla is a pet name) was the half sister of Marcus Brutus and the wife of Gaius Cassius.
58. Caesarion.
59. The first of the month.

I detest the queen. The guarantor of her promises, Ammonius, knows that my feelings are justified. Indeed, the promises concerned literary matters, appropriate to my status, and of the sort I would be comfortable discussing publicly. Moreover, Sara, in addition to the fact that he is a dishonest man, I found insulting to me. Only once I met with him at my house: when I asked him politely what his business was, he said he came seeking Atticus. I cannot recall the arrogance of the queen, when she lived on an estate across the Tiber, without great anguish. Let me have nothing to do with them; do they think I have no spirit or that I scarcely have the capacity for indignation?

APOTHEOSIS

After his death, Julius Caesar was declared a god. This was as much a strategic move on Octavian's part as an honor for a great Roman. By deifying his adoptive father, Octavian became the son of a god. Perhaps because he was not Caesar's biological son, Octavian felt the need to emphasize his relationship with Caesar in his quest for power. The fact that Caesar had, in his will, adopted Octavian and made him his heir gave Octavian legitimacy even though he was only nineteen years old in 44 B.C. Others felt they had a claim to Caesar's legacy as well. Mark Antony put himself forward as the natural successor to Caesar and called for revenge on those who had killed him. Cleopatra, of course, considered Caesarion the only true son of Caesar and presumably had hopes for his future.

3.18. Suetonius, *The Divine Julius Caesar* 88 (A.D. 119–21, Latin, prose)

For more on Suetonius, see selection 3.1. Here, Suetonius enumerates some of the posthumous honors Caesar received.

He died in his fifty-sixth year and was returned to the company of the gods, not just by nominal decree, but by the mandate of the people, because, at the games, which his heir Augustus sponsored in honor of his deification, a comet shone continuously for seven days. It rose just before sunset and was believed to be the spirit of Caesar welcomed to the heavens. For this reason, a star was added to the forehead of his statue. The senate declared that the hall in which he was killed be sealed shut, that the Ides of March be designated Parricide Day, and that the senate should never meet on that day.

3.19. Ovid, *Metamorphoses* 15.746–870 (A.D. 7, Latin, verse)

This passage reflects the Greco-Roman belief that great mortals might, after death, undergo a transformation to a divine state (apotheosis). Here, Ovid describes how and why Julius Caesar became a god, as evidenced by the appearance of the Julian Star (actually a comet) after Caesar's assassination in 44 B.C.[60] *This passage occurs near the end of Ovid's epic poem, the* Metamorphoses, *the theme of which is transformation. Ovid explores this theme from the beginnings of the universe, through Greek and Roman mythology, to the reign of Augustus.*

Caesar is a god in his own city; Caesar, who, outstanding
in military and civic life, was turned into a new star and a comet,
not so much by wars completed with triumphs and by
achievements at home and by swift renown of his deeds,
as by his offspring; for no achievement of Caesar's deeds   750
is greater than that he became the father of this man.[61]
Is it in fact greater to have tamed the British surrounded by sea
and to have led victorious ships through the seven-mouthed
streams of the papyrus-bearing Nile and to have added the
      rebel Numidians
and Libyan Juba and Pontus swelling with Mithridates' name[62]   755
to the Roman people and to have earned many triumphs,
some of which he celebrated, than to have begotten so great
      a man?
Gods, you have amply favored the human race with this man
      as a leader!
Therefore, lest this man be born from mortal stock,

60. For more on the comet, see Ramsey and Licht 1997.
61. Octavian, who was not the biological son of Julius Caesar but rather his grand-nephew. Julius Caesar revealed in his will that he had adopted Octavian (then Gaius Octavius) as his heir.
62. The Numidians lived in northern Africa. Juba II, king of Mauretania (also in northern Africa), was led in Caesar's triumph in 46 B.C. Pontus refers to the Black Sea region; Mithradates was the king from 120 to 63 B.C.

that one had to be made a god. When Aeneas's golden
  mother[63] saw this, 760
and also that the tragic death of the Pontifex[64] was being
  plotted
and that conspiratorial weapons were on the move, she grew pale
and she said to all the gods who crossed her path,
"Look, in what quantity plots are hatched against me,
what great deception seeks out that which 765
alone remains for me from Trojan Iulus.
Shall I alone be troubled by well-founded worries,
I whom now the Calydonian spear of Diomedes wounds,[65]
I whom now the walls of poorly defended Troy overwhelm,
I who see my son, driven by long wanderings and 770
tossed about on the sea, enter the home of the silent dead
and wage war with Turnus, or rather, to tell the truth,
with Juno?[66] Why do I now recall the old
misfortunes of my family? This fear forbids me to remember
my previous fears. Look, you see that criminal swords are
  sharpened. 775
I beg you, keep them away and drive off this crime and do not
put out the flames of Vesta with the priest's blood!"[67]
Venus, upset, tossed such words in vain to the whole sky
and she moved the gods, who, although they were not able to
  burst
the iron pronouncements of the aged sisters,[68] nevertheless 780
gave sure signs of the future; they say that
weapons clashing among black clouds and terrible

---

63. The goddess Venus, who bore Aeneas to a Trojan father, Anchises.

64. Julius Caesar, who held the office of Pontifex Maximus, the head priest in the Roman state religion.

65. Iulus: another name for Ascanius, son of Aeneas and, in turn, ancestor of Julius Caesar (and Augustus). The name Iulus was said to be the origin of the family name Julius. Diomedes was one of the Greeks who fought at Troy. He was said to have wounded Venus during a battle. Calydonian refers to the region in western Greece from which he came.

66. Venus refers to the trials that beset Aeneas, detailed in Vergil's *Aeneid*.

67. Vesta was the Roman goddess of the hearth. The eternal flame in her sacred precinct symbolized the life of the city of Rome. As Pontifex Maximus, Caesar oversaw the cult of Vesta.

68. The Fates.

trumpets and horns heard in the sky presaged
evil; also the mournful appearance of the sun
threw wan light on anxious lands;   785
often torches appeared to burn among the stars,
often among the clouds drops of blood fell;
the morning star was gloomy and his face spotted
with a dark rust, and the moon's chariot was sprinkled with
    blood;
in a thousand places a Stygian owl gave sad omens,   790
in a thousand places ivory wept, voices were heard
and threatening words echoed in sacred groves.
No sacrificial victim appeased, and the liver warned that
great strife loomed and a cleft lobe was discovered in the
    entrails.[69]
In the Forum and around the houses and the temples of
    the gods,   795
they say dogs howled at night and silent shades of the dead
wandered and earthquakes shook the city.
Divine warnings, however, were not able to best
the plots and the approaching Fates, and drawn swords were
    carried
into the sacred meeting place of the senate: for no place in
    the city   800
suited the crime and abominable slaughter except the senate
    house.
Then truly Venus struck her breast with both her hands
and tried to hide Caesar in the cloud in which
previously Paris was snatched from the hostile son of Atreus
and in which Aeneas had fled the sword of Diomedes.   805
Her father[70] said the following: "Do you alone, daughter,
propose to move inexorable fate? You yourself are permitted
to enter the home of the three sisters: there you will see the
    records

69. Divination by examining the entrails, especially the liver, of a sacrificed animal
was performed by a seer called a haruspex. The practice originated with the Etruscans. All
of the portents mentioned were commonly acknowledged as signs of disaster, as were
comets prior to the Julian Star.
70. Jupiter.

of events inscribed on bronze and solid iron, a huge
    undertaking,
safe and everlasting records that fear neither strife in the sky,   810
nor lightning's wrath, nor any disaster; there you will find
the fates of your descendants chiseled on lasting adamant:
I myself have read them and made note of them in my mind
and I will relate them to you, lest you be ignorant of the
    future any longer.
This man, on whose behalf you are troubled, has finished
    his time,   815
since the years he owed the earth are completed.
You and his son will bring it about that he may approach
    the sky
as a god and be worshipped in temples. And his son, heir to
    his name,[71]
alone will bear the burden placed on him and,
as the mightiest avenger of his slain parent, will have us as
    allies in war.   820
With his leadership the conquered walls of besieged Mutina
will seek peace, Pharsalia will feel his impact,
Emathian Philippi again will be wet with slaughter,
Sicilian waves will conquer a great name,
the Egyptian wife of a Roman leader will fall, since she   825
did not trust well the marriage, and she will have threatened
    in vain
that our Capitoline will be a slave to Canopus.[72]
Why should I enumerate to you the foreign land and the
    peoples lying
on each shore of Ocean? Any habitable place the earth has
will be his: the sea also will be his subject!   830
Once he has pacified the earth, he will turn his attention

---

71. Upon his adoption by Julius Caesar in 44 B.C., Gaius Octavius took the name Gaius Julius Caesar Octavianus. He took the honorary title Augustus in 27 B.C.

72. Mutina (in northern Italy) was a battle site in the civil war following the death of Julius Caesar. Pharsalia was the Thessalian town near which Caesar defeated Pompey in 48 B.C. Philippi in Macedonia was the site of Octavian and Antony's defeat of Brutus and Cassius in 42 B.C. The great name conquered near Sicily was Sextus Pompey, youngest son of Pompey the Great (member of the First Triumvirate). The Egyptian wife and Roman leader refer to Cleopatra and Mark Antony.

to civil law and he will uphold the laws as a very just statesman.
By his own example he will manage our customs and,
looking ahead to the future and to our descendants,
he will bequeath to his son, born from a chaste wife,   835
his name and his cares, but he will not touch
the heavenly abode and familial stars until as an old man
he has made his years equal to his good deeds.
I bid you meanwhile, bring it about that this spirit, snatched
from a slain body, as the divine Julius forever   840
surveys our Capitoline and Forum from his eminent temple."
Jupiter had scarcely ended his speech, when nurturing Venus,
        unseen, took her position in the middle of the senate and
        plucked
the fresh spirit of her Caesar from his limbs and did not allow it
to dissipate into the air, but brought it to the heavenly stars.   845
As she carried it, she felt it catch fire and burn
and she let it go from her bosom: it flies higher than the
        moon and,
trailing a flaming mane in its broad path, it shines as a star.
And, observing the benefactions of his son, he confesses
that they are greater than his own and he rejoices to be
        outdone by him.   850
Although the son does not allow his deeds to be elevated
        above his father's,
nevertheless his reputation, independent and obedient to
        no commands,
elevates him unwilling and in this one respect he is inconsistent.
Likewise great Atreus yields to the renown of Agamemnon,
and Theseus surpassed Aegeus, and Achilles Peleus;   855
finally, to use a sufficiently lofty example,
likewise Saturn is less than Jupiter:[73] Jupiter manages
the heavenly citadel and the three kingdoms of the universe,
but the earth is Augustus's domain; each is father and ruler.
Gods, I pray, companions of Aeneas, to whom sword and fire   860

---

73. Atreus was the father of Agamemnon, Aegeus the father of Theseus, and Peleus
the father of Achilles. In all cases the sons were greater heroes than their fathers. Jupiter
overthrew his father, Saturn, to become king of the gods.

have yielded, and native gods of Italy, and Quirinus,
begetter of the city, and Gradivus, father of Quirinus,
and Vesta, sacred among Caesarean household gods,
and you, Apollo of the house, along with Vesta of the Caesars,
and you, lofty Jupiter, who hold the Tarpeian rock,   865
and others whom it is right and pious for a bard to name:[74]
may that day be slow in coming and after our time,
on which Augustus, having left the world he rules,
enters heaven and answers prayers from afar!

74. Quirinus is another name for Romulus, the founder of Rome, who was deified after his death. Vesta was the goddess of the hearth, in the contexts of both the household and the city. Apollo was Augustus's favorite god and was associated with the sun, healing, divination, archery, poetry, and music. The Tarpeian rock was the site on the Capitoline hill where Tarpeia, a traitor to Rome in the time of Romulus, was executed. The temple of Jupiter Optimus Maximus, "Jupiter the Best and Greatest," was located on the Capitoline.

4

Antony

MARK ANTONY CAME FROM an aristocratic family that had fallen on hard times. Often portrayed as a love affair, Antony's relationship with Cleopatra largely represented a political alliance. As much as Antony needed the wealth of Egypt to support his military campaigns to the east, Cleopatra needed his help in solidifying her power, most dramatically through the murder of her sister, Arsinoe IV.

A PORTRAIT OF ANTONY

Mark Antony was known for his skill as a general as well as his penchant for drinking and womanizing. In these respects he differed from the quieter, more calculating Octavian. They did have at least one quality in common, however: ambition.

4.1. Plutarch, *Life of Antony* 4 (A.D. 110–15, Greek, prose)

For more on Plutarch, see selection 2.1. Here, Plutarch explores Antony's larger-than-life personality.

There was in addition an esteemed nobility to his features:[1] his full beard, broad forehead, and aquiline nose contributed to a manly appearance similar to paintings and statues of Hercules. There is even

---

1. I.e., in addition to his military skill and popularity with his troops.

an old story that the Antonii are descended from Hercules, since they were descendants of Hercules' son Anton. Antony believed that the tale gained credence from his appearance and his choice of clothing. For whenever he went before the public, he belted his tunic low on his hips, carried a large sword, and wore a rough cloak. But indeed, the traits that seemed vulgar to some—his boastfulness, his jesting, his open indulgence in drink, his habit of sitting with his soldiers when they ate or eating standing at the common table—gave the troops an amazing amount of good will and even love for him. He was lustful but charming as well: he captivated many people, as he often helped those in love and could make light of his own love life. Also, the liberal generosity and unthrifty indulgence he showed his soldiers and his friends afforded him an auspicious beginning to his quest for power and, once he became prominent, these tendencies increased his power manyfold, despite the hindrances posed by his many flaws. I will give one example of his generosity. He had specified that two hundred and fifty thousand drachmas be given to one of his friends (in Roman terms one million sesterces). His assistant was amazed and, in order to demonstrate to Antony how much money that was, he spread the amount before him. Antony, as he passed by, saw how much it was. When his assistant told him this was the gift he had ordered, Antony, recognizing the man as a miser, said, "I thought a million sesterces was more than that; this is too little: double it."

ANTONY'S FIRST TRIP TO EGYPT

Antony may have met Cleopatra before Caesar did. He served under Gabinius in 55 B.C. when Gabinius restored Ptolemy XII to the throne, and so it is possible that he met the then fourteen-year-old Cleopatra at the Alexandrian court.

4.2. Plutarch, *Life of Antony* 3 (A.D. 110–15, Greek, prose)

For more on Plutarch, see selection 2.1. Antony not only had great military prowess, but, as Plutarch relates, may have laid the groundwork in 55 B.C. for his later successful partnership with the Alexandrians.

When Gabinius, a man of consular rank, urged Antony to accompany his expedition to Syria, Antony said he would not participate as a private citizen, but he accepted when he was made cavalry commander. First he was sent out against Aristoboulus, who caused a revolt of the Jews. There, Antony was the first to surmount the height of the fortifications, and he routed Aristoboulus completely. After initiating the battle and with only a few men causing Aristoboulus's superior numbers to retreat, he killed all but a few of the enemy and took Aristoboulus and his son prisoner. Following these events, Ptolemy bribed Gabinius with ten thousand talents to invade Egypt and take back his kingdom.[2] Most of the commanders opposed the action and Gabinius was hesitant to engage in battle, but he was wholly taken in by the ten thousand talents. Antony, for his part, was eager to engage in great deeds and was only too happy to indulge Ptolemy's desire, and so he helped in exhorting and persuading Gabinius. The troops were more afraid of the journey to Pelusium than of the battle itself, as they would have to cross the deep sands and the desert all the way to Ecregma and the Serbonian swamp, which the Egyptians call Typhon's exhalations, but actually seems to be water from the Red Sea that flowed back and welled up where the Red Sea is divided from the Mediterranean by the narrowest isthmus. When Antony was sent ahead with the cavalry, he not only took the isthmus, but also Pelusium, great city that it was, and took its defenders prisoner, at the same time making the road safe for the army and giving sure hope of victory to the general. Even the enemy benefited from Antony's desire for glory: when Ptolemy arrived in Peleusium and was, on account of his rage and hatred, eager to execute the Egyptians, Antony opposed and prevented him. In the many great battles and conflicts that followed, Antony showed his daring and prescient leadership, the most apparent of which was encircling and outflanking the enemy from behind, thus delivering a victory to the troops meeting the enemy head on. For this, he received appropriate honor and recognition. Nor did the Egyptians fail to notice the decency he showed the dead Archelaus.[3] Antony had been his friend and guest, but declared war on him out of necessity. Nevertheless, Antony located his fallen body and gave him a royal funeral. He left

2. Ptolemy XII, the father of Cleopatra.
3. Archelaus was the son of Mithradates' general Archelaus. He married Cleopatra's sister Berenice and ruled in Egypt for six months.

behind a great reputation with the Alexandrians, and to the Roman troops he seemed to be an extremely brilliant man.

FULVIA

Fulvia, Antony's third wife, was at least as politically ambitious as her husband. She seems to have been the first Roman woman to have her portrait on a coin.[4] Also like Antony, she also came into conflict with Octavian, taking part in a revolt against his seizure of land to use as a reward for his soldiers.

4.3. Plutarch, *Life of Antony* 10.4–6, 30 (A.D. 110–15, Greek, prose)

For more on Plutarch, see selection 2.1. Here, Plutarch paints a picture of Fulvia's character.

10.4–6

It seems that Caesar did a great deal to remedy Antony's foolishness and dissolute lifestyle, as he did not accept without criticism Antony's transgressions. Antony, as a result, turned his life around and set his sights on marriage. His bride was Fulvia, the former wife of Clodius the demagogue. She had no use for women's work like spinning or housekeeping and was not interested in presiding over a husband who was not in the public eye: rather, she wanted to rule a ruler and command a general. As a result, Cleopatra should have paid Fulvia tuition for schooling Antony to obey a woman, so docile and trained to obey a woman's commands was he when she took him on.

30

Two pieces of news took Antony by surprise as he passed his time in frivolity and idleness. First, word came from Rome that his brother Lucius and his wife, Fulvia, were at war, first with each other, then with Octavian, and that finally, defeated, they had fled from Italy. The second report, no easier to bear, was that Labienus, leading a Parthian army, was conquering Asia from the Euphrates and Syria to Lydia and Ionia. Then, like one barely awakened from a drunken slumber, he hastened to oppose the Parthians and marched as far as

4. Grant 1972, 114–15.

Phoenicia, but when Fulvia sent him a letter full of lamentation, he turned toward Italy with his two hundred ships. As they went, he picked up some of his friends who had been exiled. He learned from them that Fulvia was responsible for the war, as she was by nature a rash and meddling woman and hoped to win Antony back from Cleopatra if she could create some unrest in Italy. But by chance Fulvia, as she sailed to meet him, took ill in Sicyon and died. For this reason, a treaty with Octavian became more likely. For when Antony reached Italy and Caesar was not apparently going to accuse him of anything, and he, for his part, was planning to put the blame on Fulvia for anything of which he might be accused, their friends did not allow them to scrutinize the excuses, but facilitated their reconciliation and the division of the empire. Making the Ionian Sea the boundary and allotting the eastern lands to Antony and the western to Octavian and allowing Lepidus to occupy Libya, they assigned friends of each man to hold the consulship, once it was apparent that Octavian and Antony did not desire the office.[5]

4.4. Inscriptions from the Siege of Perusia: *ILLRP*[6] 1106, 1108, 1109, 1111, 1112 (41–40 B.C., Latin, prose)

These inscriptions were written on missiles hurled during the siege of Perusia (modern Perugia), in which Antony's brother, Lucius Antonius, and his wife, Fulvia, supported those driven from their land when Octavian seized it to use as rewards for his soldiers. The conflict resulted in a siege of Perusia, the walled town where Fulvia and Lucius Antonius had taken refuge. The bitter conflict spawned not only shocking words, but, perhaps, actions as well. Octavian was said to have practiced human sacrifice after capturing the city when he executed some of the Perusians at an altar to the deified Julius Caesar.[7]

1106. I'm aiming for Fulvia's cunt.

1108. I'm aiming for Octavian's ass.

1109. Octavian, sit on this!

1111. Baldy Lucius Antonius, you're dead. Gaius Caesar: victory.

1112. Baldy Lucius Antonius and Fulvia, open your asses.

5. This agreement was the Treaty of Brundisium, concluded in September of 40 B.C.
6. Degrassi 1963, 303–4.
7. See Jones 1971, 26–28. Cf. Propertius, *Elegies* 1.21, 1.22.

4.5. Martial, *Epigram* 11.20 (A.D. 96, Latin, verse)

Martial was a writer of epigrams, short poems often devoted to light subjects. His most productive period came during the reigns of the emperors Titus, Domitian, Nerva, and Trajan. Like Catullus, Martial at times engaged in clever invective verses. Political unrest and abuses of power in Rome, particularly during the reign of Domitian, may have colored Martial's views on previous political figures.

In Epigram *11.20, Martial defends himself against the charge that his poetry is too offensive by quoting an epigram allegedly written by Octavian in 41 B.C. In the quoted poem, Octavian verbally attacks Fulvia and refers to Antony's alleged adulterous relationship with Glaphyra, the mother of the man Antony made king of Cappadocia in 41 B.C.*

Spiteful censor of the Latin language, read   1
six insolent verses of Caesar Augustus:
"Because Antony fucks Glaphyra, Fulvia has arranged
this punishment for me: that I fuck her too.
That I fuck Fulvia? What if Manius begged me   5
to bugger him? Would I? I don't think so, if I were sane.
'Either fuck or let's fight,' she says. Doesn't she know
my prick is dearer to me than life itself? Let the trumpets blare!"
Augustus, you certainly grant my clever little books pardon,
since you are the expert at speaking with Roman frankness.   10

ANTONY AND CLEOPATRA MEET IN TARSUS

The meeting has become famous as the beginning of a love affair; it also marked a historic political alliance, but visually, it was the meeting of two gods.

4.6. Plutarch, *Life of Antony* 24–27.1 (A.D. 110–15, Greek, prose)

For more on Plutarch, see selection 2.1. In the division of the provinces among the members of the Second Triumvirate, Antony had received the eastern territories. The people of Asia Minor, in recognition of his power, hailed him as the god Dionysus. While he was in Asia Minor in 41 B.C., he summoned Cleopatra to meet with him.

24. When Antony crossed into Asia after leaving Lucius Censorinus to oversee Greece, he took advantage of the riches he found there.

Kings came to his door and the wives of kings competed with one another in gift giving and sacrificed their honor to him. Octavian was in Rome wearing himself out with strife and conflict, but Antony was living the life of leisure and being impelled by his passions back into his usual habits. Men like Anaxenor, the lyre player, and Xouthos, the flute player, as well as a certain Metrodoros, a dancer, and a large troupe of Asiatic entertainers, who surpassed even the pests he brought from Italy in wantonness and boorishness, attached themselves to him and filled the court, a situation all found unbearable. For all of Asia, like that city Sophocles describes, was at once full of incense,

and at once full of hymns and laments.[8]

Indeed, when he crossed into Ephesus, women marched dressed as Bacchants, men and boys as Satyrs and Pans;[9] the city was full of ivy, thyrsoi,[10] lyres, panpipes, and flutes, and everyone hailed Antony as Dionysus, the Benefactor and the Bringer of Joy. No doubt he was for some, but for most, he was Dionysus, the Cannibal and the Savage, since he confiscated the possessions of many noble men and gave them to worthless men and flatterers. Also, some stole from the living by falsifying their deaths. There was a Magnesian man whose house Antony gave as a gift to a cook who made his reputation on the basis of one dinner, it is said. Finally, when he burdened the cities with a second round of taxes, Hybreas, speaking on behalf of Asia, dared to say the following frankly and in a way that suited Antony's own taste: "if you are able to exact tribute twice in one year, are you also able to provide us with two summers and two harvests?" This summed up the matter practically and courageously, and he then added that Asia had already paid two hundred thousand talents.[11] He said, "if you have not received this sum, demand it from those who collected it; but if it was collected and you do not have it, we are ruined."

8. The city Sophocles describes is Thebes; the line quoted is *Oedipus the King* 5.
9. Bacchants were female ecstatic worshipers of the god Dionysus; satyrs were mythical creatures mostly human in form but with some goat features. They were associated with the god Pan, himself part human and part goat and the patron of shepherds, and with Dionysus. This reception from the people of Asia associated Antony with Dionysus, who, in myth, originated in Asia and spread his worship throughout the world in a parade of revelry.
10. The thyrsus was a staff crowned with ivy carried by Bacchants.
11. The talent was a unit of currency worth six thousand drachmas.

This statement got Antony's attention, for he was unaware of many happenings, not only because he was so easygoing, but also because, out of straightforwardness, he trusted his supporters. Straightforwardness was one of his essential character traits, as was a slowness of perception. But when he did perceive his mistakes, he instantly changed his course and admitted his error to those he had treated unfairly: both atonement and punishment were substantial, but it seems that he went beyond what was appropriate more often when rewarding than when punishing. His insults involving jests and ridicule came with their own remedy, for it was appropriate to ridicule and insult him in return: he took as much pleasure in being laughed at as in laughing at others. This trait did him much harm, for he could not believe that those who exercised their freedom of speech by mocking him were in fact eager to flatter him. He was easily taken in by praise, but did not realize that some men cut the sweetness of their speech by mixing in some astringent remarks with the flattery so as not to be cloying. They made sure, through their candor and loquacity at drinking parties, to show that the support and agreement they showed for his ideas were not born of subservience, but rather of their excellent judgment.

25. For someone of Antony's nature, the love of Cleopatra that befell him was the final ruin that aroused and stirred up many feelings that had been hidden and dormant in him and, if anything good or protective remained, obliterated and destroyed it. It happened in the following way: while planning a campaign against the Parthians, Antony sent word to Cleopatra, demanding that she meet him in Cilicia to answer the charge that she had given many resources to Cassius's supporters and made contributions to the war. Dellius was the messenger Antony sent, and when he saw her face and perceived the power and cunning of her words, he knew at once that Antony could do no harm to such a woman, but rather that she would prevail over him. Dellius paid court to the Egyptian queen and urged her, in the words of Homer, "to go to Cilicia in all her splendor"[12] and not to fear Antony, since he was the kindest of leaders and the most charitable. She, for her part, believed Dellius, and, judging by her

12. Homer, *Iliad* 16.162.

previous associations with Caesar and Gnaeus, the son of Pompey, she hoped to conquer Antony even more easily. After all, those men knew her when she was still young and inexperienced; she was about to go to Antony at the age at which women are at the height of their attractiveness and at the peak of their intellectual powers. Accordingly, she prepared as many gifts and as much money and adornment to take with her as befitted her great undertaking and royal status. She placed most of her hopes, however, in herself and the charm and magic that attended her.

26. She had received many letters from Antony and his friends summoning her, but she disdained and mocked the man by sailing up the River Cydnus in a ship with its stern covered in gold, with purple sails fluttering, with rowers pulling with silver oars as flutes played accompanied by pipes and lyres. Cleopatra reclined beneath a canopy embroidered with gold, decked out to resemble a painting of Aphrodite, and boys, made to look like the Erotes[13] we see in art, stood on either side and fanned her. Likewise, her most beautiful maids, dressed as Nereids and Graces, stood, some by the rudders and some by the ropes. The marvelous scent of copious incense fills the riverbanks. Some of the men escort her from either side, directly from the river, while others come down from the city to see the sight. As the crowd thinned in the marketplace, finally Antony was left alone, sitting on the speaker's platform. The news went around that Aphrodite had come to revel with Dionysus for the good of Asia. Then he sent word inviting her to dinner; instead, she suggested he come to her. He, wishing to display his courtesy and kindness, accepted and went. He found the preparations beyond words and was struck most of all by the multitude of lights. Indeed, it is said that so many were suspended and displayed everywhere at once and were ordered and positioned at such intricate angles to one another and in such patterns, like squares and circles, that it was a sight of beauty and delight for the viewer.

27. The next day, as a way of returning the favor, Antony was ambitious to surpass her elegance and attention to detail. Outdone and bested on both counts, Antony was the first to mock the inferior and rustic nature of his banquet.

13. Cupids.

4.7. Appian, *Civil War* 5.8–5.9.2 (early 2nd c. A.D., Greek, prose)

For more on Appian, see selection 2.3. In this passage, Appian describes Cleopatra's strategy at her first official meeting with Antony.

8. When Cleopatra came to him in Cilicia, he reproached her for not participating in avenging Caesar. She did not apologize, but rather enumerated to them that she had sent her four squadrons to Dolabella right away, and that the other company, which she had ready, was prevented from going by the wind and by Dolabella himself, since he had suffered defeat rather quickly.[14] She added that she had not allied with Cassius, even though he had twice threatened her, and that, during the war, neither fearing Cassius nor guarding against Murcus, who was lying in wait for her, she had sailed to the Ionian Sea with an impressive fleet, until a storm damaged the ships and brought upon her an illness, because of which she had not set sail until the victory was already won. Antony, struck by her intelligence as well as her appearance, was captivated by her as if he were a young lad, although he was forty years old. He is said to have always been very susceptible to these things and to have fallen in love with her at first sight long before, when she was still a child and he, as a young man, went to Alexandria as a cavalry commander under the general Gabinius.[15]

9. The acute interest Antony had once shown in all things suddenly dulled; whatever Cleopatra dictated was done, without regard for the laws of man or nature.

BANQUETING IN ALEXANDRIA

Cleopatra's banquets are one of the most enduring symbols of the wealth and excess of the Alexandrian court. They provide writers and artists with rich material and, in addition, give insight into Cleopatra's character.

4.8. Plutarch, *Life of Antony* 28–29 (A.D. 110–15, Greek, prose)

For more on Plutarch, see selection 2.1. This collection of anecdotes characterizes the dynamic between Antony and Cleopatra in addition to

---

14. Dolabella was a friend of Julius Caesar who was involved in avenging Caesar's murder. Cleopatra sent help to him in the form of troops left in Alexandria by Caesar. The troops deserted to Cassius after Dolabella lost a battle (Grant 1972, 101).

15. 55 B.C.

highlighting the winter of 41–40 B.C., *the first extended time they spent together.*

28. Cleopatra captured Antony to such an extent that, while his wife Fulvia was fighting with Octavian in Rome to support her husband's interests and in Mesopotamia there loomed a Parthian army, which Labienus Parthicus had been appointed to command by the king's generals and was about to march on Syria, Antony had disappeared, spirited away by Cleopatra to Alexandria, where he enjoyed the games and pastimes of a child at play and spent and squandered what Antiphon called the most precious treasure of all, his time. They had a club they called the Inimitable Livers, and each day they hosted banquets for one another at which they squandered unbelievable sums. Indeed, Philotas of Amphissa, the physician, told my grandfather Lamprias that when he was in Alexandria learning his craft, he became friends with one of the palace cooks and was persuaded, as a young man might be, to observe the extravagant preparations for the feast. He was brought into the kitchen, where he saw many impressive sights, including eight wild boars being roasted, and marveled at the number of diners he imagined they would serve. The cook just laughed and said that there were not many diners—only about twelve—but that everything presented had to be perfect and would be spoiled by the smallest delay. Indeed, it might happen that Antony sent for the meal at the very beginning of the party or he might put it off and order a drink or fall into conversation with someone. Thus, not one, he said, but many dinners were prepared, since he could never guess the exact moment the meal would be served. These, then, were Philotas's memories; he also recalled that in subsequent years, Antony's eldest son[16] by Fulvia was his patient and that he often had dined with him and his friends, when the boy was not dining with his father. One time, a physician was there who was boasting and offering unsolicited advice to the guests, and Philotas shut him up with the following display of sophistry: "water should be given for some types of fever; every fever is some type of fever, therefore water should be given to every fever." The man was dumbfounded and fell silent; Antony's son, when he heard this, laughed and said, "As thanks, I give you all this" and indicated a table full of many large

16. Antyllus.

goblets. Philotas appreciated the gesture, but was not sure whether a child of that age had the authority to make such a gift. A little while later, one of the boy's servants brought out the goblets in a box and asked him to affix his seal. When he demurred and hesitated to take them, the man said, "What are you afraid of, you idiot? Don't you know this is Antony's son, who has the authority to give you these things, even if they were made of gold? Nevertheless, take my advice and exchange them all with us for money: it is possible his father would miss some of them, since they are antiques and exquisitely crafted." These are the stories my grandfather told me whenever he had the chance to talk about Philotas.

29. Cleopatra had command of flattery in many forms, not only the four Plato mentions,[17] and she was always able to entertain Antony, whether he was serious or playful, by inventing some new amusement and never leaving him alone day or night. Indeed, she played dice with him, drank with him, hunted with him, and watched him as he trained with weapons. At night, she accompanied him as he stationed himself outside doors and windows to mock the people inside. On these excursions, she would wear a maid's outfit, taking her cue from Antony's fondness for dressing up as a slave. He always returned having suffered insults and frequently beatings as well, but most were not fooled by the disguise. In fact, the Alexandrians delighted in his pranks and played along in a refined and cultured way, since they had a genuine affection for Antony and said that, while he wore his tragic mask in Rome, when he was with them, he put on his comic mask. To detail the many games with which Antony amused himself would be as silly as the pranks themselves. I will, however, mention one occasion on which Antony had gone fishing. Cleopatra was there and Antony was frustrated that he was not catching anything. He ordered some fishermen to dive underwater and secretly attach a previously caught fish to his line. He caught two or three in this way, but did not fool the Egyptian queen. She pretended to be impressed and told her friends, inviting them to come and watch the next day. They all got aboard boats and, when Antony cast his line, Cleopatra ordered one of her servants to dive down right away and impale on his hook a smoked fish from the Black Sea. Antony, believing he had a bite, pulled up his line and was laughed at, as was to be expected.

17. Plato, *Gorgias* 462c–66a.

But she said to him, "Emperor, leave the rod to those who rule Pharos and Canopus; your prey is cities, kingdoms, and continents."

4.9. Florus, *Abridgement of All the Wars Over 1,200 Years* 2.14.4, 2.21.1–3 (2nd c. A.D., Latin, prose)

For more on Florus, see selection 3.10. In these passages Florus describes Antony's increasing tendency to behave like a monarch, which he attributes to Cleopatra's corrupting influence.

2.14.4

Antony was indecisive and either thought Octavian an unworthy successor to Caesar or, for love of Cleopatra, surrendered to monarchy. . . .[18] For the Romans had no hope of safety other than retreating into slavery.

2.21.1–3

Since Antony's ambition could not put his madness to rest, his luxury and lust put an end to it. Indeed, when after the Parthian campaign he detested war and spent his time at leisure, captivated by love for Cleopatra, he restored himself in her embrace as if his affairs were well in order. At this point, the Egyptian wife sought the Roman Empire from the drunken leader as a price for her favors; Antony promised it to her, as if it were easier to conquer Rome than Parthia. And so Antony began to plan domination, not for himself and not secretly, but rather, forgetful of his country, name, toga, and the fasces,[19] he degenerated completely into that monster in mind as well as clothing and appearance. He had a gold scepter in his hand, a short saber at his side, and purple garments adorned with huge gems: only a crown was missing, or they would have been king and queen enjoying themselves.

4.10. Pliny the Elder, *Natural History* 9.119–21, 21.12 (A.D. 77, Latin, prose)

Pliny's Natural History *is an encyclopedia that treats geography, geology, astronomy, meteorology, zoology, and botany. The work, comprising thirty-*

---

18. There is a gap in the text.
19. The fasces were bundles of rods and axes that were the emblem of the office of consul.

*seven books, aimed to collect all of nature (*Natural History, *preface 13).
Pliny's approach to his material was influenced by Stoicism; thus, his
encyclopedia reflects a world he saw as rational and divisible into system-
atic categories. His Stoic beliefs also underlie his distrust of luxury.*[20]

*The first of the passages that follow, which is part of a discussion of
pearls, describes how Cleopatra disintegrated a pearl in vinegar in order to
win a bet with Antony. However fantastic the anecdote may seem, the
queen was exploiting real properties of pearls and vinegar, although the
timetable seems somewhat exaggerated. Pearls, which consist of calcium
carbonate in a protein matrix, react with the acetic acid in vinegar to produce water-soluble calcium acetate and carbon dioxide. The concentration
of acetic acid that occurs naturally in vinegar is ideal for the reaction. It
causes a pearl to disintegrate, leaving only a small amount of gelatinous
protein behind. A large pearl, however, takes twenty-four hours or more to
react completely. Nevertheless, the episode is a favorite of artists, for whom
it becomes a moment that defines Cleopatra's character.*[21]

*The second passage comes from a discussion of crowns made of flowers.
Pliny adds an anecdote in which Cleopatra again tricks Antony with a
drink, this time in more sinister circumstances. Just as with the pearl in
vinegar, however, Cleopatra uses her knowledge of science to outwit
Antony, thus asserting her power over him. We are left to wonder whether
she wins his trust or simply affords him no choice but to grant it.*

9.119–21

119. There were two pearls, the largest in history; and Cleopatra,
the last of the Queens of Egypt, owned them both, since they were
handed down to her through the hands of the Kings of the East.
When Antony was fattening himself every day at decadent banquets,
she with a pride both lofty and impudent, a queenly courtesan, disparaged his elegance and sumptuous display, and when he asked

---

20. French 1994, 198, 233.
21. The Italian painter Tiepolo treated the scene in a painting and a fresco, both from
the 1740s (see Walker and Higgs 2001, 351–53). The British artist Joshua Reynolds
painted a portrait of Kitty Fisher (1759) in which a goblet and a pearl were the only
details needed to determine that he was depicting his subject as Cleopatra. Frederick
Sandys, in an engraving published in *The Cornhill Magazine* (1866), depicts Cleopatra
dipping long strands of pearls into her cup (see selection *12.2* and fig. 7).

what magnificence could be added on, she replied that she would spend ten million sesterces on one banquet.[22]

120. Antony was curious, but did not think it could be done. Consequently, with bets made, on the next day, on which the trial was carried out, she set before Antony a banquet that elsewhere would be considered magnificent, so that the day might not be wasted, but that was for them ordinary, and Antony laughed and exclaimed over its cheapness. But she, claiming that it was a gratuity, and that the banquet would complete the account and she alone would consume ten million sesterces, ordered the second course to be served. According to previous instructions, the servants placed before her only a single cup of vinegar, the sharpness and power of which disintegrates pearls to a pulp.

121. She was wearing in her ears that especially unusual and truly unique work of nature. And so, with Antony eagerly anticipating what she would do, she took one off and dropped it in, and when it was wasted away she swallowed it. Lucius Plancus, the judge of the wager, put his hand on the other pearl, since she was preparing to destroy it also in a similar fashion, and declared that Antony had lost, an omen that later came true.

21.12

For in the preparation for the Actian war, when Antony feared the attentiveness of the queen herself and did not take any food unless it had been tasted beforehand, she is said to have played on his fear and dipped the tips of the flowers in his crown in poison and then put the crown on his head; soon, as the revelry proceeded, she suggested to Antony that they drink their crowns.[23] Who would thus fear treachery? Therefore with a hand put in his way as he was beginning to drink the pieces gathered into the cup, she said, "Look, I am she, Mark Antony, of whom you are wary with your new wish for tasters. If I could live without you, this is the extent to which I

22. The text is uncertain, and thus ten million may not be the price Pliny named. In addition ten million may or may not be the price of both pearls, as we see at the end of the story. At any rate ten million sesterces would have been worth about sixty thousand pounds of gold.

23. Crowns of flowers were often worn at parties, at least partly based on a belief that the scent of certain perfumes and flowers, particularly roses, retarded intoxication.

lack opportunity and motive!" She ordered a prisoner who had been
led in to drink it and he promptly expired.

OCTAVIA

In 40 B.C. the members of the Second Triumvirate forged the Treaty
of Brundisium, a reaffirmation of their political alliance. Their
bonds were in need of strengthening after Octavian's conflict with
Fulvia and Lucius Antonius at Perusia. To reinforce the political
alliance with a personal connection, Antony married Octavian's sister, Octavia.

4.11. Plutarch, *Life of Antony* 31, 53–54.5, 57 (A.D. 110–15, Greek,
prose)

*For more on Plutarch, see selection 2.1. As Plutarch suggests, Octavia was
nothing like Cleopatra. She fit the ideal of the Roman matron; she supported her husband's political goals but devoted herself to the household
and to the raising of children.*

31. These terms seemed acceptable on both sides, but a stronger
bond was needed and chance supplied one. Octavia was the elder
sister of Octavian, but by a different mother, for she was born from
Ancharia and he from Atia.[24] Octavian was very fond of his sister,
who, it is said, was a marvel of a woman. She was a widow, having
been married to Gaius Marcellus, who had recently died. Antony
too was considered a widower, now that Fulvia had died. He did not
deny his involvement with Cleopatra, but did not call it marriage,
though he still wrestled against his love for the Egyptian woman.
Everyone supported this marriage to Octavia, in hopes that she, since
she had dignity and intelligence in addition to considerable beauty,
might support and be loved by Antony, as was fitting for such a
woman, and that she would represent the salvation and harmony of
all their affairs. Thus, when the treaty was satisfactory to both men,
they went to Rome and celebrated the marriage of Octavia, not
observing the law stating that a widow may not remarry until her

24. Plutarch may confuse this Octavia with Octavian's half sister Octavia; Atia was the
mother of the Octavia who married Antony.

husband has been dead for ten months: the time was lessened for them by a decree of the Senate.

In 35 B.C. Octavia arrived in the East, forcing Antony to choose between her and Cleoapatra.

53. In Rome, when Octavia wished to sail to Antony, Octavian allowed it, many say, not for her enjoyment, but so that, if she were neglected or mistreated, he might have an appropriate cause for war. Upon her arrival in Athens, Octavia received a letter from Antony, who ordered her to remain there and told her the details of his campaign. But she, though she was upset and saw through Antony's pretext, nevertheless wrote him to inquire where he would have the things she was bringing him sent. She had brought a great deal of clothing for the troops, many beasts of burden, and money and gifts for Antony's commanders and friends; she also brought two thousand chosen soldiers, fully armed and outfitted as an official bodyguard. Niger, a friend of Antony, was sent to deliver this message to him, and he brought along with it justified and appropriate praises of her. Cleopatra perceived that Octavia was advancing on her and feared that if Octavia added to her decorum and Caesar's power the pleasure of her company and her support of Antony, she would be untouchable and would have total command of her husband. So Cleopatra feigned passionate love for Antony and made her body waste away with a strict diet. She fixed her gaze on him every time he came near and, when he left, she appeared to swoon and sink down. She contrived that he should often see her weeping, then quickly wiped away the tear and hid it, as if she wished to escape his notice. She carried out these plans while Antony was preparing to march out from Syria with the king of the Medes. Antony's flatterers were busy with him, reproaching him on her behalf, saying that he was a harsh, unfeeling destroyer of a woman who was depending on him and him alone. Octavia, they said, joined with him only out of practical considerations and to help her brother and she enjoyed the name of wife. But Cleopatra, who ruled many over many, was called Antony's mistress, and she did not avoid the term or think it beneath her, provided that she could see him and live with him. Only if she were deprived of him would she be unable to live. Finally, they wore him down and forced him into submission and he, fearing that Cleopatra would

take her own life, returned to Alexandria, putting off his expedition with the king of the Medes until the summer, even though the Parthians were reportedly in civil conflict. He did, however, go up there later and restored friendly relations. He also arranged a marriage for one of Cleopatra's sons with one of the king's daughters, who was still a young girl; he went back, already meditating war with his kinsman.[25]

54. When Octavia returned from Athens, she seemed to Octavian to have been mistreated and he ordered her to leave Antony. She, however, refused to leave her husband's house, but she asked Octavian to discount the things that had happened to her, unless he had already resolved to go to war with Antony for other reasons, since it would be intolerable if the two most powerful rulers sent the Roman people to war, one for love of a woman and the other to avenge a relative. Saying these words, she backed them up with deeds, for she lived in the house just as she had when Antony was there and devotedly and nobly cared for the children, not only those he had with her, but also those born from Fulvia. She also received those of Antony's friends who were sent to Rome on any business, political or otherwise, and helped them obtain what they needed from Octavian. In this way, she inadvertently harmed Antony, as he was hated for wronging such a woman.

In 32 B.C. Antony and Cleopatra prepared for war with Octavian with the extravagance that characterized all of their activities. This contrasted with Octavia's more sensible nature when Antony and Cleopatra arrived in Athens, the city that had recently played host to Octavia.

57. After the entertainment was over, Antony granted to the actors Priene as their home. He then sailed to Athens and returned to leisure pursuits and spectacles. Cleopatra was jealous of the honors Octavia had received in the city (for Octavia was especially loved by the Athenians) and she cultivated the people's affection with many benefactions. The Athenians voted honors to her and sent elders to her house with the decree. Antony was among them as an honorary Athenian citizen and stood before her and spoke on behalf of the city. He sent messengers to Rome to evict Octavia from his house.

25. I.e., Octavian.

They say that she left and took with her all of the children she had with Antony, but not his eldest son, whom he had with Fulvia (for that son was with his father),[26] and that she wept and was distraught at the prospect of seeming to be one of the causes of the war. The Romans did not pity her as much as they did Antony, particularly those who had seen Cleopatra and realized that she could not match Octavia's beauty or youth.

4.12. Vergil, *Eclogue* 4 (ca. 40 B.C., Latin, verse)

The Eclogues *are ten poems in the pastoral genre made famous by Theocritus (see selection 1.5). Like Theocritus, Vergil sets his poems in an idyllic rural landscape and casts shepherds as speakers in many of his poems. But while Theocritus sets his poems in real places, often in Sicily and southern Italy (the locations of Greek colonies), Vergil's setting is Arcadia, which, although it shares a name with a region in Greece, functions in the* Eclogues *as an imaginary place. Nevertheless, contemporary social issues sometimes intrude.*

Eclogue 4 concerns the impending birth of a child, whose arrival will initiate a Golden Age in which strife would no longer exist and the earth would produce crops spontaneously. The concept of a Golden Age existed prior to Vergil in Greek mythology, but always as a part of the distant past. Vergil is the first to describe the return of a Golden Age.

The theme of a child heralding a new age caused some Christian interpreters to see in the poem a prediction of the birth of Christ. Because of these interpretations, Eclogue 4 *is often called the Messianic* Eclogue. *It is more likely, however, that Vergil either alludes to the general theme of a birth initiating a new age[27] or refers to a child expected by parents known to him. The most likely candidate for this latter interpretation is the child expected to result from the marriage of Antony and Octavia. The child, as it turned out, was a girl, Antonia the Younger (mother of the emperor Claudius).[28]*

Sicilian Muses, let us sing somewhat greater songs!   1
Trees and humble tamarisks do not please everyone;
if I sing of forests, let them be forests worthy of a consul.

26. I.e., Antyllus.
27. See Clausen 1995, 128–29.
28. See Clausen 1995, 121–23.

The final age of the Cumaean prophecy is at hand.[29]

The great sequence of ages is born anew.   5

Now too the Maiden returns, as does Saturn's rule,

now a new line is sent from the lofty sky.[30]

You, chaste Lucina, bless the newborn boy, under whose
     auspices

the iron race will cease and a golden race will rise throughout
     the world:

now your brother Apollo reigns.[31]   10

And you, Pollio,[32] with you as consul, this glorious age will
     begin,

and great months will start to unfold;

under your leadership, if any traces of our fault remain,

they, nullified, will free the world from lasting fear.

That boy will have the life of the gods, he will see   15

heroes mingling with gods and be seen by them,

and he will rule a world pacified by his father's courage.[33]

But first for you, child, the earth will pour forth gifts with
     no cultivation:

ivy wandering here and there, baccaris, and

colocasia mixed with exuberant acanthus.   20

She-goats will come home unshepherded, their udders distended

with milk, and herds will not fear great lions;

your very cradle will overflow with sweet flowers for you.

---

29. Cumae was where prophecies inspired by the god Apollo were dispensed through a prophetess known as the Sibyl. The Romans had several books of *Sibylline Oracles,* which were thought to predict the future of Rome. For some examples, see selection *2.6.*

30. The Maiden refers to Astraea, the virgin goddess of justice, whom Hesiod described as leaving the earth at the end of the Golden Age (*Works and Days* 200–201). She was believed to have become the constellation Virgo. Saturn was the father of Jupiter and was believed to have ruled the universe during the Golden Age, which ended when Jupiter seized power from his father.

31. Lucina was the goddess of childbirth and was sometimes identified with Diana, the sister of Apollo.

32. Gaius Asinius Pollio, who was Vergil's patron during the composition of the *Eclogues,* held the consulship in 40 B.C.

33. These lines may contain a reference to Hercules, from whom Antony claimed descent. The future predicted for the child, to join the ranks of heroes and gods, matches Hercules' experience. As Clausen points out, the last lines of the poem may also project for the boy honors such as Hercules received. There, reference to sharing a table with a god and a bed with a goddess evokes Hercules' story in general and perhaps also specifically, via allusion to Theocritus 17.16–33 (see selection *1.5;* Clausen 1995, 123–24).

The snake will perish, as will the plant that conceals
its poison; Syrian amomum will grow like a weed.[34]   25
As soon as you can read the praises of heroes and
the deeds of your father and recognize what manliness is,
little by little the field will turn yellow with soft ears of grain
and blushing bunches of grapes will hang on wild brambles
and hard oaks will sweat dewdrops of honey.   30
Nevertheless, a few traces of the old wrong will persist,
which motivate men to test Thetis[35] with ships, to surround
     towns
with walls, to plough furrows into the earth.
Then there will be a second Tiphys and a second Argo
to carry chosen heroes; there will also be more wars   35
and again a great Achilles will be sent to Troy.[36]
Then, once strengthening time has made you a man,
even the merchant will leave the sea, and the seafaring pine will
     not exchange goods; every land will produce all things.
The ground will not suffer the rake, nor vines the pruning
     hook;   40
now too the hardy ploughman will loose the yoke from his bulls.
Wool will not learn to feign various colors,
but in the fields the ram himself will change his fleece
now with lovely red murex, now with saffron yellow;
of its own accord, vermilion will clothe the grazing lambs.[37]   45
"Hasten those ages" the Parcae, in accord
with the stable will of the fates, said to their spindles.[38]
Advance upon great honors (for the time has come),
dear offspring of the gods, great progeny of Jupiter!
Look at the universe nodding with its convex mass,   50

---

34. Amomum was an aromatic plant used in perfumes. Many spices from the East were shipped to the Mediterranean from Syrian ports (Clausen 1995, 136).

35. Thetis was a sea nymph whose name here signifies the sea.

36. The Argo was the ship sailed by Jason and his men, the Argonauts, on their quest to capture the Golden Fleece. Tiphys was the helmsman of the Argo. Achilles was the greatest of the Greek warriors in the Trojan War and the main character of Homer's *Iliad*.

37. Murex is a mollusk that yields the purple dye known in the ancient world as Tyrian purple.

38. The Parcae were originally Roman goddesses of childbirth, who came to be associated with the Fates from Greek mythology (Clausen 1995, 141). The Fates were envisioned as three old women who spun the thread of a life and then cut it off, thus ending the life.

both the earth and the expanse of the sea and the depth of
  the sky;
look, how all things rejoice in the coming age!
Then may the final phase of a long life remain for me,
and as much breath as is enough to tell of your deeds!
Neither Thracian Orpheus nor Linus will best me in singing,   55
although one has his mother's help and the other his father's
(Calliope for Orpheus and handsome Apollo for Linus).
Pan too, if he should challenge me with Arcadia as judge,
Pan too would say he was beaten with Arcadia as judge.[39]
Begin, small boy, to recognize your mother with a smile   60
(ten months have brought your mother long tedium).
Begin, small boy: the one who does not greet his parent with
  a smile
no god deems worthy of his table, no goddess of her bed.

THE DONATIONS OF ALEXANDRIA

To celebrate his successful campaign in Armenia, Antony held a ceremony, called the Donations of Alexandria. The spectacle was quite different from the Roman triumph that might have been expected after such a victory. Antony, dressed as Dionysus, presented titles and territories to Cleopatra and her children, all of whom were seated on gold thrones. As M. Chauveau notes, this ceremony did not effect any political reorganization—some of the lands were not Antony's to give, and some of the recipients were too young to rule (the children of Antony and Cleopatra were still young: the twins Alexander Helios and Cleopatra Selene were six years old, and Ptolemy Philadelphus just two).[40]

4.13. Plutarch, *Life of Antony* 54.5–9 (A.D. 110–15, Greek, prose)

For more on Plutarch, see selection 2.1. For Plutarch, the ceremony was one more example of Antony's increasing identification with the East.

---

39. Orpheus and Linus were mythical singers. Orpheus's claim to fame was the ability to move rocks and trees and to mesmerize animals with his song. Linus was Orpheus's instructor. Pan, the Greek god of flocks, shepherds, and woods, is associated with pastoral poetry as well.

40. Chauveau 2002, 60.

Antony was also hated for the distribution he made to his children in Alexandria, as it seemed dramatic, arrogant, and anti-Roman. He filled a gymnasium with the people and set up a silver platform with two gold thrones, one for himself and one for Cleopatra; for the children there were smaller ones. First, he proclaimed Cleopatra queen of Egypt, Cyprus, Libya, and Central Syria and appointed Caesarion to rule with her. Caesarion was said to be the son of Julius Caesar, who left Cleopatra when she was pregnant. Second, he decreed that his sons by Cleopatra would take the title King of Kings. To Alexander[41] he apportioned Armenia, Media, and the Parthian territory (as soon as it was conquered). To Ptolemy[42] he granted Phoenicia, Syria, and Cilicia. As he was doing this, Antony also was presenting his children to the people, Alexander wearing a Median costume with a headdress and upright tiara and Ptolemy decked out in soldier's boots, a cloak, a woolen hat, and a crown in his hand. The latter was the costume of Alexander the Great's successors, while the former was the dress of Medes and Armenians. The children then embraced their parents, and one was given a bodyguard of Armenians and the other of Macedonians. Cleopatra, on this occasion as on others, wore the sacred garment of Isis and bore the title the New Isis.

4.14. Cassius Dio, *Roman History* 49.40.2–41.4 (A.D. 202, Greek, prose)

For more on Cassius Dio, see selection 2.5. In his description of the Donations of Alexandria, Dio alludes to the political ramifications the event had at Rome.

40. Next, Antony betrothed the daughter of the Median king to his son, so that the king might be even more allied to him. Leaving the camp in Armenia, he went to Egypt, taking with him all the spoils of battle and the Armenian[43] with his wife and children. He sent them, along with the other captives, ahead, as if in a triumphal procession, and he made his entrance in a chariot. He presented

41. Alexander Helios.
42. Ptolemy Philadelphus.
43. A captive Antony had taken.

many spoils to Cleopatra, especially the Armenian and his family in golden chains. She sat in the middle of the crowd on a platform covered in silver and on a gilded chair. The barbarians failed to supplicate her or prostrate themselves before her, although they were under great pressure to do so and many attempts to persuade them were made by giving them hope; rather, they addressed her by name and thus earned a reputation for arrogance and also suffered many punishments.

41. After this, Antony held a banquet for the Alexandrians. In the assembly, he sat Cleopatra and her children next to him and, when he addressed the populace, he decreed that she should have the title Queen of Kings and Ptolemy, who was called Caesarion, King of Kings. Then, in a reorganization, he granted them Egypt and Cyprus, giving as a reason that one had been Caesar's wife and the other his son and that, therefore, he was doing these things on behalf of Caesar. In fact, however, he wished to disparage Octavian, as he was Caesar's son by adoption rather than by birth. Next, he allotted to the children he had with Cleopatra the following: to Ptolemy,[44] Syria and all the lands within the Euprates as far as the Hellespont; to Cleopatra,[45] the region of Libya around Cyrene; and to their brother Alexander,[46] Armenia and the other lands beyond the Euphrates as far as India (these last places he granted as if they were already his). He not only decreed this in Alexandria, but he also sent word to Rome, so that it might have authority there as well. None of it was read publicly there, however, for Domitius and Sosius were the consuls and, because they were loyal to Antony, they did not wish to reveal these things to the Romans, even though Octavian urged them to.

DIDO AND AENEAS

The Julian family, of which Octavian was an adopted member, claimed Aeneas as its ancestor. Reading the *Aeneid* with this fact in mind, one notices certain correspondences between Aeneas and Octavian. There are other points of contact between poem and history as well.

44. Ptolemy Philadelphus.
45. Cleopatra Selene.
46. Alexander Helios.

Dido existed as a legendary figure before Vergil, and the poet had a number of stories about her upon which he could draw in crafting his epic. Vergil chooses to portray his Dido as the queen of a city in northern Africa who, after attempting a personal and political union with Aeneas, takes her own life, becoming a casualty of Rome's destiny. These choices seem to bring the Dido legend closer to the Augustan version of Cleopatra. There are differences, however. Perhaps the most obvious is the outcome: Aeneas abandons Dido and fulfills his duty in Italy, while Antony remains by Cleopatra's side and meets his end in Alexandria. In addition, despite the threat she poses to the founding of Rome, Dido, as part of the distant past, is a more sympathetic character than Cleopatra and in the *Aeneid* is presented with pathos even as she (albeit under Cupid's spell) contrives to detain Aeneas. Vergil's portrayal of Dido became the canonical account and has influenced subsequent portrayals of Cleopatra as well.

4.15. Vergil, *Aeneid* 1.494–508, 4.160–95, 4.259–387, 4.607–62, 6.440–76 (19 B.C., Latin, verse)

Vergil's Aeneid *recounts the origins of the Roman people. After the Greeks sack Troy in the Trojan War, Aeneas, a member of the Trojan royal family, travels to Italy, marries the daughter of a local king, and becomes the ancestor of the Romans and, specifically, of the Julian family. The* Aeneid *became a Roman classic, a national epic worthy of comparison to Homer's* Iliad *and* Odyssey.

In the following excerpts, Vergil tells the story of Dido and Aeneas. After the fall of Troy, Aeneas sets out with his father, Anchises, his son, Ascanius, and a small band of followers to find the land where they are fated to settle. A storm forces them to land at Carthage, where they encounter Dido, the queen of Carthage.

1.494–508

While Dardan Aeneas observes these marvelous things,
while he stands dumbfounded and, transfixed, he gazes
    intently,[47]   495
the queen, Dido of outstanding beauty, approached the temple

---

47. Dido comes upon Aeneas as he marvels at a temple decorated with scenes from the Trojan War.

surrounded by a great crowd of young men.
Just as on the banks of the Eurotas or through the ridges of
    Cynthus
Diana leads the dances and a thousand Oreads follow her
and crowd around her on all sides;[48] she carries a quiver   500
on her shoulder and towers over all the goddesses as she goes
(Latona's silent heart thrills with joy):
so Dido appeared, and so she carried herself, happily
through their midst, overseeing the work as her kingdom takes
    shape
then, at the goddess's door, under the center of the temple's
    vault,   505
with an armed escort and enthroned on high, she took her seat.
She was granting rights and laws to the men, and she
    apportioned equally
the work to be done or she assigned tasks by lot.

Dido and Aeneas begin a love affair with the aid of Cupid, who, in order
to ensure that Dido would help Aeneas, caused her to fall in love with him.
In this excerpt, Dido and Aeneas have gone on a hunting expedition, when
a storm forces them to seek shelter.

4.160–95

Meanwhile, the sky begins to be confounded   160
with a great roar, rain follows with hail mixed in,
everywhere both the Tyrian contingent and the Trojan youths
and Venus's Dardan grandson[49] in fear seek shelter
here and there in the fields; streams rush from the mountains.
At the same cave, Dido and the Trojan leader   165
arrive. Ancestral Earth and Juno, patroness of marriage
give the sign; lightning flashes and the heavens are witness
to their marriage, and the nymphs cry out from the highest peak.
That first day was the cause of ruin and of evils;
Dido is not moved by appearances or reputation   170
and she no longer devises a secret love:

48. The Eurotas: a river in Sparta; Cynthus: a mountain on the island of Delos; Oreads:
mountain nymphs.
49. Ascanius; Venus was the mother of Aeneas.

she calls it marriage, and under this name she conceals her fault.
Suddenly, Rumor courses through the great cities of Libya,
Rumor, than which no other evil is swifter:
she thrives on motion and gains strength by going,   175
at first small with fear, soon she lifts herself into the air,
she runs on the ground and hides her head in the clouds.
Mother Earth, provoked by anger at the gods, bore her
last, they say, a sister to Coeus and Enceladus,
swift on her feet and nimble on the wing,   180
a terrible monster, huge, having as many feathers on her body
as there are watchful eyes beneath them (amazing to tell),
and as many tongues as she has, so many mouths roar, so
       many ears prick up.
At night she flies halfway between earth and sky, whirring
through the shadows, nor does she close her eyes in sweet
       sleep;   185
By day she sits watchfully on the topmost roof peak
or on high towers, and terrifies great cities,
as eager to pass on falsehood and scandal as the truth.
She gleefully filled the people with diverse reports
and gave fact and fiction equal billing: 190
she said that Aeneas had come, born from Trojan blood,
who would be a worthy husband for lovely Dido;
and that all winter long love was their only concern:
they were forgetful of their kingdoms and enslaved to base
       desire.
Everywhere the foul goddess spreads these rumors on the lips
       of men.   195

*Aeneas and Dido happily spend time together in Carthage. Jupiter, seeing
that Aeneas seems to have abandoned his mission, sends Mercury, the messenger of the gods, to tell Aeneas it is time to leave Carthage and Dido.*

4.259–387

As soon as Mercury's winged feet touched the rooftops,
he caught sight of Aeneas establishing ramparts and repairing   260
roofs. Aeneas, the hilt of his sword studded with yellow jasper,
wore a cloak that burned with Tyrian purple

draped on his shoulders, a gift Dido
had made, its fabric interwoven with fine gold thread.
He began at once: "Are you now laying the foundations   265
of lofty Carthage and building up a beautiful city,
henpecked as you are? Oh, how you forget your kingdom and
your own affairs! The ruler of the gods himself, he who guides
heaven and earth under his sway, sent me to you from bright
    Olympus.
He bids me deliver these commands through the swift breezes: 270
what are you contriving? In hope of what do you while away
    time
in Libyan lands? If fame for your own deeds does not move you
(and you do not undertake these labors for your own glory),
think of Ascanius as he becomes a man and of his hopes as your
successor; the kingdom of Italy and the land of Rome are owed   275
to him." With these words, Cyllenean Mercury[50]
abruptly vanished from human sight and he disappeared
out of sight, far off into thin air.
Aeneas, for his part, was struck dumb, shocked at the sight:
his hair stood on end, a sign of his alarm, and his voice stuck
    in his throat.   280
He burns with a desire for flight, and he wishes to leave the
    pleasant land,
so struck is he by the warning and command of the gods.
But alas, what is he to do? With what excuse would he dare to
approach the queen? What opening statement is he to employ?
His swift mind is divided now here and now there,   285
and it rushes in different directions and runs over every idea.
This solution seemed preferable to him as he vacillated:
he calls Mnestheus and Sergestus and brave Serestus,[51]
instructing them to ready the fleet quietly and to muster on
    the beach,
to prepare their weapons and to conceal the cause   290
for these initiatives; he, meanwhile, since outstanding Dido
does not know and never expected such a love to be broken,

50. Mt. Cyllene was identified as the birthplace of Mercury.
51. Trojan leaders.

will determine how to approach her and what are the easiest
    times
to speak, what is the right way in these matters. At once the men
happily obey Aeneas's orders and fulfill his wishes.   295
But the queen suspects deception (who could fool a
lover?), and she was the first to sense what was coming
and she feared all things, though they seemed safe. That same
    evil Rumor
reported to her in her madness that they were equipping the
    fleet and
charting a course. Bereft of reason, she raged and ran wild
    through   300
the whole city, like a Bacchante aroused by the shaking of
holy relics, when, every third year, the mystic rites excite her
    with the cry,
"Bacchus!" and Cithaeron calls out to her by night.[52]
Finally, she accosts Aeneas with these words:
"Did you actually hope you could conceal a crime   305
of this magnitude and secretly leave my land?
Does my love not have a hold on you, nor the pledge
you once gave, nor Dido about to die a cruel death?
Indeed you even equip your fleet in winter
and hurry to cross the deep amid stormy north winds,   310
cruel one? What if you were not seeking foreign fields
and unknown homes, and ancient Troy still stood,
would you seek Troy with your fleet over rough water?
Are you fleeing from me? I beg you by these tears, by your
    right hand
(since I myself have left nothing else for miserable me),   315
by our marriage, by the wedding we began,
if I deserved you at all, or if I was pleasing to you
in any way, pity this declining house and,
if there is still any place for prayers, put off your intentions.
Because of you the Libyan peoples and the Nomad rulers   320
hate me, the Tyrians are hostile; because of you too

---

52. The Bacchantes were ecstatic worshipers of the god Dionysus (Bacchus), whose rites were celebrated on Mt. Cithaeron, near Thebes.

my honor is ruined as well as my former reputation, by which
    alone
I was to gain glory. To whom do you leave me about to die, guest
(since this title alone remains for one once my husband)?
What am I waiting for? For my brother Pygmalion to destroy my   325
walls or Gaetulian Iarbas to lead me captive?[53]
At least if there had been some child born to me of you
before your flight, if some little Aeneas,
who might resemble you, were playing in my halls,
I would not seem so wholly conquered and forsaken."   330
So she spoke. But Aeneas was holding his eyes unmoved
    because of
Jove's warnings and, struggling, repressed his care in his heart.
At length, he replied with few words: "I will never deny, queen,
that you deserved the many things you mention,
nor will I regret remembering Elissa   335
as long as I remember myself, as long as breath rules these
    limbs.[54]
I will speak a few words to make my case. I did not hope to
    hide in stealth
this departure (do not imagine that), nor did I ever hold
the torches of marriage or enter into this contract.
If the fates allowed me to lead my life on my own   340
authority and to resolve my cares of my own accord,
I would honor first the city of Troy and the dear relics
of my compatriots, Priam's high roofs would remain,
and I would have founded a renewed Troy for the defeated.
But now Grynean Apollo and the Lycian oracles   345
ordered me to lay claim to great Italy;[55]
this is my love, this my homeland. If the towers of Carthage
and the vision of a Libyan city hold you, a Phoenician,
how can you begrudge the Trojans to settle

53. Dido left Tyre and founded Carthage after her brother Pygmalion, the ruler of Tyre, killed her husband, Sychaeus. Iarbas ruled a territory near Carthage and desired Dido's hand in marriage.

54. Elissa: another name for Dido.

55. Gryneum: a town in Asia Minor, site of an oracle of Apollo; Lycia: a country in Asia Minor.

the Ausoian land?[56] It is right for us too to seek foreign
    kingdoms.   350
A troubled vision of my father Anchises, whenever night
    cloaks the earth
in misty shadows, whenever the fiery stars rise,
warns me in my sleep and terrifies me;
my son Ascanius moves me as does the injustice I do him,
Ascanius, whom I cheat of the kingdom of Italy and the
    destined territory.   355
Now even the messenger of the gods, sent by Jove himself,
(I swear on both our heads) brought down commands
through the swift breezes: in broad daylight, I myself saw
    the god
entering the walls and I heard his voice with my own ears.
Cease to inflame both me and you with your complaints;   360
I do not pursue Italy of my own accord."
The whole time he was speaking she averted her gaze,
turning her eyes here and there, and she surveyed everything
with silent eyes and, inflamed, she spoke out:
"No goddess was your mother, nor was Dardanus the founder
    of your people,   365
liar, rather the Caucasus, rough with harsh crags
bore you and Hyrcanian tigers offered you their teats.[57]
Why should I pretend, for what greater wrongs am I saving
    myself?
Did he groan at the sight of my tears? Did he even look?
Overcome with sorrow, did he shed tears or pity his lover?   370
What should I do first? Already, already greatest Juno
and the Saturnian father look upon these events with biased
    eyes.[58]
Trust is never safe. When he was cast out on the shore, destitute,
I took him in and, insane as I was, made him a partner of my
    kingdom.
I restored his lost fleet; I saved his companions from death   375

---

56. Phoenicia: the region of Tyre, the city of which Carthage was a colony; Ausonia: Italy.
    57. Caucasus: mountain range between Europe and Asia; Hyrcania: a region near the
Caspian Sea.
    58. Saturnian: the son of Saturn, i.e., Jupiter.

(alas, inflamed, I am possessed by Furies!): now Apollo the
    prophet,
now the Lycian oracles, now even the messenger of the gods sent
from Jove himself brings terrible commands through the air.
Doubtless this is a task for the gods, this care disturbs
their calm. I don't detain you or contradict your words: 380
go, follow the winds to Italy, seek your kingdom over the waves.
I truly hope, if pious divinities have any power, in the middle
of reefs and rocks you will drink in punishment and often
    cry out
for Dido. I will pursue from a distance with black torches
and, when cold death has robbed me of my limbs,   385
I will be omnipresent as a shade. You will pay, cruel one.
I will hear and the report will come to me among the shades
    below."

*As Dido commits suicide, she curses Aeneas and his descendants, foretelling
the persistent enmity between Rome and Carthage that culminated in the
Punic Wars.*

4.607–62

Sun, you who survey all the achievements of the world with
    your rays,
and you, Juno, agent and witness of my cares,
and Hecate, whose name is shrieked by night at crossroads
    throughout the city,
and vengeful Furies and gods of dying Elissa, hear these things,   610
and bring to bear the divine power I deserve upon my
    misfortunes
and heed my prayers. If the evil man must
reach his port and gain a landing
and thus the fates of Jove dictate, this end is fixed:
but may he, harassed by war and the arms of a bold nation,   615
plucked from the borders of his exile and his son's embrace,
beg for help and see the undeserved deaths
of his people: nor, when he has yielded to the provisions
of an unjust peace, may he enjoy his kingdom or the life he
    desired,
but may he die before his time, unburied on the sand.   620

These things I pray, this final voice I pour out with my blood.
Then, Tyrians, pursue his descendants and the entire future race
with hatred, and send these offerings to my ashes.
Let there be no love or treaties between our peoples.
Rise, some avenger from my bones,   625
to harass the Trojan colonists with iron and fire,
now, later, whenever strength presents itself.
I invoke our shores against their shores, our waves against their
    waves,
our arms against their arms: let them and their descendants
    fight."
She spoke, and turned her mind in every direction,   630
seeking to leave as quickly as possible the hated light.
Then she addressed Barce, Sychaeus's nurse, with few words,
for of her nurse only black ash remained in the ancient
    homeland:
"Dear nurse, call my sister Anna here to me:
tell her to hurry and sprinkle her body with river water,   635
and to bring with her animals and the things required for
    sacrifice.
So may she come; you must cover your head with a holy fillet.
To Stygian Jove[59] I wish to present offerings, which I have
    ritually begun
and prepared, and I wish to impose an end on my cares
and to surrender to flames that Trojan's pyre."   640
So she spoke. Barce hastened her step with energy belying
    her age.
But Dido, fearful and out of her mind with these terrible
    undertakings,
turning a bloodshot gaze, her trembling cheeks
flushed and pale with approaching death, bursts
into the palace's inner courtyard and mounts the high   645
steps to the pyre in a frenzy and unsheathes a sword—
the Trojan's, though she had not requested the gift for this
    purpose.
Here, when she caught sight of the Trojan garments and the
    familiar

59. The Jove of the Underworld, i.e., Pluto.

bed, she hesitated a little in tearful reflection;
she lay down on the bed and spoke these final words: 650
"Sweet relics, while the god and the fates allowed,
receive this spirit and release me from these cares.
I have lived and I have completed the course fortune set for me,
and now my great shade will go under the earth.
I founded a renowned city, I saw my walls rise,   655
I avenged my husband and made my hateful brother pay:
happy, alas, too happy would I have been, if only
Dardan ships had never touched our shores."
She spoke, and pressing her mouth to the bed, said,
"I will die unavenged, but let me die. Thus, thus it pleases me   660
to go to the shades below. May the cruel Trojan drink in this
    fire with his eyes
as he sails away, and let him carry with him the omens of my
    death."

When Aeneas journeys to the Underworld, he encounters the shade of
Dido. In the afterlife, she inhabits the Fields of Mourning, home to those
who died for love.

6.450–76

Among these, Phoenician Dido, her wound still fresh,   450
wandered in the great forest; as soon as the Trojan hero
approached and recognized her shadowy form among
the shades, just as one who sees or thinks he sees
at the beginning of the month the moon rising through the
    clouds,
he shed tears and spoke with fond love,   455
"Unhappy Dido, were the reports true, then, that you
were dead, that you sought your own end with a sword?
Alas, was I the cause of your death? I swear by the stars,
by the gods and by whatever faith exists beneath the earth,
unwilling, queen, I left your shores.   460
But the decrees of the gods now dictate that I go now
among these shades, through places rough with neglect,
    through the deep night;
then, too, gods drove me with their commands; I could not
    believe

that I brought you such grief with my departure.
Stay your feet and do not take yourself from my sight.   465
Whom do you flee? This is fated to be the last time I speak
    to you."
With such words, Aeneas tried to soothe her as she flashed
    burning eyes,
And he tried to move her with his tears.
She turned away, her eyes fixed on the ground,
and her face showed no more emotion at his speech   470
than if she were hard flint or a Marpesian cliff.[60]
Finally, she snatched herself away and, hostile, fled
into the shady grove, where her first husband, Sychaeus
sympathizes with her cares and returns her love.
Still, Aeneas, anguished at Dido's unjust fate, weeping,   475
trailed behind her and pitied her as she went.

---

60. Marpesus: a mountain famous for its marble quarries.

5

Octavian

OCTAVIAN PLAYED QUITE A different role in Cleopatra's story from Julius Caesar and Mark Antony. Seemingly immune to her charms, Octavian desired Cleopatra as a trophy rather than as a mistress.

A PORTRAIT OF OCTAVIAN

While Antony was a great general, Octavian was much more the shrewd politician. Of somewhat weak health, he relied more on intellect than on physical capabilities. His vision of Rome was a return to the old ways—self-sufficiency, simplicity, and piety. He made a show of leading by example, but his own indiscretions when it came to women made it difficult for him to impose a return to old Roman morals.

5.1. Suetonius, *The Divine Augustus* 72–84 (A.D. 119–21, Latin, prose)

For more on Suetonius, see selection 3.1. In this passage Suetonius describes Octavian's appearance and character.

72. In other aspects of his life, it is well known that he valued moderation and was without suspicion of any vice. At first, he lived next to the Roman Forum just above the Ringmakers' Stairs in a house formerly owned by the orator Calvus. Later, he lived on the Palatine, but in a modest dwelling that had been Hortensius's and that stood out neither for its spaciousness nor for its refinement: the

porticoes had squat columns of Alban stone and the rooms had no marble or mosaic flooring. For more than forty years, he slept in the same bedroom, winter and summer, even though he did not find the city conducive to good health in winter and he always wintered in the city. If he ever needed to do anything in private or without interruption, he had a secluded place on the top floor, which he called "Syracuse" or "little studio": he would retreat to this place or to the suburban estate of one of his freedmen. When he was sick, he would stay at the home of Maecenas.[1] His vacations frequently took him to the coast and the islands off Campania, or to various towns near the city such as Lanuvium, Praeneste, and Tibur, where he administered justice in the portico of Hercules' temple. Roomy and elaborate country houses annoyed him. He even razed to the ground a house his granddaughter Julia had lavishly built. His own estates were modest: they were notable not so much for the statues and paintings that decorated them as for the terraces and groves and items of interest for their age and rarity, such as, at Capri, giant bones of huge beasts and brutes, which were known as the bones of giants and the weapons of heroes.

73. The economy of his decor and furnishings is evident from the couches and tables still in existence, of which most are scarcely of a quality suitable for a private citizen. They say he would only sleep on a bed if it were low and modestly made up. He scarcely ever wore clothing that was not homemade by his sister and wife and daughter and granddaughters; his toga was neither fitted nor loose, the stripe neither wide nor narrow, his shoes were somewhat high soled, so that he would appear taller than he was. He always kept in his room a set of business clothes and shoes, in case of sudden and unexpected occasions.

74. He entertained guests at dinner often and always with a formal occasion: he was very aware of the status and character of his guests. Valerius Messala relates that he never invited freedmen to dinner with the exception of Menas, who had been decreed freeborn after he deserted Sextus Pompey's fleet to join Augustus. Augustus himself

---

1. Maecenas was one of Octavian's close associates, to whom he delegated some responsibilities, including the patronage of poets. The poet Horace mentions Maecenas's house on the Esquiline as a healthful place (*Satires* 1.8.14).

writes that he once invited a freedman in whose house he had stayed and who had once been one of his bodyguards. Sometimes at dinner parties he would both arrive late and leave early; his guests would start their drinking and dining before he was seated and continue after his departure. He served a dinner of three courses, or, if he was entertaining lavishly, six. There was no excessive elegance, but always good company because he encouraged those who kept silent or spoke only softly to join the general discussion. He also provided entertainers, actors, or even roving circus performers and storytellers on many occasions.

75. He celebrated religious holidays lavishly and sometimes light-heartedly. At the Saturnalia, and whenever else it pleased him, he would vary his gifts in value: now giving clothing, gold and silver, now coins of every type, even ancient ones from the monarchy and foreign ones, but then nothing more than blankets made from goat hair, sponges, pokers, tongs, and other things of that type, all labeled with misleading and ambiguous tags. At dinner parties, he was also fond of selling lottery tickets for items of vastly unequal value or auctioning off paintings turned toward the wall. Buyers either had their hopes dashed or fulfilled on the gamble, as the occupants of each couch offered a collective bid and shared either loss or gain.

76. As for food—for I should not omit this topic—he was a light eater and almost common in his tastes. He preferred coarse bread, small fish, soft handmade cheese, and green figs from the second crop; he ate between meals, whenever and wherever his appetite dictated. These quotations come from his own letters: "I ate some bread and dates in my chariot" and "as I returned home in my litter from the Regia, I had an ounce of bread and a few fruits from a cluster of hard-skinned grapes" and "not even a Jew, my dear Tiberius, observes the Sabbath fast so carefully as I have fasted today: only after six o'clock in the evening while at the baths did I eat two mouthfuls before my rubdown." Because of these erratic eating habits, he sometimes dined alone, either before or after the meal, and touched nothing at the dinner table.

77. He was by nature very moderate in his drinking. Cornelius Nepos tells us he usually took no more than three drinks at dinner at the Battle of Mutina. Later, he often indulged himself more freely, but did not exceed a pint, or, if he did exceed it, he would rid himself

of it with an emetic. He was fondest of Raetian wine, but rarely drank during the day. Rather than drinking he would have some bread soaked in cold water or a piece of cucumber or the stalk of a young lettuce or a ripe or dried sour apple.

78. After his midday meal, he used to rest a little without removing his clothes or shoes and with his feet uncovered, shading his eyes with his hand. After dinner, he retired to his study couch; there he remained late into the night until he completed the remainder of the day's business or at least most of it. Then he went to bed and slept no more than seven hours at the most, and even those hours were not continuous: in that interval of time he would awaken three or four times. If, as often happened, he was not able to fall asleep again, he would summon readers or storytellers and, when he fell asleep, he would not wake until after first light. He never stayed up at night unless someone was with him. He did not like to rise early: if some official or religious ceremony required him to be up early, he would stay with any member of his household who lived near the location, lest he be inconvenienced while performing his duty. Even so, he often did not get enough sleep and, while he was being carried in his litter, he would fall asleep anytime there was a delay and the litter was put down.

79. He was quite handsome and carried himself gracefully even in old age, although he paid no attention to personal adornment. He was so careless of his hairstyle that he gave the task of hairdressing to several barbers working hastily at the same time, now cutting his hair, now shaving his beard, while he would read or write something at the same time. Whether he was speaking or silent, he had such a calm expression that one of the leaders of the Gauls admitted to his men that had he not been restrained and softened by the sight of Augustus, he would have gone through with his plan to push him off a cliff when he was admitted to the princeps's presence on the pretense of meeting with him as he crossed the Alps. Augustus's eyes were bright and clear: he flattered himself there was a kind of divine radiance in them and he was thrilled if anyone whose gaze he met quickly dropped his eyes as if he had looked into the sun. As he aged, he lost some of the vision in his left eye; his teeth were few, small, and decayed; his hair was somewhat blonde and wavy; his eyebrows met; his ears were medium sized; his nose was prominent at the top and somewhat curved at the tip; his coloring was between dark and pale;

he was not tall—his freedman and record keeper Julius Marathus gives his height as five feet seven inches—but the proportion and symmetry of his build disguised his short stature to the extent that it was only noticeable if someone tall stood next to him.

80. He reportedly had blemishes on his body: birthmarks were scattered across his chest and stomach similar in shape, layout, and number to the stars of the constellation the Great Bear; there were hard patches all over his skin that resulted from an itching of the skin as well as constant and vigorous use of the strigil,[2] though they resembled eczema. His left hip, thigh, and leg were not very strong, and so he often limped slightly. The sand and reed cure helped, however.[3] His right index finger often was so weak from being stiffened and shrunken by cold that it could scarcely hold a pen even with the aid of a horn splint. He also complained of bladder pains, although they were eased when he passed stones in his urine.

81. He experienced a number of serious and dangerous illnesses during his life, the most severe following his conquest of Cantabria, when, reduced to despair by abscesses afflicting his liver, he underwent a treatment opposed to the prevailing medical advice. Since hot poultices were not effective, he found relief in cold ones under the care of his physician Antonius Musa. He also suffered on a yearly basis from certain seasonal complaints: around his birthday,[4] he often was listless; in early spring, he suffered from swelling of the diaphragm; in hot weather, he caught colds. As is evident, his weakened constitution tolerated neither cold nor heat well.

82. In winter, he warded off cold with four tunics, a thick toga, a wool undershirt and chest protector, thigh coverings, and leggings. In summer, he slept with his bedroom door open or often slept in the courtyard with someone fanning him and water leaping from the fountain. He could not stand the sun even in winter: he never walked outside without a broad-brimmed hat, even at home. He made journeys by litter and at night, so slowly and in stages that it took two days to reach Praeneste or Tibur. If it was possible to go by

2. The strigil was a curved implement made of bone or metal used to scrape the skin of perspiration, oil, and dirt.

3. The sand and reed cure may have been a poultice made of sand and crushed reeds, or it may have been a splint of some sort.

4. September 23.

sea, he preferred to sail. Truly, he guarded his health with great care: in particular he bathed only rarely; more often he anointed himself with oil or took a sauna and then doused himself with water either warmed or allowed to stand in the sun. But whenever he had to use hot salt water or water from the Alban hot springs for his rheumatism, he was content to sit on the wooden seat (which he called "dureta"—its Spanish name) and alternately dip his hands and feet.

83. After the civil wars, he stopped his practice military maneuvers and instead took up playing catch and handball. Soon he only rode or walked. At the end of his walk he would run by leaps and bounds, though wrapped in a mantle or blanket. To relax his mind, he would go fishing or play dice, marbles, or nuts with little boys, whom he sought out for their appearance and conversation, especially Moors and Syrians. He disliked dwarves or those with any type of deformity, as he considered them nature's pranks and a bad omen.

84. From his earliest youth, he studied rhetoric and the liberal arts with great enthusiasm and diligence. It is said that, even in the hectic conditions of the Battle of Mutina, he read, wrote, and declaimed daily. From then on, he never spoke before the Senate, the people, or the soldiers without a planned and prepared address, even though he was not without talent in speaking extemporaneously. He adopted the practice of reading from a prepared text so as not to be betrayed by his memory or waste time in memorization. He did not even make statements to individuals, or even to his wife Livia, except by writing them down and reading them aloud, lest he say too much or too little by speaking casually. His speech had a pleasant tone and a distinctive sound, for he trained regularly with a teacher of elocution. Nevertheless, when at times his voice was too weak, he addressed the people through a herald.

ACCOMPLISHMENTS

For much of his reign, Augustus was concerned with his legacy. Near the end of his life, he composed an account of his accomplishments. While he is selective about what he includes and how he portrays events (for instance, Antony is never named), he is bound to a certain degree of accuracy because many readers would have lived through the events about which he writes.

5.2. Augustus, Res Gestae 1–2 (A.D. 13, Latin, prose)

Augustus wrote the Res Gestae *("things done") to be inscribed on bronze panels and displayed outside his mausoleum after his death. The text of the inscription as we have it comes from copies displayed in the Roman province of Galatia (modern Turkey). The* Res Gestae *is part of the genre of grave inscriptions and eulogizing speeches given at funerals.[5] In it Augustus treats his military accomplishments, honors he received, benefactions to the Roman people, and his restoration of the Republic. The following passage treats the events of 44–42 B.C., the period in which Octavian competes with Antony for the legacy of Julius Caesar, defeats Antony at Mutina,[6] is elected consul for the fist time, forms the Second Triumvirate, and defeats Brutus and Cassius at Philippi.*

1. At age nineteen, on my own authority and at my own expense, I marshaled an army, with which I liberated the Republic, when it was oppressed by the rule of a faction.[7] As a result, the senate elected me to membership by honorary decree in the year of consuls Gaius Pansa and Aulus Hirtius and granted me consular status for giving my opinion and gave me the power of a commander. They charged me as propraetor, along with the consuls, to see that the Republic came to no harm. Moreover, in the same year the people made me consul and triumvir for establishing the Republic, when both consuls had been killed in battle.

2. Those who assassinated my father I expelled to exile, avenging their crime with legal judgments. Afterward, when they brought war upon the Republic, I defeated them twice in battle.

The Propaganda War

In addition to military conflict, Octavian and Antony waged a battle of words. Because the winners write the history, we have much more information about the accusations Octavian brought against Antony

---

5. Brunt and Moore 1990, 2–3.

6. At Mutina (Modena) in 43 B.C., Antony was fighting Caesar's assassins and also Octavian, his rival in the quest to be Caesar's successor. Later in 43 B.C., the Second Triumvirate was formed, consisting of Octavian, Antony, and Lepidus.

7. The "faction" was Antony's.

than we do about Antony's rejoinders; nevertheless, it is possible to uncover and reconstruct some of Antony's verbal arsenal. The passages that follow present some of the charges the two sides made against one another.

5.3. Cassius Dio, *Roman History* 50.24–28 (A.D. 202, Greek, prose)

For more on Cassius Dio, see selection 2.5. Here, Dio presents a speech in which Octavian exhorts his troops and details his reasons for declaring war on Cleopatra. Dio would not have had access to Octavian's words from that occasion, so he composes a speech that captures what Octavian is likely to have said.

24. "Since I have observed, soldiers, both from what I have learned through hearsay and from what I have tested by experience, that the majority and the greatest deeds of war, or rather of all affairs of men, favor those who think and act justly and reverently, I have carefully considered this truth and I urge you to heed it as well. Accordingly, even if we have extremely numerous and impressive forces, with which even a man who chose the less just cause might hope to conquer, nevertheless I have much more courage based on the causes of the war than on these forces. Indeed, for us as Romans, rulers of the largest and best part of the world, to be disparaged and downtrodden by an Egyptian woman is unworthy of our fathers, who conquered Pyrrhus, Philip, Perseus, and Antiochus, who routed the Numantians and the Carthaginians, who slaughtered the Cimbri and Ambrones; it is also unworthy of ourselves, who subdued the Gauls, mastered the Pannonians, reached the Ister, crossed the Rhine, and voyaged to Britain. How could all those who accomplished the deeds I have mentioned not be greatly aggrieved, if they heard that we had been overthrown by a ruinous woman? How would we not be behaving indecorously if, after surpassing everyone everywhere in excellence, we should then mildly endure these outrages of these people, who—Hercules—are Alexandrians and Egyptians (for what else would be more shameful or more true to call them?), who honor as gods lizards and other creatures, who preserve their bodies to make them appear immortal, who are very rash in boasting but very weak in courage, and, what is worst of all, who are slaves to a woman instead of a man, but dared to try to take our goods and to take

possession of them with our help, so that we willingly yield to them the wealth that is ours?

25. "Who would not be dismayed to see the queen of the Egyptians with Roman bodyguards? Who would not lament to hear that Roman knights and Senators fawn over her like eunuchs? Who would not moan to hear and see Antony himself, twice a consul, many times a commander, to whom, along with me, leadership was entrusted and so many cities, so many legions—who would not weep to see that he has now left behind his ancestral customs, that he has imitated foreign and barbaric ones, that he does not respect the laws or gods of his ancestors, but bows before that woman like Isis or Selene, names her children Helios and Selene, and finally calls himself Osiris and Dionysus, and, after all these things, he gives as gifts whole islands and parts of continents, as if he were the lord of the whole earth and sea? These things seem unbelievable and amazing to you soldiers, I know; and because of that, you should be even more outraged. Indeed, if what you do not believe when you hear it turns out to be true, and if that man commits crimes of luxury at which anyone would shudder to learn, then how is it not appropriate for your anger to know no bounds?

26. "And yet, at first, I was so enthusiastic about him that I shared with him my command, married my sister to him,[8] and gave him legions. After this, I was so sympathetic and kind to him that I did not wish to go to war with him because he insulted my sister, or because he did not care for the children he had with her, or because he honored the Egyptian woman instead of her, or because he gave that woman almost all the things that are rightfully yours, or because of anything else. I considered the first reason to be that the same approach should not be taken with both Cleopatra and Antony, for she was clearly an enemy because of what she did and also because she was a foreigner, but he, as a citizen, might possibly be reasoned with. Secondly, I hoped that, even if he did not want to, he might, under duress, change his mind because of the decrees passed against Cleopatra. Because of this, I did not declare war on him. But he, since he despises and disparages these favors, he will not receive pardon, even if we wish to grant it, and will not receive pity, even if

8. Octavia.

we feel it. He is either irrational or insane (for I have heard this and believe that he is under that abominable woman's spell) and has no respect for our magnanimity and kindness, but, since he is enslaved to that woman, he brings war and its dangers, which he voluntarily incurs on her behalf, against us and against his fatherland. Therefore, what choice do we have but to defend ourselves against him and Cleopatra?

27. "Therefore, let no one consider him a Roman, but rather an Egyptian; let no one call him Antony, but rather Serapion; let no one believe that he was at one time a consul or commander, but rather a gymnasiarch.[9] He himself has chosen willingly the latter rather than the former titles; casting off all the respectable titles of his homeland, he has become a cymbal player of Canopus. Let no one fear that he will turn the tide of the war, for previously he was nothing outstanding, as those of you who beat him at Mutina know well. But even if at one time he had some success in an expedition when he was on our side, be confident that now he has destroyed his abilities through his change in lifestyle: it is not possible for someone living in royal luxury and being treated like a woman to think or act like a man, because it is always true that one's behavior reflects one's way of life. As evidence, I submit that he, having fought one battle in all this time and having engaged in one campaign, lost many citizens in the battle, shamefully retreated from Praaspa, and lost many more in the flight. As a result, if this were a contest of dancing ridiculously or comic buffoonery and one of us had to compete against him, our man would surely lose, for Antony is the expert in these skills; since, however, the contest is one of weapons and battle, what could anyone fear from him? The fitness of his body? He is over the hill and thoroughly effeminate. His mental powers? He has the mind of a woman and the physical desires of one too. His respect for our gods? He fights against them as he does against our homeland. His loyalty to his allies? Who does not know that he deceived the Armenian and put him in chains? His fairness to his friends? Who has not seen those whom he has wickedly destroyed? His reputation among the

---

9. A gymnasiarch was a Greek official who supervised the gymnasium, the facility used for athletic training and competitions. The gymnasiarch would organize contests and contribute money to support training (see Plutarch, *Life of Antony* 33, on Antony's holding this office).

soldiers? Who among them has not condemned him? This is evident because crowds of them desert to our side on a daily basis. Indeed, I think that all of our citizens will follow suit, just as has happened previously, when he went from Brundisium to Gaul. As long as the men expected to enrich themselves without risk, some were very happy to be among his troops, but they will not wish to fight against us, their fellow citizens, on behalf of things that are not theirs, especially it is possible for them to be safe and to get rich without danger if they join us.

28. "But someone will say that he has many allies and great wealth. How, then, were we able to conquer the inhabitants of the Asian continent? Scipio Asiaticus knows, as do fortunate Sulla, Lucullus, Pompey, my father Caesar, and you yourselves who conquered those who fought with Brutus and Cassius.[10] If this is true, then, insofar as you think that the riches of Antony and his allies is greater than that of others, you should desire even more to take it for yourselves: to win the greatest prizes, one must undertake the greatest contests. And I can honestly tell you that there is no other prize for you greater than to protect the reputation of your ancestors, to preserve your own way of thinking, to punish those who rebel against us, to avenge the outrages against us, to vanquish and rule over all people, and to overlook no woman who would consider herself equal to a man. Against the Taurisci, the Iapydes, the Dalmatians, and the Pannonians you, who are now present, have fought bravely, often over a few walls and some deserted land, and you conquered all these peoples, even though they are extremely hostile. By Jupiter, you also contended with Sextus Pompey, with only Sicily as a prize, and with Antony himself, with only Mutina as a prize, and you conquered both of them. Will you be less determined against a woman plotting against everything that is yours, or against a man who has given your property away to her children, or against their illustrious companions and dinner guests, whom they themselves refer to as buffoons? What reason would you have? Their superior numbers? No number of bodies can compete with courage. Their race? They are used to carrying loads, not carrying

---

10. Scipio Asiaticus: brother of Scipio Africanus and consul in 190 B.C. In the same year he defeated Antiochus III, ruler of the Seleucid Empire in Asia Minor. Sulla: Roman consul who fought Mithradates Eupator, the king of Pontus, in 88 B.C. Lucullus: an officer in Sulla's army.

on wars. Their experience? They know how to row, not how to fight at sea. I am embarrassed that we are to fight such people: if we conquer them, we will not enhance our reputation, but if we are defeated, we will bring shame upon ourselves."

5.4. Plutarch, *Life of Antony* 36, 55, 58–59 (A.D. 110–15, Greek, prose)

For more on Plutarch, see selection 2.1. Antony made a number of impolitic moves in his dealings with Cleopatra, and these hurt his reputation at Rome. Octavian took full advantage of these circumstances.

36. The calamity that had been dormant for a long time, his love for Cleopatra, lulled to sleep and enchanted by better reasoning, again blazed up and roused itself as he approached Syria. Finally, like the horse Plato describes as hard to control and unresponsive to the whip,[11] Antony shook off all noble and redemptive things and sent Fonteius Capito[12] to bring Cleopatra to Syria. He rewarded her when she arrived and granted her no small prizes, but Phoenicia, Central Syria, Cyprus, and much of Cilicia. In addition to these, he granted her the part of Judaea that produces balsam and as much of Nabataean Arabia as borders the outer sea.[13] These gifts to her annoyed the Romans. Previously, Antony had granted tetrarchies[14] and kingships over great peoples to many private individuals; he had taken kingdoms away from many rulers like Antigonus of Judaea, whom he had brought out and beheaded, although none of the other kings had ever been punished in this way. But the shameful thing was the extremely distressing honors given to Cleopatra. He increased the scandal by acknowledging the children he had with her, calling one Alexander Helios and one Cleopatra Selene.[15] But Antony was skilled in putting a positive spin on disgraceful acts and said that the greatness of Rome was shown not through taking kingdoms, but granting them, and that, if one has a noble ancestry, it should be spread by begetting heirs from many sovereigns. It was thus, he claimed, his ancestor had been begotten from Hercules, who did not place his successors in a

11. Plato, *Phaedrus* 254a.
12. A close friend of Antony.
13. The Red Sea.
14. A tetrarch was a member of a board of four rulers.
15. Alexander the Sun and Cleopatra the Moon.

single womb, and did not respect Solon's laws of legitimate concep-
tion, but gave license to his nature to leave behind many beginnings
and foundations.

55. Octavian publicized these events in the Senate and, by frequently
criticizing Antony before the people, he provoked the majority against
Antony. Antony, too, sent word condemning Octavian in return. The
greatest accusations were: first, that Octavian had failed to give
Antony a share of Sicily after capturing it from Pompey;[16] second,
that Octavian had used Antony's ships for the war and not returned
them; third, that Octavian had removed their colleague Lepidus
from power, dishonored him, and then took his army, territory, and
income; on top of it all, that Octavian had distributed almost all available Italian land to his own soldiers, leaving nothing for Antony's men.
Octavian responded to these charges by saying that he had termi-
nated Lepidus's command on the grounds that he was abusing his
power, that he would share what he had conquered in war with
Antony once Antony shared Armenia with him, and that he would
not give any share of Italy to Antony's soldiers, for they had Media
and Parthia, which they had won for the Romans by fighting nobly
with their commander.

58. Octavian was distressed, when he heard of the speed and size
of Antony's preparations, at the prospect of being forced into war
that summer. He still lacked many supplies and the Romans were
resentful over the taxes he had imposed, for some were required to
pay one quarter of their income and freedmen one eighth of their
net worth. Both groups rebelled and there were protests throughout
Italy over the measure. For this reason, people say that putting off
the war was Antony's biggest mistake, since he gave Octavian time to
prepare and the Italians' tempers time to cool: in the thick of the
controversy, they were angry, but once it was behind them and they
had paid the taxes, they became calm. Titius and Plancus, friends of
Antony of consular rank whom Cleopatra offended (they vehemently
opposed her accompanying the expedition) deserted and went over
to Octavian, sharing with him some details of the contents of Antony's
will, which they knew. The will was kept by the Vestal Virgins, who,
when Octavian asked for it, refused to give it to him, but told him

16. Sextus Pompey.

that if he wished to take it, he could come and do so. Thus, he went and took it. First, he went through the document himself in private and put a mark beside passages he could attack easily. Then, he gathered the Senate and read it, though most of the Senators did not support his actions. It seemed to them monstrous and terrible that someone still living should have to submit to an audit of his accounts, when he did not wish it done until after his death. Octavian attacked the document in particular where Antony's burial was concerned. Indeed, Antony had ordered that his body, if he died in Rome, be carried in a procession through the Forum and then conveyed to Alexandria and placed in Cleopatra's care. Calvisius, a friend of Octavian, brought additional charges against Antony relating to his treatment of Cleopatra, saying that he had made a gift to her of the libraries at Pergamum, in which there were two hundred thousand volumes; during a banquet at which there were many guests, he had gotten up and massaged her feet like a slave, in order to fulfill some wager or agreement; he had permitted the Ephesians to recognize Cleopatra as their queen while he was present; frequently, when he was dispensing justice to tetrarchs and kings from the speaker's platform, he would receive love letters from her inscribed on onyx or crystal and he would read them; when Furinus, who was the most skilled and most famous orator of all the Romans, was speaking in court and Cleopatra came though the square in her litter, Antony, when he saw her, jumped up, left the trial, and followed her, clinging to her litter.

59. It seems, however, that Calvisius lied about most of these events. Antony's friends went around in Rome entreating the people and they sent one of them, named Geminus, to ask Antony not to allow himself to be voted out of power and declared an enemy of the state. Geminus sailed to Greece, where Cleopatra suspected that he was acting on behalf of Octavia and consistently mocked him at dinner and disrespected him by always seating him in the position of lowest status, but he held up well and waited for a chance to speak with Antony. But when ordered to state the reason for his visit, they were at dinner, and so he said that he would tell the rest when he was sober, but that, drunk or sober, he knew one thing, that all would be well if Cleopatra returned to Egypt. Antony was upset at this, but Cleopatra just said, "You have done well, Geminus, as you

told the truth without our having to resort to torture." After a few days, Geminus fled and returned to Rome. Cleopatra's flatterers also drove off many of Antony's other friends, who could not stand the drunken antics and clowning around. Among those who left were Marcus Silanus and Dellius the historian. Dellius even said that he feared that Cleopatra was plotting against him, of which Glaucus the physician informed him. Glaucus had quarreled with Cleopatra at dinner, when he said that sour wine was poured for Antony's friends, while in Rome Sarmentus was drinking Falernian;[17] Sarmentus was one of Octavian's boy toys, which the Romans call *deliciae*.

5.5. Plutarch, *Comparison of Demetrius and Antony* 3.3 (A.D. 110–15, Greek, prose)

For more on Plutarch, see selection 2.1. Each of Plutarch's biographies is part of a pair in which the biography of a Greek is paired with that of a Roman. Following each pair, Plutarch gives a brief analysis of the two figures, highlighting the features they have in common and pointing out any differences between them. Plutarch pairs the Life of Antony *with his biography of Demetrius, one of the successors of Alexander the Great because both men experienced reversals of fortune. The anecdotes in this passage illustrate one of their shared traits, a love of luxury.*

But Antony—just as in paintings of Omphale[18] taking away Hercules' club and removing his lion skin—frequently surrendered his weapons to Cleopatra and was bewitched by her. She succeeded in persuading him to cast aside his important affairs and essential campaigns and instead to wander on the shores of Canopus and Taphosiris and play with her. Finally, like Paris, fleeing from battle, he sank into a woman's bosom.[19] To be exact, however, Paris fled to the bedroom after his defeat, but Antony fled in pursuit of Cleopatra and sacrificed his victory.

---

17. Falernian was a fine Italian wine.
18. Omphale was the queen of Lydia to whom Hercules was enslaved as a punishment for murder. Some sources (e.g., Ovid, *Heroides* 9.53–118) claim that Omphale forced Hercules to dress in women's clothes and perform stereotypically female tasks such as spinning and weaving.
19. Paris, son of the Trojan king Priam, caused the Trojan war by stealing Helen, the wife of Greek general Menelaus.

5.6. Suetonius, *The Divine Augustus* 68–70, 17.1–2 (A.D. 119–21, Latin, prose)

For more on Suetonius, see selection 3.1. In these passages Suetonius relates a number of unflattering stories that circulated about Octavian, some of them instigated by Antony, along with some of Octavian's counterattacks against Antony, which led to the final break in their alliance before the Battle of Actium.

68. Augustus was the subject of rumors involving various disgraceful acts going back to his youth. Sextus Pompey accused him of being effeminate; Mark Antony claimed that his adoption was a reward for serving the homosexual desires of his uncle;[20] likewise, Lucius the brother of Mark Antony said that after being deflowered by Caesar, he had prostituted himself to Aulus Hirtius in Spain for three thousand gold coins and that he was in the habit of singeing his legs with a burning walnut shell to make the hair grow softer. In addition, one time the people, all assembled in the theater on a festival day, applauded enthusiastically at a line that they took as mocking Augustus. One actor portrayed a tambourine-playing eunuch priest of Cybele, while another proclaimed:

Do you see how the catamite's finger governs the orb?[21]

69. Even his friends do not deny that he was guilty of adultery, but they justify it by claiming that he acted not out of lust but rather as a calculated strategy: he could more easily learn the strategies of his enemies through their wives. Mark Antony reproached him for marrying Livia in too much haste and for absconding to the bedroom with the wife of a consul, before the eyes of her husband and at a dinner party he was hosting no less. She returned to the party blushing and with her hair in disarray. Antony also complained that Augustus divorced Scribonia for criticizing him too openly for keeping a mistress and that Augustus's friends set up his affairs, depriving families of mothers and making girls of marriageable age strip for inspection as if they stood before Toranius the slave dealer. Antony even wrote frankly in a letter to Augustus (before they were estranged by private and public feuds):

20. Julius Caesar.
21. The line's double meaning, "beat the drum" and "rule the world," is difficult to capture in English.

What changed you? That I'm sleeping with the queen?[22] She's my wife. I've been seeing her for nine years. Do you sleep only with Livia Drusilla? Good for you if, when you read this, you haven't been sleeping with Tertulla or Terentilla or Rufilla or Salvia Titisenia or all of them. What does it matter where and with whom you get it on?

70. Another topic of gossip was the rather exclusive dinner party he held, called the "Twelve Gods," at which guests would recline dressed as gods or goddesses (Augustus was always Apollo). We know this not only from a letter in which an embittered Antony names the twelve participants, but also from these well-known anonymous verses:

> Once the impious banqueters found a stage manager,
> Mallia saw six gods and six goddesses,
> while Caesar makes a mockery of the role of Phoebus,
> and hosts novel debaucheries of the gods.
> Then all the gods turn away from the earth,
> and Jupiter himself flees his golden throne.

What made the rumored dinner even more scandalous was the fact that it took place at a time of poverty and starvation in the city. The following day there was a public outcry: "the gods have eaten all the grain!" "Caesar is surely Apollo, but Apollo the Torturer." For Apollo was worshiped with that epithet in a certain part of the city. It also has been noted that he was quite fond of indulging in expensive furniture, Corinthian bronzes, and gambling, as evidenced by a graffito written on the base of his statue during the proscriptions:[23]

> My father traded in silver, I in Corinthian bronzes,

implying that he had proscribed certain men because they owned vases of this type. Then there was this epigram, made public during the Sicilian War:[24]

> After two fleets lost in defeats at sea,
> he plays dice all day to win just one victory.

22. Cleopatra.
23. Proscription was the publication of a list of enemies marked for execution, whose property was confiscated. The Second Triumvirate (Octavian, Antony, and Lepidus) instituted proscriptions in 43–42 B.C.
24. Octavian's forces suffered severe losses in the conflict with Sextus Pompey in 38 B.C.

17. Finally Octavian broke off his alliance with Mark Antony—it had always wavered and had been kept alive with difficulty through various reconciliations. In order to prove that Antony had abandoned the conduct worthy of a Roman citizen, Octavian arranged for a will that Antony had deposited at Rome to be opened and read publicly. It named as Antony's heirs the children he had fathered by Cleopatra. Although Antony was declared a public enemy, Octavian allowed all his friends and relatives, including current consuls Gaius Sosius and Titus Domitius, to go to him. Octavian also excused the people of Bononia from joining the rest of Italy in swearing an oath of loyalty to his party, since the Antonian family had long been benefactors of Bononia.

6

Actium

THE BATTLE OF ACTIUM HAS, in retrospect, been seen as Octavian's definitive victory over Antony and Cleopatra. In fact the war continued for nearly a year after Actium, until Antony and Cleopatra committed suicide in 30 B.C. Actium, however, was the beginning of the end, and Cleopatra's dramatic departure from the battle made it a popular moment in the conflict for poets and artists to portray.

PREPARATIONS

Octavian's preparations for Actium included a formal declaration of war on Cleopatra, performed according to an archaic, native Italian ritual. Antony and Cleopatra prepared for battle as they did everything, with a great deal of extravagant celebration.

6.1. Cassius Dio, *Roman History* 50.4.3–6 (A.D. 202, Greek, prose)

For more on Cassius Dio, see selection 2.5. Politically, Octavian had to walk a fine line as he prepared to engage in open hostilities with Antony. He was careful to minimize associations with civil war, as the Roman people had already suffered through many years of civil conflict and Octavian would risk losing support if he declared war on a fellow citizen.

4. The Romans stripped Antony of his consulship, to which he had been elected, along with all his other authority. They did not,

however, use the term *enemy,* as they feared that it would also be necessary to consider his supporters as enemies if they did not desert him. Their actions, however, more than anything else indicated their feelings: they voted to pardon and praise his supporters if they would desert him, and they unequivocally declared war on Cleopatra. They donned military cloaks as if he were nearby, and, going to the temple of Bellona, they performed all the rites for declaring war according to custom, with Octavian acting as priest. In word, war was declared on Cleopatra, but in fact the declaration was aimed at Antony.

5. Indeed, Cleopatra had enslaved Antony to such a degree that she persuaded him to take the office of gymnasiarch in Alexandria.[1] He called her queen and mistress; she had Roman soldiers in her bodyguard and her name was inscribed on all their shields. She would go to the marketplace with him, organize festivals with him, dispense justice with him, and ride with him even in the cities or be carried in a litter as Antony followed her on foot along with the eunuchs. Antony named his general's tent the palace; there were times when he carried a Persian dagger in his belt; he wore foreign clothing; he was seen even in public on a gilded couch or chair. He also had portraits painted and statues sculpted of him with Cleopatra: he appeared as Osiris or Dionysus and she as Selene or Isis. Because of this more than anything else, he seemed to have been put under her spell, for she so bewitched and captivated not only him but also all his advisors that she hoped to rule the Romans and, whenever she swore any oath, she swore by her intent to dispense justice on the Capitol.

6. Because of these things, they voted to declare war on Cleopatra, but they declared no such thing against Antony, as they knew that he would become an enemy on his own (for he was not about to betray Cleopatra and take Octavian's side). They also wished to hold the following against him: that he of his own accord went to war against his own country on the Egyptian queen's account, although his countrymen had not provoked him at all.

Therefore, young men were assembled hurriedly on both sides, money was amassed from all sources, and all the machines of war were swiftly assembled. The whole undertaking was by far the largest

1. On gymnasiarch, see chapter 5, note 9.

of any up to that time, so many peoples cooperated with one another in the war. Italy was controlled by Octavian (he had also enlisted those Antony had settled in colonies, in part by frightening them because of their numerical weakness, and partly by granting them favors: for example, he re-established the colony in Bononia, so that they would seem to have been settled by him). In addition to Italy, Gaul, Spain, Illyricum, the Libyans (both those who had been Romanized for a long time, except those around Cyrene, and those who were ruled by Bogud and Bocchus), Sardinia, Sicily, and the other islands lying near the continents mentioned above all fought with Octavian. Antony had those on the Asian continent who were subject to Rome, Thrace, Greece, Macedonia, the Egyptians, the people of Cyrene and the surrounding area, the islanders near them, and almost all the kings and dynasts of regions bordering the parts of the Roman empire Antony controlled either came themselves or sent representatives. Both sides equally enjoyed such enthusiastic support that oaths of allegiance were sworn to both leaders.

6.2. Plutarch, *Life of Antony* 56, 60–64 (A.D. 110–15, Greek, prose)

For more on Plutarch, see selection 2.1. Antony and Octavian had been trading accusations (see selections 5.3–5.6) as the hostilities between them escalated toward the outbreak of war.

56. Antony heard these things while busy in Armenia; immediately, he ordered Canidius to take sixteen legions and go down to the coast.[2] Antony took Cleopatra and went to Ephesus. This was where his fleet was coming together from many locations: eight hundred ships including merchantmen, of which Cleopatra contributed two hundred along with twenty thousand talents and resources for the whole army during the war. Antony was persuaded by Domitius and some of his other associates to request that Cleopatra sail to Egypt and there await the end of the war. But Cleopatra, fearing that these conflicts might be resolved by Octavia, persuaded Canidius by bribery to intercede for her with Antony on the grounds that it was not right to banish from the war a woman who made such contributions and that it was not advantageous to dishearten the Egyptians, since they

---

2. 33 B.C.; Canidius was the commander of Antony's land army.

were a large part of the naval force, and, in addition, that Cleopatra was no less intelligent than any of the kings fighting alongside Antony—for some time, she had been governing a great kingdom by herself and she had been with Antony and learned from him many things about affairs of state. Since Caesar was destined to prevail, Canidius's persuasion was successful and, when the forces had assembled, they sailed to Samos and celebrated.[3] Accordingly, just as all the kings, dynasts, tetrarchs, peoples, and cities from Syria to Lake Maeotis, to Armenia and Illyria were asked to send or bring resources to the war, likewise the call went out to all the performing artists demanding that they report to Samos. At this time, almost the whole world was lamenting and grieving, but one island resounded with flutes and lyres for many days, theaters were full, and choruses competed. Each city sent an ox for a collective sacrifice, and kings competed with one another in sponsoring entertainments and giving gifts. As a result, the rumor spread: what will they do as a victory celebration if they entertain so lavishly to prepare for war?

60. When Caesar had prepared sufficiently, he successfully passed a declaration of war on Cleopatra and had Antony stripped of his power, since he had handed it over to a woman. Caesar also accused Antony of being out of control because he was under the influence of drugs and claimed that the true enemies were Mardian, the eunuch; Pothinus; Iras, Cleopatra's hairdresser; and Charmion, since they seemed to have the greatest power.

It is said that the following signs occurred before the war. Pisaurum, a colony near the Adriatic founded by Antony, was swallowed up by a chasm that opened up. One of Antony's marble statues in Alba Longa[4] dripped with sweat for many days and, although it was wiped down, the flow did not stop. When Antony was spending time in Patras, a temple of Hercules was struck by lightning. The Dionysus from the Athenian sculpture known as the *Battle of Gods and Giants* was broken off by the wind and hurled into the theater. Antony associated himself with Hercules through his ancestry and with Dionysus in his lust for life. The same storm overturned statues of Eumenes and Attalus, which the Athenians had inscribed with

3. Spring, 32 B.C.
4. A city in Italy thirteen miles southeast of Rome.

Antony's name, although other statues were unharmed. Cleopatra's lead ship was called *Antonias,* and a terrible omen appeared on it: swallows had built nests under the stern, and other swallows attacked them and drove them out and killed their chicks.

61. When they were prepared for the war, Antony had no less than five hundred warships, among which many were eights or tens and were adorned magnificently and festively; he had one hundred thousand infantry and twelve thousand cavalry. Subject kings fighting with him included Bogud, the king of the Libyans; Tarcondimotus, the king of Upper Cilicia; Archelaos, king of Cappadocia; Philadelphus, the king of Paphlagonia; Mithradates of Commagene; and Sadalas of Thrace. These marched with him and Polemon of Pontus sent him soldiers, as did Malchus of Arabia, Herod of Judaea, and Amyntas, the king of the Lycaonians and Galatians; aid was also sent by the king of the Medes. Octavian had two hundred fifty warships, eighty thousand infantry, and a force of cavalry about equal to his adversary's. Antony controlled territory from the Euphrates and Armenia to the Ionian Sea and Illyria, Octavian that lying between Illyria and the western ocean[5] and that from the ocean back to the sea that washes Etruria and Sicily.[6] Octavian controlled the part of Libya facing Italy, Galatia, and Iberia up to the Pillars of Hercules;[7] Antony held the territory from Cyrene up to Ethiopia.

62. Antony was so much a pawn of Cleopatra that, although he exceeded Octavian's capabilities on land, he wished the victory to be a naval one, with Cleopatra instrumental, even though he knew that a lack of sailors necessitated his commanders' drafting travelers, mule drivers, reapers, and underage boys from long-suffering Greece. Even then, the ships were not full, but understaffed and incompetently sailed. Octavian, on the other hand, had ships not constructed ostentatiously for height or mass, but they were fully manned and fitted out especially for maneuverability and speed; the fleet was stationed at Tarentum and Brundisium, and Octavian sent word to Antony urging him not to delay, but to approach with his forces. Octavian promised to leave the approaches and harbors unblocked for Antony's fleet and to withdraw his infantry from the coast the distance of a

5. The Atlantic Ocean.
6. The Mediterranean west of Italy.
7. The Straits of Gibraltar.

day's ride from the sea, until Antony had disembarked safely and set up camp. Antony challenged him in return to a single combat, even though Antony was older, saying that if Octavian refused, their forces should engage at Pharsalus, where Caesar and Pompey had previously contested. Octavian, however, preempted him: while Antony was hastening to Actium, the site where the city of Nicopolis now stands, Octavian crossed the Ionian Sea and occupied a town in Epirus called Torone, which means ladle. Antony's associates were disturbed by this development (for their infantry had not arrived), but Cleopatra joked, "Why is it so terrible if Caesar is sitting on a ladle?"

63. At dawn, when the enemy sailed toward his fleet, Antony feared that they might capture his ships before his soldiers had manned them. He therefore stationed armed rowers on the decks to create an illusion; he had the oars raised like wings on each side, the ships facing out of the harbor towards Actium, as if they were manned and equipped to defend themselves. Octavian was out-strategized and withdrew. Antony also seemed shrewd when he deprived the enemy of water by putting up some bulwarks, since springs in the area were few and meager. He treated Domitius[8] generously, against the advice of Cleopatra: when Domitius, who had a fever at the time, took a small boat and deserted to Octavian, Antony took it hard but sent over all of Domitius's possessions, his supporters, and his servants. Almost immediately after his desertion, Domitius died, as if repenting his faithlessness and betrayal. There were other desertions too: some of the kings, including Amyntas and Deiotarus, went over to Caesar. Since the fleet was a failure in all respects and was too late to be of any help, Antony had to rely on his infantry. Canidius, the commander of the land force, had a change of heart when he saw the severity of the situation and advised that Cleopatra be sent away and that they should move the army to Thrace or Macedonia and resolve the conflict with a land battle. After all, Dicomes, the king of the Getae, had promised to come to their aid with a large army. Canidius pointed out that there was no shame in yielding the sea to Octavian, who had been trained in the Sicilian War, but that it would be terrible

8. Domitius Ahenobarbus, who fought against the Second Triumvirate in 44–42 B.C. but then joined Antony. He opposed Cleopatra's participation in the conflict with Octavian.

if Antony, an expert in land battles, did not exploit the strength and readiness of so many foot soldiers and instead divided and wasted his strength among ships. Despite these arguments, Cleopatra prevailed and chose to decide the war in a naval battle, although she was already looking to flee and arranged matters not for their conduciveness to victory, but for ease of flight in case of defeat. Two long walls stretched from Antony's camp down to the harbor, and Antony was accustomed to walk between them without fear. One of Octavian's slaves told his master that it would be possible to ambush Antony as he walked between the walls, and so Octavian sent men to lie in wait for him. They came close—jumping up a moment too soon, they seized the man walking in front of Antony, while Antony narrowly escaped at a run.

64. When he resolved to fight a naval battle, he burned all the ships except sixty of the Egyptian vessels. He filled with soldiers the best and largest ones that had between three and ten banks of oars, putting twenty thousand foot soldiers and two thousand archers on board. It was then, they say, that one of the infantry commanders who had fought many battles alongside Antony, and whose body bore many scars, began to lament as Antony passed and said, "General, why do you despise my wounds and my sword, instead placing your hopes in these wretched planks? Let the Egyptians and Phoenicians fight at sea; give us the land, on which we are accustomed to stand and either die or conquer the enemy." Antony had no answer for these arguments, but only indicated by gesture and expression that the men should be of good courage as he passed by. He did not have high hopes, for, when the captains wished to leave their sails behind, he ordered them to take them on board, saying that it was necessary to keep anyone of the enemy who was fleeing from making good his escape.

6.3. Velleius Paterculus, *Histories* 2.82.4 (A.D. 30, Latin, prose)

Velleius Paterculus performed military service under Julius Caesar and held the praetorship in A.D. 15. He wrote a history in two volumes, covering a span of time beginning with events from Greek mythology and continuing to A.D. 29. Much of the first book is lost, but it is evident that Velleius was

*a summarizer of history, although in the second book he devotes a dispro-
portionate amount of space to Julius Caesar, Augustus, and Tiberius.*[9] *In
the following passage, he describes Antony in a way that leaves no doubt
about his assessment of the situation.*

Next, as the flames of his passion for Cleopatra were increasing
along with the extent of his vices (these things always gain strength
from ability, license, and adulation), he prepared to wage war on his
country. Before this, he had decreed that he should be called the
New Father Liber, when he had entered Alexandria wearing a crown
of ivy, a robe of gold, and Greek boots, carrying a thyrsus, and riding
in a chariot just like Father Liber.[10]

THE BATTLE

On September 2, 31 B.C., Antony and Cleopatra engaged Octavian's
forces at Actium in western Greece (see map 2). Octavian's strategy
was to lure Antony's fleet out of the Gulf of Ambracia into open
water, where he could outflank them. The two fleets had joined battle
in open water when Cleopatra's flagship, with the queen on board,
exited the gulf, passing through Antony's line and Octavian's, and
headed south toward Egypt. Shortly thereafter, Antony followed her.
Most accounts describe this move as motivated by Cleopatra's cowardice, but it may have been a strategy. Antony and Cleopatra were
unlikely to beat Octavian and his admiral Agrippa in a naval battle.
They may have realized that their best hope was to break out of the
blockade and escape to Egypt so that the war could continue on
land, where their forces were more equally matched with Octavian's.

6.4. Plutarch, *Life of Antony* 65–69 (A.D. 110–15, Greek, prose)

*For more on Plutarch, see selection 2.1. There is debate over the strategy of
Antony and Cleopatra in the Battle of Actium. Most of the ancient sources,
influenced by Octavian's point of view, portray their departure from Actium
as cowardly flight.*

---

9. Syme paints Velleius as a panegyrist for Augustus (1978, 45–63).
10. Liber: another name for Dionysus, the god of wine, irrationality, and theater. In
Greek myth Dionysus spreads his worship by conducting a band of revelers in a celebra-
tory procession through Asia Minor and the rest of the world.

65. For that day and the next three, the sea, disturbed by a great wind, held up the battle. On the fifth day, when there was a windless, waveless calm, the fleets came together. Antony had command of the right wing along with Publicola; Coelius led the left wing and in the middle were Marcus Octavius and Marcus Insteius. Octavian stationed Agrippa on the left and commanded the right wing himself. Canidius was in charge of Antony's land army and Taurus of Octavian's; both marshaled their troops on the shore and waited. Of the two generals, Antony traveled around on all sides in a small boat, exhorting his men to fight as if they were on land, since their ships were heavy, and ordering the captains to take the missiles of the enemy as if they were at anchor and to maintain their position at the mouth of the gulf.[11] Octavian, on the other hand, is said to have left his tent before dawn to inspect the fleet. He met a man driving a mule and asked his name. The man, recognizing him, said, "My name is Fortunate and my mule is named Victor." For this reason, after the war, when he erected a monument on the spot, he set up a bronze statue of a mule and a man. When he had examined the arrangement of the rest of the fleet, he was taken in a small boat to the right wing, where he was surprised to see the enemy lying still in the narrows: their ships appeared to be at anchor. For a while Octavian believed that they were and kept his ships approximately eight stades away.[12] Around noon, a sea wind came up and Antony's men, impatient with the delay and trusting that the height and size of their own ships would make them unassailable, went for the left wing. Octavian rejoiced seeing this and backed off his right wing, hoping to lure the enemy out of the gulf and the narrows and, by surrounding them with his lighter ships, to entrap them, since his forces would be superior to Antony's ships, which were sluggish and ungainly because of their size and lack of sailors.

66. Once the fight began, there were no charges or ramming of ships: Antony's ships, because of their weight, did not have the speed that makes the blows of the ram effective; Octavian's not only guarded against being struck with the bronze-reinforced rams, but also were not willing to make attacks on the sides of Antony's ships, since their

11. The Gulf of Ambracia.
12. Eight stades was about a mile.

rams broke off easily when they hit the ships, which were made of great beams fastened with iron and secured to one another. Therefore, the fight was like a land battle or, to be more precise, a siege. Three or four of Octavian's ships would surround one of Antony's and attack with wicker shields, spears, stakes, and firebrands. Antony's ships launched missiles from catapults on wooden towers. Agrippa extended his left wing to outflank Antony's formation, forcing Publicola to advance against him, leaving the center vulnerable. When these ships had been disrupted and surrounded by those under Arruntius's[13] command, success was shared equally by both sides. Suddenly, Cleopatra's sixty ships were seen raising their sails to sail away and fleeing through the middle of the battle line. These had been stationed behind the massive ships and created chaos as they burst through the line. Their opponents marveled at the sight of Cleopatra's ships offering their sails to the wind and heading toward the Peloponnese. With that, Antony made it clear that he was not governed by the reasoning of a commander or of a man or, indeed, by his own reasoning at all. Rather, as is said in jest, that the soul of a lover lives in someone else's body, he was dragged around by a woman as if he had become one with her and was carried with her. He rushed after her ship when he saw it sailing away; he left everything behind, betrayed and forsook the men fighting and dying on his behalf, and, taking only Alexas the Syrian and Scellius with him, he pursued the woman who had already ruined him and would kill him besides.

67. When Cleopatra recognized him, she gave a sign from her ship. When Antony approached and was taken aboard, he neither saw her nor was seen by her, but went alone to the bow and sat silently by himself, holding his head in both his hands. Then, some Liburnians from Octavian's side were seen pursuing.[14] Antony commanded that the ship be turned toward them and resisted the attacks of all except the one with which Eurycles the Spartan haughtily pressed him and brandished a spear from the deck as if he was prepared to throw it at Antony. Antony stood in the bow and said, "Who is this man pursuing Antony?" The answer: "I am Eurycles,

13. Arruntius was the commander of the center of Octavian's fleet.
14. Liburnians were light ships with two banks of oars.

son of Lachares, and I am avenging my father's death with Caesar's fortune." Lachares had been accused by Antony of piracy and had been beheaded. Eurycles did not ram Antony's ship, instead striking the other commander's ship with his ram (there were two commanders) and spinning it around like a top. As the ship swung around sideways, he seized it, along with one of the others, on which were expensive furnishings for banquets. As Eurycles departed, Antony sat down in place and remained there; for three days he stayed alone in the bow, either out of anger or shame, and then anchored at Taenarum.[15] There, Cleopatra's maids first brought the two together to talk with one another and then to eat and sleep together.

Already, a number of the transport ships and some of their allies had gathered around them from the rout and brought news that the fleet had been destroyed, but that they thought the land army remained. Antony sent messengers to Canidius ordering him to retreat through Macedonia to Asia with all possible speed. Antony planned to cross from Taenarum to Libya; before departing, he chose one transport ship filled with much money and expensive items of gold and silver from the palace and presented it to his friends, telling them to divide it and save themselves. When they tearfully declined, he comforted them with great kindness and warmth and, asking them to accept, he sent them away after writing to Theophilus, his assistant in Corinth, that he should provide for their safety and conceal them until Octavian could be appeased. This Theophilus was the father of Hipparchus, the most powerful man on Antony's side and the first of Antony's freedmen to defect to Octavian; afterward, he lived in Corinth.

68. This was how it was with Antony. At Actium, his fleet resisted Octavian for a long while and most of the harm was done by high winds that buffeted the prows; they finally surrendered in the late afternoon. No more than five thousand died, but three hundred ships were captured, as Octavian himself wrote. Not many people realized that Antony had fled, and those who found out did not believe it at first, that he had departed and left behind nineteen undefeated legions and twelve thousand cavalry. Antony had experienced both good and bad fortune and had trained for the reversals

15. Taenarum was at the southern tip of the Peloponnese.

that happen in battles and wars. His soldiers had such a desire and expectation that he would appear somewhere or other and they displayed such faith and courage that, even when it became clear that he had fled, they remained together for seven days and refused Octavian's overtures to them. Finally, when Canidius deserted by night and left the camp, did they, bereft of everything and betrayed by their commanders, surrender to the victor.

After this, Octavian sailed to Athens and settled affairs with the Greeks. He divided the grain left over from the war among the cities, since they were suffering terribly after being plundered of money, slaves, and beasts of burden. Indeed, my great-grandfather, Nicharchus, used to tell how all the citizens of Chaeronea[16] were compelled to carry on their shoulders a set amount of wheat to the harbor at Anticyra, hurried along by the whip, and how, when they had carried down one load and were about to take a second, it was announced that Antony had been defeated, news that saved the city, for once Antony's assistants and soldiers had fled, they divided the grain among themselves.

69. When Antony arrived in Libya and sent Cleopatra into Egypt from Paraetonium,[17] he enjoyed copious solitude and wandered and roamed with two friends, Aristocrates, a Greek scholar of rhetoric, and Lucilius, a Roman about whom I have already written.[18] At Philippi, Lucilius, to help Brutus escape, pretended to be Brutus to deceive those who came in pursuit, for which he was pardoned by Antony and remained faithful and loyal to him until the end. When the man entrusted with the forces in Libya defected, Antony tried to kill himself, but was prevented by his friends and was brought to Alexandria, where he found Cleopatra undertaking a dangerous and monumental task. Since the isthmus that separates the Red Sea from the sea bordering Egypt and that is taken to divide Asia and Libya is pressed a great deal by the seas and is, at its narrowest, about forty miles across, Cleopatra planned to raise the fleet from the water and transport it overland, launching the ships into the Arabian Gulf at great expense, in order to settle outside her territory and escape from slavery and war. The Arabs living near Petra burned the first

16. Plutarch was from Chaeronea.
17. Paraetonium was a city to the west of Alexandria.
18. Plutarch, *Life of Brutus* 50.

ships dragged across. Antony thought that the army at Actium still remained, and so she stopped and guarded the approaches to Egypt.

Antony left the city and the companionship of his friends and took up residence on the island of Pharos, where he had built a mole into the sea. There, he lived in exile from society, saying that he desired and envied the life of Timon,[19] since he had suffered similar things: he had been wronged by his friends and distrusted, because of which he distrusted and disliked all men.

6.5. Cassius Dio, *Roman History* 50.31–35 (A.D. 202, Greek, prose)

For more on Cassius Dio, see selection 2.5. Here, Dio gives a detailed description of Octavian's strategy in the Battle of Actium.

31. Next, Octavian planned to let the enemy pass by, so that he might take them from behind as they fled (he was hoping that if he sailed quickly, he would soon overtake Antony and Cleopatra and, when it was clear they were attempting to flee, he thought he could, as a result, attach the rest to himself without a fight). But he was prevented by Agrippa's fear that they would not be able to catch Antony and Cleopatra, who were planning to use sails, and also by his own confidence that he would win easily in a battle because a furious rainstorm with heavy winds had fallen upon Antony's fleet, and only Antony's fleet, and thrown it all into confusion. Because of this, Octavian gave up his strategy, put many foot soldiers aboard his ships, and placed his companions in tenders, so that they might sail about quickly and give needed advice to those fighting the battle and deliver the appropriate messages to him. He then watched for them to sail out. When they set out at the trumpet call, stationed their ships in a thick mass a little outside the narrows, and held their position, Octavian hastened forth as if to engage them if they remained or to force them to retreat. When they neither came forth nor turned around, but stood their ground and, in addition, greatly reinforced their formation, Octavian held off in hesitation and, commanding his sailors to stay their oars in the water, waited for some time. Next, at the signal, he suddenly led out both wings and arranged them in a

19. Timon was an Athenian man who became proverbial: when he lost his money his friends deserted him, and then, when they returned to him after he became rich again, he drove them away.

semicircle, in hopes of surrounding their opponents or at least breaking through their battle line. Antony, who feared being surrounded and encircled, led out his fleet as much as possible and, against his will, engaged with Octavian.

32. Thus, rushing together, they fought at sea. Both sides encouraged their men to show their skill and passion; those on the shore also called out orders to the fighting men. The two armies did not fight in similar ways: Octavian's men, since they had smaller and swifter ships that were reinforced all over to prevent damage, rushed up and rammed the opposing ships. They might sink a ship, but if not, they could retreat before engaging in close combat and either suddenly hit the same ships again or leave those and attack others, in order to attack as much as possible those who were not anticipating it. Because they feared the strength the enemy ships had in fighting at long range and also in close engagements, they spent as little time as possible in the approach and the engagement; instead, they would approach suddenly, so as to elude the enemy archers and do some harm or just throw the enemy into confusion so that they could escape capture, and then they would retreat out of missile range. The enemy, however, launched at Octavian's ships as they approached many volleys of stones and arrows. They also threw iron grappling hooks at the attackers. If they hit Octavian's lighter ships, they prevailed, but if they missed, their ships' hulls would be punctured and they would sink or, if they spent time trying to avoid this fate, they became vulnerable to attack by other ships, for two or three of Octavian's ships would attack the same ship of Antony's, some of them doing damage while the others received it. On one side, the pilots and rowers suffered most, on the other, the soldiers; one side acted like cavalry, sometimes charging and sometimes retreating thanks to their maneuverability, while the other side resembled hoplites[20] who were warding off attackers and trying their best to hold their line. As a result, both sides had advantages: one side would fall upon the enemy's oars and break them, while the other side, since they were taller, would sink their opponents with stones and other devices. Each side also had disadvantages: the one because they were not able to harm their attackers and the other because, if they failed to

---

20. Hoplites were the heavily armed infantry of the Greek army.

sink a ship they had hit, they were not able at close range to equal their opponents' strength.

33. The sea battle was nearly equal for a long while and neither side was able to prevail, but this is how it ended. Cleopatra, anchored behind the battle line, could not bear the uncertainty and the waiting, but, exhausted (for she was a woman and an Egyptian) by the long and painful suspense and by the fearful anticipation of either result, she suddenly hastened to flee and sent up a signal to her followers. And so, immediately raising their sails, they put out to sea, aided by a favorable wind that happened to blow. Antony, thinking that their flight was not ordered by Cleopatra but motivated by fear that they were beaten, followed them. When this happened, the remaining soldiers were worried and confused and, wishing to somehow join the retreat, they raised their sails and tossed their towers and other items into the sea in order to be lighter as they fled. The enemy attacked them as they were busy with these things (the enemy, being without sails and prepared only for a naval battle, had not pursued the others who fled). Many fought against each ship both from a distance and in close engagement, so that the contest was most varied and fierce on both sides. Octavian's troops destroyed the ships from below on all sides: they broke oars, damaged rudders, climbed onto the decks, seized men and dragged some down, pushed some back, and fought with some, now that their numbers were equal. Antony's men drove the attackers back with poles, slashed at them with battle-axes, threw stones and heavy weights designed for this tactic down upon them, pushed off those who climbed up, and lay hands on those who approached them. Someone observing these events would have thought, comparing small things to great, that it was like forts or many closely packed islands being besieged from the sea. Thus, some men would try to climb onto the boats as if they were climbing out of the sea onto the land or a fort, eagerly employing all the tools for such a task. The others would drive them back, employing whatever tends to be used for such a purpose.

34. When they continued to fight without either side gaining the advantage, Octavian, not knowing what to do, sent for fire from the camp. Before this, he had not wanted to use it, so that he might take Cleopatra's treasure, but seeing that it would otherwise be impossible for him to be victorious, he resorted to this as their only hope. Then,

it became another sort of battle. Octavian's men, sailing up to their opponents from all sides at once, shot flaming arrows at them, hurled torches like javelins, and, aided by siege engines, threw from afar clay vessels full of coal and pitch. Antony's men averted the missiles as they came, and when some hit their ships and ignited the wood, at once starting a fire, as tends to happen on a ship, they first used the drinking water they had brought on board to extinguish some of the fires, and when that was used up, they hauled up seawater. And if they used a great deal at once, they were able to quench the fire by force. They were, however, unable to do this everywhere (for they did not have many buckets or large ones and, since they were in a panic, they brought them up half filled). As a result, they did not help matters, but contributed to the conflagration, for saltwater, if a little is poured on a flame, makes it flare up. Therefore, when they were losing on this front as well, they threw upon the flames their thick cloaks and the dead bodies; for a while, the fire was controlled by them and it seemed to die down, but then, especially when a strong wind came up, the fire blazed even more, fueled by the very things they had thrown upon it. As long as only part of a ship was burning, some men would stand on it and jump up and down, breaking off and knocking away the burning planks. Then some tossed them into the sea and others threw them at the enemy, on the chance they might somehow cause injury. Others, going to the sturdy parts of the ship, studiously used their hooks and long spears to fasten an enemy ship to theirs and, ideally, boarding it, but otherwise setting it on fire as well.

35. When the enemy did not approach, as they were defending themselves against these tactics, and the fire spread to the outer walls and went down into the hold, then the most terrible things happened to them. Some, especially the sailors, were killed by the smoke before the fire even got near them; others burned in the middle of the flames, as in an oven; others melted with their burning armor. Others, before they suffered such a fate or when they were half incinerated, tore off their armor and were wounded by the missiles coming from afar, or jumped into the sea and drowned, or were hit by enemy fire and their ships sank, or were torn apart by sea monsters. The only ones who died bearably, given the intolerable conditions,

were those who, before they could suffer these things, either killed one another or themselves. They did not endure any torture and, as corpses, they were burned on the ships just as on a pyre.

Octavian's men, observing these events, at first did not engage with the enemy, as some of them were still able to defend themselves, but when the fire attacked the ships, and the men were neither able to help themselves nor harm an enemy, they eagerly sailed up to them, in case they could take the treasure, and tried to put out the fire, which they had started. As a result, many of them were destroyed by the flames and by their own greed.

6.6. Florus, *Abridgement of All the Wars Over 1,200 Years* 2.21.4–9 (2nd c. A.D., Latin, prose)

For more on Lucius Annaeus Florus, see selection 3.10. In this passage, he summarizes the events surrounding the Battle of Actium.

At the first report of revolutionary uprisings, Caesar crossed from Brundisium in order to confront the approaching war, and, once he had pitched camp in Epirus, he surrounded the entire Actian shore, the island of Leucas, Mount Leucate, and the gulf of Ambracia with his fleet's dangerous flank.

(5) Our ships numbered more than four hundred, the enemy's less than two hundred; but their size outweighed their number. Indeed, they had between six and nine banks of oars and stood tall with towers and platforms that gave the impression of fortresses or cities and caused the sea to groan and the winds to labor as they were carried along. Their massive size, however, was their downfall.

(6) Caesar's ships were equipped with between two and six banks of oars at the most and so were suited for anything the occasion might demand: attacking, retreating, turning. Whenever they wished, they put to flight those ships that were heavy and hindered every maneuver: several of Caesar's ships would attack one of the enemy ships with missiles and with their prows at the same time and also with firebrands launched at it.

(7) The multitude of enemy troops was never more obvious than after the victory. For the battle had caused wreckage of the huge fleet to float on the whole expanse of the sea and, as the winds ruffled

the water, the spoils of the Arabs and Sabaeans and the thousand peoples of Asia, purple and adorned with gold, kept surfacing.

(8) The first leader of flight was the queen, who headed for open water in her gilded ship with its purple sails. Soon Antony followed, with Caesar hot on his trail.

(9) And thus neither their premeditated flight into the ocean nor their garrison fortifying both promontories of Egypt, Paraetonium and Pelusium, profited them at all: they were within Caesar's reach.[21]

6.7. Velleius Paterculus, *Histories* 2.85–86 (A.D. 30, Latin, prose)

For more on Velleius Paterculus, see selection 6.3. In this passage he describes the events of September 2, 31 B.C., in dramatic fashion.

85. Then the day of the great conflict arrived, on which Caesar and Antony marshaled their fleets and contended, one for the safety of the world, the other for its ruin. The right wing of the Julian fleet was commanded by Marcus Lurius, the left by Arruntius, and Agrippa oversaw the entire naval conflict; Caesar, resolved to participate in the part of the battle to which fortune called him, was present every-where. Antony's fleet was commanded by Publicola and Sosius. On land, Taurus led Caesar's army and Canidius commanded Antony's. When the fight began, one side had it all: commander, oarsmen, soldiers; the other side had nothing but soldiers. Cleopatra was the first to flee; Antony preferred to accompany the fleeing queen than his own fighting men and, as a commander, whose responsibility it should have been to punish deserters, he became a deserter of his own army. Even without their commander, Antony's army endured bravely for a long time and, despairing of a victory, fought to the death. Caesar, eager to defeat with words those whom he could have slain with the sword, called out to them and noted that Antony had fled. He asked them for whom and with whom they were fighting. And they, when they had fought for a long time on their absent leader's behalf, reluctantly laid down their arms and conceded the victory; Caesar granted them pardon and spared their lives even before it occurred to them to ask. It was clear that the soldiers played the role of the excellent general and the general the part of the cowardly soldier, and

---

21. Paraetonium and Pelusium were located on either side of the mouth of the Nile.

so it is not clear whether he would have achieved the victory on his own counsel or Cleopatra's, since it was her counsel that chose flight. The land army surrendered just as easily, since Canidius had taken an opportunity for a hasty retreat to join Antony.

86. Who would dare to describe in so concise a work what that day accomplished for the world, how it caused the fortunes of the state to arrive at their current state? Truly the victory was most humane: no one was killed except for a very few who could not stand to ask for mercy. Caesar's leniency is an indication of the character his victories would have had, if it had been possible, at the beginning of his triumvirate or on the battlefield of Philippi. But Sosius owed his life to the faith displayed by Lucius Arruntius, who was well known for his adherence to the ancient principle of dignity, and also to Caesar, who relented after long wrestling with his merciful tendencies. Asinius Pollio's memorable word and deed should not be overlooked either. For although he remained in Italy after the Treaty of Brundisium and never had seen Cleopatra nor involved himself in Antony's faction once Antony had become weakened by love, when Caesar requested his service in the Battle of Actium, he said, "I have a greater loyalty to Antony and he is known to be my benefactor and so I will remain impartial in your conflict and make myself the victor's reward."

CLEOPATRA AND ACTIUM IN ROMAN POETRY

Several Roman poets treat the Battle of Actium. Their poems offer a more personal perspective on Cleopatra and reflect some of the ambiguities of Octavian's conflict with Antony and Cleopatra.

6.8. Horace, *Epodes* 1 and 9 (41–30 B.C.), *Ode* 1.37 (30 B.C., Latin, verse)

Before his poetic career began, Horace had joined Brutus's army and fought against Octavian's forces at Philippi. He returned to Rome after receiving amnesty from the triumvirs in 41 B.C.. In 38 B.C. he met the patron Maecenas through Vergil. Maecenas was a close associate of Octavian, and thus Horace, along with Vergil, had the most powerful patron in Rome.[22]

22. Conte 1999, 292.

Horace's poetry treats a wide variety of themes, among them subjects pertaining to the reign of Augustus. Profoundly affected by the civil wars, Horace brings to bear a private perspective and voice upon public and political matters. The terms ode and epode both refer to relatively short poems written in a variety of meters. Horace's Epodes tend to be in iambic meters and to have a satirical tone, while his Odes employ a variety of lyric meters.

Epode 1, addressed to Maecenas, expresses Horace's intention to accompany his patron as he joins Octavian's military efforts against Antony and Cleopatra, which will culminate in the Battle of Actium. It is not known whether Maecenas and Horace were actually present at the battle. Epode 9 and Ode 1.37 also celebrate Octavian's victory at Actium.

Epode 1

You will go in Liburnian craft among	1
the high turrets of their ships,	
Maecenas my friend, ready to share	
with Caesar in every risk.[23]	
But what will I do? My life is sweet	5
if you survive, but bitter otherwise.	
Should I pursue leisure at your command,	
although it is not pleasant unless you enjoy it also,	
or should I pursue this trial, which I would endure	
with the type of mind brave men have?	10
I will endure it, and whether I follow you	
through Alpine ridges and the inhospitable Caucasus	
or all the way to the furthest inlet of the western ocean,	
I will do so with a brave heart.	
Would you ask how I might help your labor by adding my own,	15
when I am unwarlike and infirm?	
I will be your companion and fear less,	
since one who is far away fears more.	
Just as a bird sitting on featherless chicks	
fears the slithering approach of snakes	20
more when the young are left alone, although,	

23. Liburnian ships, the choice of Octavian at Actium, were lightweight and maneuverable, as opposed to the heavier warships of Antony and Cleopatra. Cf. *Ode* 1.37.

were she present, she would be no more help.
Willingly will this and every war
be fought in hope of your favor,
not to increase my herds to the point that   25
plows groan with the pull of so many oxen,
or to move my flock from Calabrian
to Lucanian pastures before the dog days,
or to have an outstanding villa in Tusculum
that touches Circean walls.[24]   30
Enough and more than enough your generosity
has enriched me: I will not hoard my possessions
in the earth like the miser Chremes,
nor will I squander them like a loose-belted spendthrift.

Epode 9

When will I, delighting in the victory of Caesar,   1
drink Caecuban[25] wine stored up for festive banquets
with you—since it pleases Jove—in your lofty house
fortunate Maecenas, as the lyre
mingles its song with flutes,   5
combining Dorian with Phrygian?
Just so, recently, when the son of Neptune
fled, pursued on the deep in burnt ships,
after threatening the city with chains, the same ones
he took off the lying slaves he had befriended.[26]   10
The Roman soldier (alas!)—though posterity will deny it—
enslaved to a woman,
marches carrying weapons and fence posts and
obeys the commands of wrinkled eunuchs.
The sun witnesses mosquito nets (shameful)   15
among the military standards.
Toward the sun two thousand Gauls turn

24. In summer flocks were moved from Calabria to the higher elevations of Lucania
to graze. Tusculum was a popular location for the villas of the wealthy. The town was said
to have been founded by Telegonus, son of Circe and Odysseus.

25. Caecuban was a famous wine produced in southern Latium.

26. Sextus Pompey, defeated at Naulochos in 36 B.C., referred to himself as the son of
Neptune.

their snorting horses, as they chant "Caesar!"[27]
Enemy ships, steered to the left,
hide in the harbor.   20
Hail, Triumph! Are you saving
your golden chariot and untouched oxen?
Hail, Triumph! No general this great from
the Jugurthine War did you bring home,
not even Africanus, to whom Courage   25

dedicated Carthage as a monument.[28]
The enemy, beaten on land and sea,
replaces his purple cloak with a drab one.
He either plans to sail against the winds
to Crete distinguished by a hundred cities,   30
or he seeks the Syrtes harassed by the south wind,
or he is carried on an uncertain sea.
Boy, bring larger cups here to me
and some Chian wine or Lesbian,
or mix us some Caecuban   35
to calm our nausea.
It is pleasant to find release from care and fear
over Caesar's affairs in sweet Bacchus.

Ode 1.37

Now there must be drinking, now the earth   1
must be pounded with a free foot, now it is long past
time to decorate the couch of the gods
with Salian feasts, my friends.[29]

Before this time, it was not right to bring out   5
the Caecuban wine from ancestral cellars, while the queen
plotted insane ruin for the Capitol
and death for our rule
with her flock of base men

---

27. Mosquito nets would have been considered shameful in a Roman military context, because they represented the eastern luxury for which Egypt was known. "Caesar!" refers to Octavian.

28. Marius was the Roman general who conquered Jugurtha; Scipio Africanus won a victory against Hannibal in the Second Punic War.

29. The Salii were priests of Mars, famous for their banquets.

polluted by disease. She was mad 10
to hope for anything at all and
drunk on good fortune. But scarcely one ship

safe from the fires cooled her fury,
and Caesar snatched her mind,
crazed with Mareotic wine, back to 15
true fears; Caesar who flew from Italy

bearing down on her with oars, like a hawk
chasing soft doves or a swift hunter tracking
a rabbit on the snowy plains
of Thessaly, so that he might deliver 20

the deadly monster into chains. The queen,
seeking to die more nobly, did not, womanish,
shrink from the sword, nor did she retreat
in her swift fleet to hidden shores.

She dared, too, to look upon her fallen palace 25
with a calm face, and to handle
poisonous snakes, so her body
might drink black venom.[30]

More defiant in a deliberate death,
begrudging the cruel Liburnian ships 30
to be led, a queen no longer,
but never humbled, in a showy triumph.

6.9. Propertius, *Elegies* 3.11 and 4.6 (23 and 16 B.C., Latin, verse)

Propertius's family suffered losses when, in 40–41 B.C., Octavian confiscated land in Italy to give as a reward to his troops. Propertius was a member of Maecenas's literary circle, but ideas subversive to the Augustan moral program surface quite frequently in his poetry. Many of Propertius's elegies focus on his tumultuous love affair with the woman he calls Cynthia. The poems follow the conventions of Latin love elegy, in which the poet claims to be the slave of his mistress (who is not a woman he can marry)

---

30. Cf. chapter 7 on Cleopatra's death by the bite of an asp.

and to prefer a life of love to the traditional Roman career in the military and in politics. Indeed, for the elegist, love is his military service.

In addition to these highly personal poems, Propertius writes poems on Roman themes, including the early history of Rome and the Battle of Actium. These poems evoke Callimachus's Aetia *both in subject matter and in style. While* Elegy *3.11 invites comparison between Cleopatra and the women of elegy,* Elegy *4.6 presents an account of Actium more epic in scale but still in the meter of elegy.*

3.11

Why are you amazed if a woman runs my life   1
and drags me, a man, captive under her yoke,
and why do you trump up base charges of cowardice against me
just because I cannot burst the chains and break the yoke?
"The sailor best predicts the ways of the winds;   5
the soldier learns fear through wounds."
In my bygone youth, I tossed off boasts like yours:
you now learn fear by my example.
The Colchian drove fire-breathing bulls under a yoke of adamant
and she sowed in the ground battles bearing crops of soldiers,   10
and she closed the savage, gaping mouth of the guardian serpent
so that the golden fleece might go home with Jason.[31]
Once, fierce Maotian Penthesilea on horseback dared
to attack Greek ships with arrows;
her brilliant beauty bested the triumphant man   15
after the golden helmet uncovered her forehead.[32]
Omphale, the Lydian girl who bathed in the Gygean Lake,
attained such heights of beauty
that he, who had erected pillars in a world he had pacified,
drew out soft wool with so rough a hand.[33]   20

31. Medea (here referred to by her homeland, Colchis) helped the hero Jason capture the Golden Fleece by bewitching the dragon that guarded it. In most versions it is Jason who yokes the bulls and sows dragon's teeth to produce a crop of warriors (Richardson 1977 *ad* 3.11.9).

32. Lake Maotis (modern Sea of Azov) was the home of Penthesilea, an Amazon. She fought Achilles in the Trojan War, and post-Homeric legend has it that he fell in love with her at the moment he killed her.

33. Hercules was enslaved to Omphale, queen of Lydia. During his servitude, she forced him to dress in women's clothes and perform women's tasks.

Semiramis established Babylon, the Persian capital,
so that it rose as a solid structure with walls of baked brick,
and two chariots sent through its walls in opposite directions
would not hit one another's sides because their axles touched;
she also led the Euphrates through the center of the city she
    founded 25
and she commanded Bactra to bow its head to her rule.[34]
For why should I cite heroes, why should I haul the gods into
    court?
Jupiter disgraces himself and his house.
What about that woman who just now heaped abuse
upon our forces, and had trysts with her slaves? 30
She demanded as an indecent bride price the walls
of Rome and the senators captive in her kingdom.
Guilty Alexandria, a land best suited to deception,
and Memphis so often bloodied by our crime,
where the sand stripped three triumphs from Pompey: 35
no day will lift this stain from you, Rome.
Better if your funeral had proceeded on the Phlegraean plain,
or if you were destined to offer your neck to your father-in-law.[35]
Indeed, the whore-queen of incestuous Canopus,
a singular stain branded on Philip's blood, 40
dared to foist barking Anubis on our Jove,
and to compel the Tiber to endure the Nile's threats,
and to rout the Roman trumpet with the chattering sistrum,[36]
and to chase Liburnian prows with a poled raft,
and to string up vile mosquito-nets on the Tarpeian rock, 45
and to pass laws among the statues and the trophies of Marius.
What good is it now that the axes of Tarquin were broken,
Tarquin whose arrogant life marks him with that same epithet? 48
What good are Hannibal's spoils and the trophies of
    conquered Scyphax, 59

34. According to Diodorus Siculus, Semiramis was believed to have designed Babylon from a master plan (2.7.2). Her first great exploit was the conquest of Bactra (Diodorus 2.6.2–8).
35. Allusions to ways in which Pompey might have ended his life rather than being murdered in Egypt. He might have died of an illness he contracted in Naples in 50 B.C. or perished in the battle of Pharsalus in 48 B.C.
36. Sistrum: a rattle associated with the worship of Isis.

and Pyrrhus's glory crushed by our feet?   60
Now where are the fleets of Scipio, or the standards of Camillus,   67
or you, Bosporus, newly captured by Pompey's men,   68
if a woman must be endured? Cheer on the triumph, Rome,   49
and, safe, pray for Augustus's long life![37]   50
And yet you fled to the meandering streams of the cowardly Nile,
your hands accepted Romulus's chains.
I saw your arms bitten by sacred snakes,
and the hidden course of sleep overtake your limbs.
"You need not have feared me, Rome, when you had such a
    citizen   55
protecting you!" She spoke, though strong wine had
    overwhelmed her tongue.
The lofty city with its seven hills, the city that presides over the
    world,
did this city, terrified by female aggression, fear her threats?   58
Curtius made a monument of himself after filling in the chasm;   61
Decius burst the battle line when he charged through on his
    mount;
Cocles' path bears witness to the bridge he severed;
and then there's the man who got his name from a raven:[38]

37. Scholars have rearranged the lines in this passage to produce a sensible train of
thought. The order in which the manuscripts transmit the lines is indicated by the line
numbers. Marius was a highly successful military commander in the late second and early
first centuries B.C. Tarquinius Superbus, "Tarquin the Proud," was the last king of Rome
(534–510 B.C.). He was removed from power and the Republican system of government,
which had two consuls as its highest officials, was instituted. The fasces, bundles of five-foot
elm or birch rods and an ax, were symbols of royal power. Hannibal led the Carthaginians
against the Romans in the Second Punic War; Scyphax was among his allies. Pyrrhus, king
of Epirus, won a "Pyrrhic victory" against the Romans in 275 B.C., when he won the battle
but lost two-thirds of his army. Richardson (1977) points out that while Pyrrhus certainly
did not enjoy great success, he was not completely defeated. Thus Propertius may be
referring to a descendant of Pyrrhus, Perses of Macedon, who was conquered by Aemilius
Paullus in 167 B.C. (Richardson 1977 *ad* 3.11.60). Scipio Africanus defeated Hannibal to
win the Second Punic War. Camillus saved Rome from an invasion of the Gauls in 387 B.C.
    38. Marcus Curtius closed a chasm that had opened in the Roman Forum by riding
into it fully armed. An oracle specified that the chasm would be closed by an offering of
Rome's most important resource, which Curtius took to mean the city's young men. The
Decii (father and son) secured a victory for the Romans at Sentinum by conducting a ceremony in which they devoted themselves and the Roman army to the spirits of their
ancestors and to the Earth and then charged on horseback into the enemy battle line
(Richardson 1977 *ad* 3.11.62). Horatius Cocles saved Rome from an Etruscan invasion
by burning the bridge the Etruscans would have to cross to reach the city then swimming
across the Tiber to safety. A raven (*corvus*) assisted Marcus Valerius in combat with a
Gaul. Marcus Valerius then added Corvus to his name.

The gods established these walls, the gods will preserve
    them too;   65
Rome would scarcely fear Jupiter, as long as Caesar lives.   66
Leucadian Apollo will commemorate the routed troops: 69
one day overcame such a force of war.[39]   70
But you, sailor, whether you seek the harbor or leave it,
Be mindful of Caesar on the Ionian Sea.

4.6

The priest makes sacrifice:[40] may you keep reverential silence,   1
and may the heifers fall stricken before my hearth.
Let Roman tablets strive decked with Philetas's ivy,
and let the urn offer waters of Cyrene.[41]
Give me soft perfume and offerings of alluring incense,   5
and thrice let the woolen fillet encircle the hearth.
Sprinkle me with water, and at new altars let the ivory flute pour
a libation of song from Mygdonian vessels.[42]
Go far off, crimes; likewise may punishments be remote;
pure laurel softens the priest's new path.   10
Muse, we will present the temple of Palatine Apollo;
the topic is worthy, Calliope, of your approval.[43]
My songs are composed for the glory of Caesar; to Caesar,
I think, while he is celebrated, even you, Jupiter, pay attention.
There is a harbor of Phoebus extending inland to the shores   15
of the Athames, where a gulf silences the roar of the Ionian Sea,[44]
the Actian Gulf, a memorial to the Julian ships,
a path not troublesome for sailors' prayers.
Here the forces of the world converged: hulls of pine

---

39. Leucas is the island just off the promontory of Actium, where there was a temple of Apollo.

40. The term *vates,* translated "priest" in this line and in line 10, can mean "poet," "priest," or "prophet."

41. Philetas and Callimachus were Hellenistic poets; Philetas came from Cos and Callimachus from Cyrene.

42. Mygdonian: Phrygian, a musical style from Asia Minor associated with worship of the Magna Mater.

43. Augustus vowed the temple of Apollo would be built on the Palatine in 36 B.C., while he was at war with Sextus Pompey. The temple was dedicated in 28 B.C. and was part of a complex of buildings including Augustus's house as well as two libraries, one housing Greek and one Latin literature.

44. The Athames lived northeast of Actium.

stood still on the water, but equal fortune did not bless their oars.   20
One fleet was cursed by Trojan Quirinus,[45]
and javelins flew shamefully under a woman's command;
on the other side Augustus's ship, its sails full with Jove's favor,
and its standards already taught to conquer for their homeland.
At last Nereus arrayed the fleet in twin arcs,   25
and the water rippled reflecting the glint of arms,
when Phoebus, leaving Delos that rests securely under his
    protection,
(that island alone did not resist the South Wind's fury),
stood above Augustus's stern, and three times a strange flame
flashed, bent into an angular bolt.   30
The god had not come with hair flowing over his neck
or with the peaceful song of the tortoise-shell lyre,
but just as he came to face Agamemnon, son of Pelops,
as a pallbearer, transferring the Doric army to greedy pyres,[46]
or how he looked when he slew the serpent Python and loosed 35
its coils, terrifying to the peaceful Muses.
Soon he spoke: "Savior of the world, Augustus from
Alba Longa, more famous than your Trojan ancestors,
conquer the sea; the earth is yours already; this bow fights
for you and this burden on my shoulders favors you.   40
Release your homeland from fear, since it now depends on you
as savior and your ship carries the people's prayers.
Defend your country, lest Romulus prove a poor founder
    of walls,
when he observed birds flying over the Palatine.[47]
Look, they dare come too close with their oars; shameful   45
that, with you in charge, the Latin waves must endure the
    queen's sails.
Don't let it frighten you that their fleet flies on a hundred oars;
they sail an unwilling sea;

45. After his deification, Romulus was known as Quirinus.
46. In the *Iliad,* Apollo sends a plague to punish Agamemnon for taking Briseis from Achilles.
47. Twin brothers Romulus and Remus took omens from bird flight in order to decide on which hill to found a city. First Remus saw six vultures from the Aventine, and Romulus subsequently saw twelve from the Palatine. A fight ensued, in which Romulus killed Remus.

and, although the prows carry centaur figureheads threatening
    with boulders,
you will find they are hollow wood and painted-on monsters.   50
A soldier's cause makes or breaks his strength;
unless the cause is just, shame dashes the weapons from
    his hands.
The time is at hand, engage the ships; I will choose the moment
and, with laurel in hand, will lead the Julian ships."
So he spoke, and his bow relieved his quiver of its weight;   55
after the volley of arrows, Caesar was the first to hurl his spear.
With Phoebus's assurance, Rome conquered; the woman paid
    the price;
Ionian waves carried broken scepters.
Father Caesar marvels from his Idalian star:[48]
"I am a god; your victory proves your ancestry."   60
Triton follows with a song, and all the sea
goddesses greeted the liberated standards with applause.
She, however, trusting unwisely in her fleeing skiff, sought
    the Nile.
Her one prize: not to die by execution.
The gods knew better! How great a triumph could one woman
    provide,   65
paraded through streets where once Jugurtha was led![49]
For this Actian Apollo received his monuments, because
each arrow he shot laid low ten ships.
I have sung enough of war; now Apollo the victor
requests my lyre and lays down his arms for peaceful dances.   70
Now may toga-clad banqueters enter the mild grove;
may delightful roses cascade over my neck,
and may wine made in Falernian presses be poured,
and three times may Cilician saffron perfume my hair.[50]
Let the Muse inspire poets who recline at the feast;   75

48. A reference to the Julian Star, a comet that appeared after Julius Caesar's death and was interpreted by Augustus as proof that Caesar had become a god. Idalium: a city in Cyprus sacred to Venus, from whom the Julian family claimed descent.

49. Jugurtha was a Numidian king conquered by Marius and led in his triumphal procession in 106 B.C.

50. Falernian was judged to be one of the best wines. Cilicia: a region in southern Asia Minor.

Bacchus, you have been known to inspire your companion
  Phoebus.
Let one relate how the marsh-dwelling Sycambri were taken
  hostage,
let another sing of Cephean Meroe and its dark realms,
let another recall how the Parthians admitted defeat in a
  belated treaty
(Let them return Remus's standards, soon they will surrender
  their own;   80
or if Augustus temporarily spares the quivers of the East,
let him leave those prizes for his sons.
Rejoice, Crassus, if the knowledge can reach you under the
  black sands;
now we can cross the Euphrates and visit your grave.)[51]
Thus I will spend the night drinking to the god and singing,
  until   85
the rays of dawn hit my wine.

6.10. Vergil, *Aeneid* 8.675–731 (19 B.C., Latin, verse)

For background on the Aeneid, *see selection* 4.15. *In* Aeneid 8, *Aeneas
leaves the battlefield where the Trojans are fighting the Latins, the native
population of Italy, and travels upstream on the Tiber to seek aid from a
local king, Evander. There, Evander leads Aeneas on a tour of the future
site of Rome. Later, Aeneas's mother, Venus, presents him with arms crafted
by the god of the forge, Vulcan. The shield shows scenes from Roman history,
culminating in the Battle of Actium, the depiction of which occupies the
center of the shield.*

In the middle, fleets of bronze were visible—the Battle of
  Actium—   675
and you could see all of Leucate surge,
troops arrayed, and the waves flash with gold.[52]

---

51. A series of Augustus's accomplishments. He defeated the Sycambri, a German
tribe who had invaded Gaul in 16 B.C. Meroe, an island in the Nile, was controlled by the
Ethiopians, who raided Egypt and were defeated by the Romans in 22 B.C. A diplomatic
mission in 20 B.C. reclaimed the Roman army standards that Crassus had lost to the
Parthians on the expedition that cost him his life. Augustus adopted his grandsons, Gaius
and Lucius, in 17 B.C. and was clearly grooming them as potential successors.
52. Leucate: the bay located off the promontory of Actium.

Here, Augustus Caesar, leading the Italians into battle,
along with the senate and people, the household and
   Olympian gods,
stands on the high stern. Twin flames pour from his blessed
   temples 680
and his father's star shines from the top of his head.[53]
Elsewhere, mighty Agrippa, with winds and gods favorable,
leads the battle line; his temples, clad in prows,
gleam with the naval crown, a magnificent decoration of war.
Next there was Antony with barbaric wealth and varied troops, 685
just come as a victor from the peoples of the East and the
   Red Sea;
he carries with him Egypt and the might of the East
and farthest Bactria, and (sinfully) his Egyptian wife follows
   him.
At once, they all charge and the whole sea foams,
heaving with straining oars and three-pronged prows. 690
They seek the deep; you would think the Cyclades,
torn from their foundations, roamed the sea or high mountains
slammed into mountains, so immense were the towered ships
   they manned.
They toss torches of flax and darts of iron;
the fields of Neptune grow red with freshly spilled blood. 695
In the midst of it all, the queen summons her troops with her
   native sistrum;[54]
not yet does she glance back at the twin serpents in her wake.
All sorts of monster-gods and barking Anubis
brandish weapons against Neptune and Venus and Minerva.
In the middle of the contest, Mars rages, 700
embossed in iron. Dire Furies descend from the sky
and Discord advances, reveling, her cloak in tatters,
as Bellona follows her with a bloody whip.[55]

---

53. "His father's star" refers to the Julian Star, a comet that appeared after the death of Julius Caesar and was believed to be evidence of his apotheosis. Augustus used this symbol on coins to advertise his link to his deified adoptive father.

54. The sistrum was a kind of rattle used in the worship of Isis.

55. Anubis was an Egyptian god associated with the dead and was often depicted with a jackal's head. Bellona was a Roman goddess of war.

Actian Apollo sees all this and aims his bow
from above; all Egypt and the Indians,   705
all Arabia and all the Sabaeans turned their backs on this
    terror.[56]
The queen herself was seen summoning the winds,
unfurling her sails and frantically paying out the slackened ropes.
The lord of fire had fashioned her, pale with approaching death,
amid the slaughter, impelled by the waves and the Northwest
    wind.   710
Opposite, the mourning Nile with open arms
receives the conquered into his folds,
into his blue embrace and sheltering streams.
But Caesar, carried inside the walls of Rome in triple triumph,
fulfills an everlasting vow to the Italian gods,   715
as he dedicates three hundred shrines throughout the entire city.
The streets echo with revelry, celebration and applause;
there was a chorus of mothers at every temple, every altar.
Before the altars sacrificed cattle strewed the ground.
Caesar, sitting on the white marble threshold of gleaming
    Apollo,   720
acknowledges the offerings of various peoples and affixes them
to the proud doorposts. Conquered races march in long
    procession,
as varied in their languages as in their dress and weapons.
Here Mulciber had fashioned the Nomad tribe and the
    loose-robed Africans;
here were the Leleges, the Carians and the arrow-bearing
    Geloni.[57]   725
The Euphrates flowed with waves now tamer. Then came
the Morini, the furthest of men, the two-horned Rhine,
the wild Dahae and the Araxes resentful of its bridge.[58]
Aeneas marvels at such scenes on Vulcan's shield, his
    mother's gift.

56. The Sabaeans lived in Arabia.
57. Mulciber: another name for Vulcan. The Leleges and Carians were from Asia
Minor. The Geloni were from Scythia.
58. The Morini lived in northern Gaul. The Dahae were Scythian nomads. Augustus
bridged the river Araxes in Armenia after the river broke the bridge Alexander the Great
had built.

Unfamiliar with the content, he delights in the depiction,   730
as he shoulders the renown and fate of his descendants.

6.11. Martial, *Epigram* 4.11 (ca. A.D. 88, Latin, verse)

*For more on Martial, see selection 4.5. Here, he references the Battle of
Actium in a poem addressed to another Antonius. Lucius Antonius Sat-
urninus commanded an army in Upper Germany during the reign of
Domitian. In A.D. 89 Saturninus and his army revolted. The governor of
Lower Germany, remaining loyal to the emperor, put down the revolt,
killing Saturninus in a battle at the Rhine.*[59]

While pompously rejoicing too much in an empty name   1
and being ashamed, you wretch, to be Saturninus,[60]
you incited treasonous war under the Parrhasian bear,[61]
like the one who carried the arms of a Pharian wife.[62]
Had you so forgotten the fate of this name,   5
which the dire wrath of the Actian Sea overwhelmed?
Or did the Rhine promise you that which the Nile did not grant
him, and would the Northern waters have been more
    permissive?
That Antonius also fell to our arms,
and he, compared to you, faithless one, was a Caesar.   10

59. See Suetonius, *Life of Domitian* 6; Cassius Dio 67.11.
60. The empty name refers to Antonius, the name Saturninus shares with Mark
Antony. He is ashamed, however, of "Saturninus," the part of his name that distinguishes
him from Mark Antony.
61. The constellation Ursa Major. Parrhasia is another name for Arcadia, the region
of Greece that was home to Callisto, who was transformed into the constellation by
Jupiter. Here, the constellation is a way of specifying the North.
62. "Pharian wife" indicates Cleopatra by referencing Pharos, the lighthouse of
Alexandria.

7

The Death of Cleopatra

CLEOPATRA'S SUICIDE BY THE bite of an asp (according to most sources) is one of the most dramatic and most often recounted parts of her story. Her final moment encapsulates much of her character: too proud to be displayed in Octavian's triumph, she prefers death to life as a prisoner; under close guard, she devises a means of taking her life; mentally equipped for any situation, she knows what method of suicide will be least painful. It is no wonder that Cleopatra's death has captured the imagination of authors and artists for centuries.

THE FINAL DAYS IN ALEXANDRIA

After the Battle of Actium, Antony and Cleopatra continued their resistance against Octavian's troops in Alexandria. As the situation became increasingly desperate, Antony attempted suicide under the impression that Cleopatra had died. Having succeeded only in wounding himself, he learned that she was alive, demanded that he be carried to her, and died in her arms. Octavian occupied Alexandria and took Cleopatra prisoner. Try as he might to keep her alive for his triumphal procession, she succeeded in wresting control of her life from him by her suicide.

7.1. Plutarch, *Life of Antony* 71–84 (A.D. 110–15, Greek, prose)

For more on Plutarch, see selection 2.1. As Plutarch relates, Antony and Cleopatra are aware that their situation is becoming desperate.

71. Canidius[1] came as his own messenger, bringing Antony word of the loss of his forces at Actium, and Antony also heard that Herod of Judaea had gone over to Octavian, taking some cohorts and legions with him, and that the other dynasts likewise were deserting him and that nothing remained for him outside Egypt. This sort of news no longer distressed him, as if he was glad to give up hope so that he might also give up his cares, and he left the island abode he called the Timonium.[2] Cleopatra received him in the palace and the city's attention turned to banqueting, drinking, and extravagant gift giving. Antony had the son of Caesar and Cleopatra enrolled in the list of ephebes[3] and granted to Antyllus, his son with Fulvia, the toga of manhood that does not have a purple stripe. The drinking parties, banquets, and entertainments given to celebrate these events occupied Alexandria for days. They dissolved the society of Inimitable Livers and founded another, in no way inferior to the first in elegance, extravagance, and luxury, which they called the Partners in Death. Their friends enrolled, resolving to die together, and spent their time in rounds of banquets. Cleopatra assembled an assortment of powerful and deadly poisons and, in order to determine how painless each was, she tested them on men condemned to death. When she observed that the fastest acting poisons brought the most painful deaths and that the gentler ones were not swift, she tested various beasts by having one set on one man and another on another man while she observed. She did this every day and in almost all cases, she discovered that the bite of the asp produced deep and comatose sleep without moaning or seizures and with only light perspiration of the face and a decrease in perception as the victims gradually grew weak and became difficult to awaken or rouse, just like people in a deep sleep.

72. At the same time, they sent ambassadors to Octavian in Asia, requesting that the kingdom of Egypt go to her children and that Antony be allowed to go to Athens, if he could not remain in Egypt, and live as a private citizen. Because of their lack of and distrust of friends, many of whom had deserted them, they sent Euphronius, their children's tutor. The reason for this was that Alexas of Laodicea, whom Timagenes had introduced to Antony in Rome, became more

---

1. The commander of Antony's land army.
2. See Plutarch, *Life of Antony* 69 (selection *6.4*).
3. Ephebes were youths who received military training.

influential over Antony than any other Greek. Alexas had become the most powerful of Cleopatra's tools against Antony: he cast out any arguments for reconciling with Octavia. Antony had sent him to deter Herod of Judaea from deserting Antony, but Alexas, after staying with Herod and betraying Antony, dared to obtain an audience with Octavian, relying on Herod's protection. Herod, however, did not help him at all, and Alexas was apprehended at once and brought to his homeland in bonds, and there he was executed at Octavian's command. Alexas paid this penalty for treachery to Antony while the latter was still living.

73. Octavian refused to entertain requests made on Antony's behalf, but he replied that Cleopatra would not be refused any reasonable requests if she destroyed Antony or sent him away. Then Octavian sent over one of his freedmen, Thyrsus, who was not unintelligent and would speak persuasively on behalf of a young commander to a haughty and magnificent woman who took great pride in her beauty. This man met with her for longer than the others and was honored so conspicuously that Antony was seized by suspicion and had him arrested and whipped before sending him back to Octavian with a letter to the effect that Thyrsus's arrogance and insolence had provoked him, since his troubles made him easy to provoke. "If you do not think my actions appropriate," he said, "you have my freedman Hipparchus. You may hang him up and whip him so that we will be even." After this incident, Cleopatra, in an attempt to redeem her errors and suspicions, entertained Antony lavishly: she celebrated her own birthday in a manner commensurate with their current status, but she celebrated Antony's by putting on such a lavish and elaborate event that many of the guests who came to the party as poor men left wealthy. Caesar was called away by Agrippa, who kept writing from Rome that matters there required his presence.

74. At that time the war was delayed; when winter ended, however, Octavian at once attacked via Syria and his generals via Libya. They took Pelusium and word went around that Seleucus surrendered it with Cleopatra's approval.[4] She, however, allowed Antony to execute

4. Pelusium: a city across the Nile delta from Alexandria; Seleucus: Cleopatra's general at Pelusium.

Seleucus's wife and children. Meanwhile, she had constructed tombs and monuments notable for their beauty and height, which were located near the temple of Isis. There, she collected the most valuable of the royal treasures: gold, silver, emeralds, pearls, ebony, ivory, cinnamon, and, in addition, much wood and tow.[5] Octavian was apprehensive about these preparations and feared that she would give in to despair and destroy and burn her wealth and so, as he surrounded the city with his army, he sent her encouraging and hopeful messages. But when he had pitched camp near the hippodrome,[6] Antony went on the offensive, attacked brilliantly, and routed Octavian's cavalry, driving them back to their camp. Exulting in his victory, Antony returned to the palace, embraced Cleopatra while still wearing his armor, and presented to her the bravest of all his soldiers. She gave a gold breastplate and helmet to the man, who took them and then, in the night, deserted to Octavian.

75. Antony again sent word to Octavian challenging him to fight one-on-one. When Octavian replied that there were many ways for Antony to kill himself, Antony realized that there was no better way for him to die than in battle, and so he decided to attack on land and sea at the same time. It is said that at dinner he ordered his slaves to fill his cup and entertain him more lavishly than usual, for it was unclear whether they would be doing the same tomorrow or serving other masters while he lay as a corpse and became nothing at all. Seeing that his words brought his friends to tears, he said that he would not lead them into battle, for he was seeking from it a noble death rather than safety and victory. It is said that on this night, around midnight, when the city was silent and sorrowful due to the fear and anticipation of the things to come, suddenly harmonious sounds of every type of instrument were heard, along with the shout of the crowd mixed with Bacchanalian cries and the leaping of Satyrs, as if a Dionysiac procession was departing tumultuously. The march went almost through the center of the city to the gate nearest

---

5. These last items were presumably to be used to set fire to the treasure to prevent its falling into Octavian's hands.
6. Hippodrome: a track for horse races.

to the enemy camp, where the clamor became loudest and then came to an end. It seemed to those interpreting the sign that the god to whom Antony likened himself and to whom he claimed to be related was deserting him.

76. When day broke, Antony stationed his infantry on the hills in front of the city, observed his ships moving out and heading toward the enemy, and waited and stood to watch how they fared. But when the ships approached the enemy, they saluted Octavian with their oars and, when he returned their salute, the fleet, becoming one with all these ships, set sail pointing their prows toward the city. As Antony saw this, he was deserted by his cavalry, who went over to the enemy, and, his infantry bested, he returned to the city, crying that he had been betrayed by Cleopatra to the men he was fighting on her account. And she, fearing his anger and despair, fled to her mausoleum and closed the doors, which were reinforced with bars and bolts; she sent word to Antony that she was dead. He, believing it, said to himself, "Why do you still put it off, Antony? Chance has removed the one remaining reason to live," and went into his quarters. He unfastened and removed his armor. "Cleopatra," he said, "I am not pained to be bereft of you, for at once I will be where you are, but it does pain me that I, as a commander, am revealed to be inferior to a woman in courage." He had a trustworthy slave named Eros. He had made this man promise to kill him, should it be necessary, and now he demanded that the promise be fulfilled. Eros drew his sword and raised it as if about to strike Antony, but instead turned away and killed himself. When he fell at Antony's feet, Antony said, "Well done, Eros, for, not being able to carry it out, you have taught me what I must do." Striking himself through the belly, he fell onto a couch. But the blow was not fatal. When the bleeding stopped, he sat on the couch and asked those nearby to strike a second, fatal blow. But they fled from the room as he wailed and writhed, until Cleopatra's secretary Diomedes, on her orders, brought Antony to her mausoleum.

77. When Antony realized that Cleopatra was alive, he eagerly ordered the slaves to lift his body up and he was carried by hand to the doors of the building. Cleopatra did not open the doors, but she appeared in a window and sent down ropes and cords. They fastened

Antony to these and Cleopatra and her two maids, who were the only ones she allowed in the mausoleum with her, raised him up. Those who were there say that no scene was sadder than this one, for bloodstained and dying, he was lifted up, extending his hands to her as he was suspended alongside the building. The task was not easy for a woman, but Cleopatra just managed to pull the rope up, clinging to it with her hands and distorting her face with the effort, as the onlookers encouraged her from below and shared her struggles. When she received him into the mausoleum and laid him on a couch, she tore her clothing over him, beat her breast and scratched it with her hands, covered her face with his blood, called him her husband and master, and almost forgot her own misfortunes as she pitied his. Antony stopped her lament and requested a drink of wine, either because he was thirsty or because he hoped it might hasten his end. He drank it and then advised her to consider her own safety, provided she could do it with no loss of honor, to trust Proculeius, Octavian's associate, most of all, and not to mourn the change of fortunes that accompanied his last days, but rather to rejoice in the good fortune he had experienced, since he was the most illustrious of men and had held great power and now he, as a Roman, was conquered honorably by a Roman.

78. When he was at the very moment of death, Proculeius came from Octavian. When Antony had stabbed himself and was being taken to Cleopatra, Dercetaeus, one of Antony's bodyguards, took the sword and, keeping it hidden, slipped away and went to Octavian in order to be the first to deliver the news of Antony's death and show the bloody sword. Octavian, when he heard the news, withdrew into his tent and wept for the man who was his brother-in-law, fellow ruler, and companion in many battles and situations. Next, he took their letters and, calling his friends together, read them to show how fairly and justly he had written and how vulgarly and arrogantly Antony had always replied. After this, he sent Proculeius, ordering him to capture Cleopatra alive if at all possible, for he feared for her treasure and thought that leading her in his triumph would increase its glory. She did not wish to hand herself over to Proculeius, but words were passed as he stood outside the building on the ground; the door was stoutly reinforced, but voices could pass

through. They conversed, Cleopatra asking that her children inherit her kingdom and Proculeius advising her to be optimistic and trust Octavian.

79. When he had seen the place, Proculeius reported back to Octavian and Gallus was sent back to meet with Cleopatra. He approached the doors and deliberately dragged out the conversation. At the same time, Proculeius set up a ladder and entered through the window through which the women had received Antony. He immediately rushed to the doors where Cleopatra was standing, along with her two maids, and talking with Gallus. The women came to Cleopatra's aid and cried, "Unfortunate Cleopatra, you are captured!" When Cleopatra turned and saw Proculeius, she attempted to stab herself, for she happened to have hidden in her clothing a thief's dagger. But Proculeius ran quickly to her, grabbed her with both his hands, and said, "You will wrong both yourself and Caesar, if you deprive him of the chance to show his clemency and erroneously assume that this most kindly ruler is faithless and merciless." As he spoke, he took the dagger from her and searched her clothing in case she was hiding any poison. Octavian sent Epaphroditus with instructions that he should be extremely vigilant to keep her alive, but otherwise to allow her anything she wished for her comfort and happiness.

80. Octavian himself entered the city, conversing with Areius[7] the philosopher and offering him his right hand, so that Areius would be instantly well regarded by the Alexandrians and respected for the well-deserved honor Octavian showed him. When Octavian entered the gymnasium and ascended the platform built for the occasion, the citizens were inspired with awe and prostrated themselves. He ordered them to rise and said that the city was free from blame, first because its founder was Alexander the Great, second because he admired the beauty and size of the city, and third because of his esteem for his companion Areius. Areius received this honor from Octavian, as well as numerous individual pardons for others. One of these was Philostratus,[8] a man more proficient at extemporaneous speaking than any Sophist alive, but who had falsely claimed to be a

7. Areius Didymus was a philosopher and one of Octavian's teachers.
8. Another philosopher.

member of the Academy.[9] Because of this, Octavian, who detested
the man's way of life, refused him a pardon. Therefore, Philostratus
grew his white beard long, wore all black, and followed behind
Areius, continually repeating this verse:

> The wise will save the wise, if they are wise.

When Octavian found out about this, he pardoned Philostratus,
more because he wished to relieve Areius's embarrassment than to
relieve Philostratus's fear.

81. Of Antony's children, Antyllus the son of Fulvia died after his
tutor Theodorus betrayed him;[10] when the soldiers beheaded him,
the tutor took a precious stone the boy wore around his neck and
stitched it up in his belt and, although he denied taking it, he was
crucified. Cleopatra's children and their nurses were closely guarded,
but treated with respect. Caesarion, said to be Cleopatra's son with
Caesar, was sent by his mother with ample funds to India, via Ethiopia.
Another tutor like Theodorus, Rhodon, persuaded him to go back,
saying that Octavian would call upon him to take the throne. As
Octavian was considering what to do with Caesarion, Areius is said
to have paraphrased:

> It is not good to have too many Caesars.[11]

82. Octavian had Caesarion killed later, after Cleopatra's death.
Many kings and generals asked to bury Antony, but Octavian did not
deprive Cleopatra of his body; she buried him with her own hands
lavishly and royally, as she was granted the right to use all the
resources she wished. Because of her grief and pain—for her chest
was inflamed and lacerated where she had beaten it—she was feverish
and embraced the excuse to refrain from eating and, unimpeded,
free herself from living. A doctor named Olympus was attending her
and she told him truthfully what she was doing and obtained his
help and council in reducing her body, as Olympus himself recounts in
the book he published on these events. Octavian found out and hurled
threats at her and made her fear for her children. She was undermined

---

9. Plato's philosophical school.
10. Antony's other children by Fulvia were in Rome with Octavia.
11. Homer, *Iliad* 2.204.

by these threats as surely as by siege engines and allowed her body to be cared for and nourished by those whose job it was.

83. Octavian came in person after a few days to meet with her and discuss matters. She met him lying humbly on a mat wearing only a tunic, but when he entered, she leapt up and prostrated herself; her hair was in disarray and her face had a crazed expression, but her voice trembled and her eyes were lifeless. Her chest showed signs of the injuries she had inflicted upon it; in all, her body seemed no better off than her mind. Her charm and the vigor of her beauty were not at all diminished, but although it lay beneath the surface, it shone forth from within and was evident in her changing expressions. Octavian proposed that she lie down and then sat down nearby. Cleopatra offered some rationalizations, portraying her actions as motivated by necessity and fear of Antony. When Octavian disagreed with her on every point, she quickly changed her approach and appealed to his pity and begged, as if she still was desperate to live. Finally, she gave him a list that inventoried her wealth, but when Seleucus, one of her assistants, claimed that she was hiding and stealing away several things, she leapt up, grabbed him by the hair, and rained down blows on his face. When Octavian smiled and stopped her, she said, "Is it not terrible, Caesar, if you think it worthwhile to come and speak with me in my current state, that my slaves accuse me, if I put aside some womanly items, not to adorn myself, alas, but so that I might give a few small tokens to Octavia and your wife, Livia, in hopes of finding you more mild and gentle?" Octavian approved of these words and believed that she truly desired to live. He said that he entrusted those matters to her and that he would treat her better than she could hope; he then departed, thinking that he had deceived her, but in fact having been deceived by her.

84. An illustrious young man named Cornelius Dolabella was among Octavian's associates. He was not unreceptive to Cleopatra's charms and so, as a favor to her, since she asked him, he notified her by sending word in secret that Octavian was leading his infantry through Syria and that he had decided to take her and her children to Rome on the third day. When she heard this news, she first asked Octavian to allow her to pour libations for Antony. When he agreed, she was carried to the mausoleum, along with her maids, where she fell upon the coffin and said, "My dear Antony, not long ago I

buried you with the hands of a free woman, but now I pour libations as a prisoner, under guard so that I will not harm this slave's body by beating it or by lamenting and so that I may adorn their triumphs over you. Do not expect any further honors or libations; these are your final rites from the captured Cleopatra. In life, nothing could separate us from each other, but in death we will be forced to change places: you, a Roman, will lie here, while I, unfortunate, will be in Italy, but will have at my disposal only a small part of your land. But if any of the gods there have strength and power—for those here have betrayed us—do not desert your wife as long as she lives, nor allow me to be led in a triumph over you, but conceal me here and bury me with you, for the myriad evils I have endured are nothing as great or terrible as this short time I have lived apart from you."

7.2. Velleius Paterculus, *Histories* 2.87 (A.D. 30, Latin, prose)

For more on Velleius Paterculus, see selection 6.3. In this passage Velleius summarizes the events of the year after the Battle of Actium.

Over the next year, he pursued Antony and the queen to Alexandria and tied up the loose ends of the civil wars. Antony lost no time in ending his own life and, as a result, he atoned with his death for his indolence in life; Cleopatra deceived the guards and had an asp smuggled in and relinquished her life to its bite nobly and without womanly fear. It is a testament to Caesar's fortune and clemency that no one who had taken up arms against him was executed by him or at his decree: Antony's cruelty sealed the fate of Decimus Brutus;[12] likewise, Sextus Pompey,[13] although it was Caesar who conquered him, was killed by Antony, despite Antony's promise to preserve not only his life but his honor as well; Brutus and Cassius seized upon a voluntary death before they even learned their conquerors' plans; we have already described the deaths of Antony and Cleopatra. More cowardly was Canidius in his actions at the end of his life than in the brave statements he was always making.[14]

---

12. Decimus Brutus was one of the conspirators against Julius Caesar.
13. The son of Pompey the Great; he was conquered by Octavian, who accused him of violating an agreement.
14. Canidius is said to have deserted his troops and fled back to Antony after they were defeated in the fighting that followed the Battle of Actium.

7.3. Florus, *Abridgement of All the Wars Over 1,200 Years* 2.21.9–11 (2nd c. A.D., Latin, prose)

For more on Florus, see selection 3.10. In this passage Florus discusses the motives behind Cleopatra's suicide.

Antony fell on his sword first; the queen, throwing herself at Caesar's feet, tried to work her charms on him. But it was all in vain: for her beauty was no match for the virtue of the Princeps.[15]

(10) She was not angling for her life, which he willingly granted her, but rather for a share in her kingdom. When she despaired of convincing the Princeps and realized that she was spared only for display in his triumph, she took advantage of a rather lax guard and escaped to the mausoleum (this is what they call the royal tomb).

(11) There, she dressed herself in her richest attire, as was her custom, and settled herself next to her Antony in a sarcophagus filled with aromatic perfumes. She then put snakes to her veins and slipped into death as if into sleep.

7.4. Cassius Dio, *Roman History* 51.11–13 (A.D. 202, Greek, prose)

For more on Cassius Dio, see selection 2.5. Here, Dio narrates the events following Antony's suicide.

11. And so Antony died there in the embrace of Cleopatra; she felt confident about Octavian and made it clear to him right away what had happened, but she did not completely trust that she would suffer no harm. Therefore, she remained inside so that, even if nothing else should save her, she could obtain amnesty and her kingdom by exploiting Octavian's fear of losing her treasure. Even then, amid such calamity, she was so mindful of her sovereignty that she preferred to die with her name and status intact rather than to live as a private citizen. To be sure, she also had fire for her treasure and for herself asps and other reptiles, which she had tested on men to determine how each of them killed. Octavian was eager both to control her treasury

---

15. Princeps was the title Octavian chose for his position as the most powerful individual in Rome after his defeat of Antony. The term, which means "first man," had been applied to the senator who had the right of expressing his opinion first during deliberations.

and to take her alive and lead her in his triumph, but having given her, in some sense, his word, he did not want to seem to have deceived her, since he intended to have her as a prisoner taken captive against her will. So he sent to her Gaius Proculeius, an equestrian, and Epaphroditus, a freedman, with instructions detailing what should be said and done. They met with Cleopatra and, while discussing some reasonable options, suddenly grabbed her before completing the negotiation. They next removed any things with which she might be able to kill herself and permitted her to remain in place for some days preparing Antony's body for burial. Next they led her to the palace, not depriving her of the attendants or servants to whom she was accustomed, in order to give her hope that she would accomplish her plans and to prevent her harming herself. Accordingly, when she desired an audience and a hearing with Octavian, it was granted. To complete the deception, he pledged to come to her.

12. She readied her quarters, set up a sumptuous couch, presented herself as if she did not care (for she looked stunning in her mourning clothes), and took her place on the couch. She arranged next to her all sorts of images of his father and clutched to her breast all the letters his father had sent her. Then, when Octavian entered, she leapt to her feet gracefully and said, "Greetings, my lord (for a god has given you this power and taken it from me). You see your father, how he was when he often came to me, and you have heard the other things he did to honor me, especially making me queen of the Egyptians. Take these letters and read what he wrote in his own hand and let him introduce me to you."

With that, she read out the letters' many passionate words. Then, weeping, she kissed the letters and fell to her knees before the images of Caesar and venerated them. She turned her eyes to Octavian and, lamenting melodiously, addressed him languishingly, on one occasion saying, "What good are your letters doing me, Caesar?" and on another, "But you still live for me in this man," and then, "I wish I had died first," but then, "But having him, I have you."

She employed these sorts of variations of speech and comportment as she looked at him and spoke to him sweetly. Octavian recognized her appeal to his emotions and bid for sympathy, but did not let on; rather, he lowered his eyes to the ground and said only, "Take courage, woman, and retain your good spirits: no harm will come to you." Then she, despairing because he neither looked at her nor mentioned her kingdom, nor expressed any fondness, threw herself at his knees and wailed, "Caesar, I neither wish nor am able to live; I entreat you, grant me this favor in honor of your father's memory: since the gods sent me Antony after him, let me die with Antony. For I wish I had died right after Caesar. Since, however, I was destined to endure this misfortune, send me to Antony and do not begrudge me a tomb in common with him so that, just as I die with him, so too may I live with him in Hades."

13. She spoke such words to arouse his pity, but Octavian made no response to them, but, fearing that she might do herself in, he urged her again to take courage. He did not take away her servants and he even paid special attention to her, so that she might be the centerpiece of his triumph. She, suspecting that this was the case and considering it a fate worse than a thousand deaths, became truly eager to die. She both beseeched Octavian on many occasions that she be allowed to perish in some way and devised many of her own strategies. When she met with no success, she pretended that she had changed her mind and now placed great hope in him and in Livia. She said she would sail willingly and readied some prized ornaments as gifts in order to gain trust through these actions that she would not kill herself and, as a result, to be less closely guarded and to have the opportunity to commit suicide. Her plan was a success. For when the others and Epaphroditus, to whom she was entrusted, believed that she meant what she said, they were less concerned to guard her closely and she had the opportunity to prepare to die with as little suffering as possible. She wrote a letter, in which she entreated Octavian to have her buried next to Antony, sealed it, and gave it to Epaphroditus so that he might take it to Octavian in the belief that it contained some other content and, thus, be absent while she performed the deed. Dressing herself in her finest clothing, positioning herself in the most appropriate pose, and taking in her hands the royal symbols, she died.

7.5. Martial, *Epigram* 4.59 (ca. A.D. 88, Latin, verse)

For more on Martial, see selection 4.5. Here, he compares Cleopatra unfavorably to a viper.

While a viper crept among the weeping boughs of the Heliads,[16] 1
a drop of amber flowed onto the beast as it stood still:
while it was amazed that it was held fast by the thick liquid,
it grew stiff, suddenly fettered by solid ice.
Do not, Cleopatra, be pleased with your royal tomb, 5
if a viper lies in a finer sepulcher.

POST MORTEM

Most of the sources agree that Octavian was dismayed at Cleopatra's
death, but there are conjectures that although he would have like to
have displayed her in his triumph, he was not unhappy to have her
out of the way.

7.6. Plutarch, *Life of Antony* 85–86 (A.D. 110–15, Greek, prose)

*For more on Plutarch, see selection 2.1. Here, he describes the careful
orchestration of Cleopatra's suicide.*

85. Such was the mourning of Cleopatra for Antony: she placed a
garland on his coffin and kissed it, then ordered a bath to be drawn
for her. After bathing, she reclined and enjoyed an outstanding meal.
Someone came from the countryside, bringing a basket. When the
guards asked what it held, he opened it, parted the leaves on top and
showed that the basket was full of figs. The guards wondered at the
size and beauty of the figs and so he smiled and offered that they
could take some. Trusting him, they let him in. After her meal,
Cleopatra picked up a letter, already written and sealed, and sent it
to Octavian. She then sent away all of her attendants except two
women and closed the doors. When Octavian opened the letter and,
encountering prayers and laments requesting that she be buried with
Antony, at once realized what she had done, at first, he wanted to
rush to her himself and save her, but then he decided to send some
people to quickly find out what had happened. The tragedy, however, was over too quickly. When the messengers arrived at a run,

---

16. Amber was said to have been created by the tears of Phaethon's sisters, who were
transformed into weeping willows as they mourned Phaethon's death after he fell from the
chariot of the sun (see Ovid, *Metamorphoses* 2.1–400).

they found the guards still suspecting nothing. Opening the doors, they found her dead, lying on a golden couch, dressed in royal attire. Of her maids, the one called Iras lay dying at her feet and Charmion, already failing and hardly able to hold up her head, was arranging Cleopatra's crown on her head. One of the men asked angrily, "Are these things well done, Charmion?" "Very well done indeed," she said, "and fitting for one descended from so many kings." She said no more, but fell right there beside the couch.

86. It is said that the asp was brought in with the figs, hidden under the leaves, just as Cleopatra had commanded, so that the creature would alight on her body without her knowledge. But they say she saw it as she picked up some of the figs and she said, "So there it is, then," and offered her bare arm to its bite. Others say that the asp was kept enclosed in a pitcher and that Cleopatra excited and provoked it with a golden distaff until it struck and fastened itself to her arm. No one knows the truth: it is also said that she carried poison in a hollow hairpin, which she kept hidden in her hair. There was, however, no sign of a rash on her body or any other indication of poison. Also, no snake was found in the mausoleum, although they say some tracks could be seen leading from there to the sea on the side that faced that direction and where the windows were. And some claim to have seen two light and indistinct pricks on Cleopatra's arm. It seems that Octavian believed this, for in his triumph he had a statue of Cleopatra carried that showed an asp clinging to her. These events are said to have happened in this way. Octavian, although he was pained by Cleopatra's death, admired her courage and ordered her body to be buried with Anotny in a lavish and regal funeral. He also honored her maids with appropriate funerals.

Cleopatra died at age thirty-nine, having ruled for twenty-two years and shared her power with Antony for more than fourteen.[17] Some say Antony was fifty-six when he died and others say he was fifty-three. Statues of Antony were removed, but those of Cleopatra remain throughout the land, since Archibius, a friend of hers, paid Octavian two thousand talents to save them from the fate Antony's suffered.

---

17. This number seems to be incorrect, since they met at Tarsus in 41 B.C. and died in 30 B.C.

7.7. Cassius Dio, *Roman History* 51.14 (A.D. 202, Greek, prose)

For more on Cassius Dio, see selection 2.5. Here, we pick up the story begun in selection 7.4 as Dio speculates about the means by which Cleopatra committed suicide.

No one knows for sure how she died; small punctures on her arm were the only evidence found. Some say that she applied an asp concealed in a water jar or among flowers, but others claim that she had applied to one of her hairpins some poison, the sort that would not harm the body unless it touched the smallest drop of blood, in which case it killed extremely swiftly but without suffering; that she had been wearing it in her hair as usual; and that after scratching her arm somewhat, she dipped the pin into the blood. In this manner, or very similarly, she died along with her two servants—the eunuch had willingly offered himself to the reptiles at the time Cleopatra had been apprehended and, once they had bitten him, had leapt into a waiting coffin. Caesar was astounded to hear of Cleopatra's death: he inspected her body and called for drugs and Psylli, in case they could save her. These Psylli are men (for no female Psylla is born) who are able to suck out the poison of any reptile immediately, before it proves fatal, and who suffer no harm themselves from any of these creatures. They are born from one another and they test their offspring by casting them as newborns among snakes or by throwing their swaddling to the snakes: for the snakes either do not harm the child or are anesthetized by the clothing. That is the nature of the phenomenon. But when Caesar was not able in any way to revive Cleopatra, he marveled at her and pitied her too; he was exceedingly pained for himself, since he was robbed of the full splendor of his victory.

7.8. Galen, *On Antidotes* 8[18] (ca. A.D. 200, Greek, prose)

Galen was born in Asia Minor, where he was a doctor who treated gladiators. He ended his career in Rome, serving as court physician during the reign of Marcus Aurelius. Galen also wrote on many subjects, including

18. Kühn 1821–33, vol. 14, 235–37.

*grammar, philosophy, and medicine. He offers a physician's perspective on
the death of Cleopatra in the context of a discussion of snakebites.*

Of the asps, the one called ptyas[19] extends its throat, estimates the
length of the interval and then, like a rational being, the creature
spits venom from its body with perfect aim. They say that it was by
means of one of these creatures (for there are three kinds of asps, the
one mentioned above, the one called chersaea, and the one known as
chelidonia)[20] that Queen Cleopatra, wishing to foil her guards, died
swiftly and without arousing suspicion. For Augustus, after conquering
Antony, wished to take her alive and wished very much to keep her
alive, as is reasonable, so that he might exhibit to the Romans in his
triumph so famous a woman. But she, they say, perceived this and,
choosing to leave the human race still a queen rather than to appear
before the Romans as a private citizen, engineered her own death by
this beast. And they say that she called her two most trustworthy
maids to her—they were the ones who attended to her toilette and
cared for her body; their names were Naera and Carmione. The one
arranged her hair becomingly and the other dexterously trimmed the
tips of her nails. Then Cleopatra ordered the creature brought in
hidden among grapes and figs, so that, as I have said, she might
elude the guards. She tried this method beforehand on these women
to determine whether it could cause death quickly, and after they
perished swiftly, she turned it upon herself, and they say that, on this
account, Augustus was greatly amazed, in part because of the affection these women had to die with their queen, and in part because
she did not wish to live in slavery, but preferred to die nobly. Indeed,
they say that her right hand was found resting on her head, holding
her crown, as was appropriate, so that she might appear to those
who saw her to be a queen even in death. Just so, the tragic poet tells
us, Polyxena, although she was dying, nevertheless had the foresight
to fall with grace.[21] Those who wish to explain to us the woman's skill
in deception and creature's speed in killing say that she wounded
her own arm with a deep bite and poured into the wound venom

19. Literally, "spitter."
20. Chersaea: "living on land"; chelidonia: "reddish-brown."
21. Polyxena was a daughter of the Trojan king Priam and Hecuba. In Euripides'
Hecuba, the son of Achilles sacrifices Polyxena at his father's tomb.

brought to her in a container. Not long after receiving this aid, she foiled the guards and died contentedly. But let this tale be told not only for pleasure, because you are interested in every topic, but also so that we understand how quickly these creatures can kill, for they are truly swift in taking a life. Often in great Alexandria I have seen the speed with which death results from their bite.[22] For when someone is sentenced to punishment under the law and must be executed quickly and humanely, they put a snake on his chest and make him walk around a little, thus swiftly removing the man from their midst. Therefore, you see how I properly use none of these creatures in medicine because they have such destructive power in their bodies.

7.9. Strabo, *Geography* 17.1.10 (A.D. 18–23, Greek, prose)

For more on Strabo, see selection 1.4. Strabo adds one more possible means of suicide that Cleopatra may have employed.

After crossing through the hippodrome, one comes to Nicopolis, a settlement on the coast no smaller than a city; it is thirty stades[23] from Alexandria. Augustus Caesar honored this place because there he conquered in battle those who fought against him under Antony's leadership. As soon as he had taken the city, he forced Antony to kill himself and Cleopatra to be taken alive. Shortly afterward, however, she secretly killed herself while under guard by the bite of an asp or with a poisonous ointment (two versions of the story exist), and, as a result, the rule of the Lagids[24] ended, although it had survived for many years.

THE FATE OF EGYPT

After Cleopatra's death, Octavian annexed Egypt but did not make it a Roman province in the usual fashion. For the same reasons that Julius Caesar had been unwilling to make Egypt a province, Octavian also hesitated. Rather than allowing Egypt to be governed as a province, he kept it more closely under his own control, appointing a

22. Some of Galen's medical education took place in Alexandria.
23. A stade is about six hundred feet.
24. The Ptolemies.

prefect to govern there as his representative. The first prefect of Egypt was Cornelius Gallus, who was forced to take his own life after he overstepped his bounds.

7.10. Cassius Dio, *Roman History* 51.15–17 (A.D. 202, Greek, prose)

For more on Cassius Dio, see selection 2.5. Dio continues the narrative begun in selection 7.7, here summing up the paradoxical natures of Antony and Cleopatra. He also details the fates that befell their children.

15. Antony and Cleopatra, who were responsible for many misfortunes both for the Egyptians and for the Romans, thus fought a war and died; they both were embalmed in the same way and were buried in the same tomb. I will describe the nature of their souls and the fortunes of their lives. No one was better than Antony at understanding what had to be done, but he did many foolish things; he was conspicuous for his bravery at times, but frequently faltered due to cowardice; he had equal parts noble heart and slavish spirit; he plundered what belonged to others, but wasted his own resources; he showed mercy to many for no particular reason, but even more were censured unjustly. As a result, although he went from the greatest weakness to the greatest power and from the greatest poverty to the greatest wealth, he had the enjoyment of neither, but rather his hopes of being powerful and the sole ruler of the Romans ended when he killed himself. Cleopatra had both overwhelming charm and overwhelming riches; she often displayed admirable ambition, but just as often arrogant rashness. She won the throne of Egypt by love; hoping to become queen of the Romans by the same method, she failed and lost Egypt as well. She mastered the two most powerful Romans of her time, and, because of a third, she was destroyed. This is the sort of people they were and the way they met their end. Of their children, Antyllus, who was engaged to Caesar's daughter, had fled to the shrine Cleopatra had built for his father, but was immediately murdered. Caesarion fled to Ethiopia but was intercepted on the road and killed.[25] Cleopatra married Juba, the son of Juba, to whom, since he had been raised in Italy and had fought alongside him, Caesar

25. Antyllus was the son of Antony and Fulvia; Caesarion was the son of Julius Caesar and Cleopatra.

gave the princess and the right to keep his ancestral kingdom, and did them the favor of sparing Alexander and Ptolemy.[26] He apportioned to his nieces, whom Octavia had borne to Antony and brought up, their inheritance from their father. To Iullus, the son of Antony and Fulvia, he ordered that whatever the laws dictate for citizens to leave their children should be given to him right away.

16. Of the others who had aligned themselves with Antony, he punished some and others he let go, either because he wished to or because his friends lobbied him. A number of children of rulers and kings were discovered being raised at the court, some serving as hostages and some the result of a wanton display of might. Of these, he sent some home, some he married to one another, and some he kept there. I will pass over most of these, and mention only two by name. He voluntarily returned Iotape to the Median ruler who, when defeated, had taken refuge with him. He did not send Artaxes his brothers, despite his requests, because he had executed Romans left behind in Armenia. This is what happened to the others; as for the Egyptians and Alexandrians, he spared all of them so that none were killed. The truth of the matter was that he did not think it reasonable to do anything irreversible to them, as they were strong in numbers and likely to be useful. He gave as an excuse, however, the god Serapis, their founder Alexander, and thirdly the citizen Areius, whose philosophical inquiries and friendship he enjoyed. He delivered the speech in which he granted them this reprieve in Greek, so that they would understand him. Afterward, he viewed the body of Alexander and even touched it; as a result, the nose, they say, was broken. He did not view the bodies of the Ptolemies, despite the Alexandrians' eagerness to show them to him; he said, "I wanted to see a king, not corpses." For the same reason, he did not wish to visit Apis, saying that he was used to worshipping gods, not cattle.

17. Next, he made Egypt pay taxes to Rome and entrusted it to Cornelius Gallus.[27] Because of Egypt's large population, both in its cities and in the surrounding countryside, the irresponsible and

---

26. These were the children of Antony and Cleopatra: Cleopatra Selene, Alexander Helios, and Ptolemy Philadelphos. Juba was a Numidian prince.

27. Egypt was not made a province in the usual manner, but rather it remained more closely under the control of the princeps. Cornelius Gallus, a man of the equestrian order,

impressionable nature of the people, and the abundance of grain and money, he did not dare to appoint any senator to govern, and would not even let them live there, except those to whom he gave express permission; nor did he permit Egyptians to be members of the senate in Rome. He settled matters in the other cities as befitted each, but he dictated that the Alexandrians run their city without a senate, presumably because he considered there to be significant risk of a revolution. Their government was at that time set up in this way. Other aspects of it are certainly maintained even now, but they now have a senate both in Alexandria, begun under the emperor Severus, and in Rome, with the first senators enrolled under Severus's son Antoninus. In this way, Egypt was enslaved. All who engaged in rebellion were in time brought under control, as the divine spirit clearly foretold: it rained not only water in places where it never had before, but also blood; at the same time as this blood fell from the clouds, weapons were seen in the sky. Elsewhere, drums sounded, cymbals rang out, the sounds of pipes and trumpets were heard, a sort of giant serpent suddenly was seen, and it hissed unbelievably loudly. At the same time, comets were observed and the ghosts of the dead materialized; cult statues adopted angry expressions and Apis lowed laments and wept. That is the way these things happened. Great riches were found in the palace (for Cleopatra, by removing almost all the offerings from even the most sacred temples, increased the Romans' spoils while preventing pollution from settling on any of their households). Large fines were collected from anyone accused of anything. As for all the rest, against whom no charge could be brought, two thirds of their property was confiscated. From these goods, all the troops received what they were owed; those who were in Caesar's company at that time received two hundred and fifty drachmas for not plundering the city. Those who had made loans were paid in full, and both senators and equestrians who had supported the war received large rewards. Finally, the Roman Empire got richer and its temples gained ornaments.

---

was a poet and a close associate of Octavian. He served as the prefect of Egypt, a position that carried less authority than that of provincial governor. His role was to act as Octavian's representative.

7.11. Suetonius, *The Divine Augustus* 17.3–18 (A.D. 119–21, Latin, prose)

For more on Suetonius, see selection 3.1. In this passage Suetonius describes the end of Cleopatra's reign, focusing on Octavian and his forces.

17.3. After leaving Actium, Octavian retreated to his winter quarters on the island of Samos, where disturbing news of a rebellion reached him: following the victory, he had sent troops from every division to Brundisium, where they were demanding rewards and honorable discharge. As he returned to Italy, he was twice hindered by foul weather, once between the promontories of the Peloponnese and of Aetolia and again near the Ceraunian mountains. On each occasion some of his light warships were lost and his own ship suffered damage to its rigging and helm. He remained in Brundisium no more than twenty-seven days, just as long as was necessary to meet demands of his soldiers. Next, he headed for Egypt via Asia and Syria. After laying siege to Alexandria, where Antony had fled along with Cleopatra, he quickly occupied the city. Antony made a belated attempt to negotiate a treaty, but Octavian gave him no choice but suicide and even looked upon his corpse. Octavian wanted so badly to take Cleopatra alive for display in his triumph that he even employed snake charmers to suck the venom from her wounds, as the cause of death was thought to be the bite of an asp. Octavian granted the pair proper burial in a shared tomb and ordered the mausoleum, the construction of which they had begun, completed. He had Antony's elder son by Fulvia[28] dragged from the statue of the divine Julius Caesar, to which he had fled after making many unanswered prayers for mercy, and executed. The same fate awaited Caesarion, whom Cleopatra claimed to have conceived with Julius Caesar: Octavian recalled him from his flight and put him to death.[29] He spared the remaining children of Antony and the queen, treated them as he did his own relatives, and brought them up in a manner appropriate to their status.

---

28. I.e., Antyllus.
29. Caesarion was on his way to India; Cleopatra had sent him away from Alexandria in the hope that his life would be spared.

18. Around the same time, when he laid eyes upon the sarcophagus and body of Alexander the Great, which he had ordered brought out from its resting place, he honored it by placing a gold crown upon the head and scattering flowers. When asked whether he wished to see the tomb of the Ptolemies, he replied that he had wanted to see a king, not dead men. Egypt was reduced to a Roman province and, to increase the production of grain for tax purposes, Octavian sent a military detachment to dredge the irrigation canals into which the Nile flood overflowed, as they had, over time, become clogged with mud. To ensure that the Actian victory continued to be remembered and celebrated in the future, he founded the city of Nicopolis[30] at Actium and established games to be held there every five years. He expanded an ancient temple of Apollo and adorned the spot where his camp had been with naval trophies and dedicated the site to Neptune and Mars.

CLEOPATRA'S AUTOGRAPH

For all the histories, legends, and rumors about Cleopatra, it is difficult to uncover her voice. We do, however, seem to have some of her handwriting.

7.12. Papyrus with Declaration of Tax Exemption[31] (February 23, 33 B.C., Greek, prose)

In 2000 Peter van Minnen published a new interpretation of a papyrus from Ptolemaic Egypt.[32] Originally thought to be a private contract, the document, van Minnen demonstrates, is a royal decree (see fig. 6). The date at the top of the text indicates that the decree was received in Alexandria on February 23, 33 B.C., during the reign of Cleopatra VII. The text details various tax exemptions granted to a Publius Canidius. Van Minnen argues that the only person with the authority to issue such a document in Egypt at the time would have been the ruler.[33] In addition Publius Canidius can be

---

30. Nicopolis means "Victory City."
31. P. Bingen 45.
32. van Minnen 2000, 30.
33. Ibid.

Fig. 6. Papyrus with declaration of tax exemption of the Roman citizen Q. Cascel-lius, probably bearing the signature of Queen Cleopatra VII, February 23, 33 B.C. Photo: Margarete Buesing. Bildarchiv Preussischer Kulturbesitz / Art Resource, NY.

*identified as Mark Antony's land commander in the Battle of Actium; thus,
the tax exemptions were probably designed to ensure his loyalty to Cleopatra.*[34]

Below the text of the decree, the papyrus contains a single word, written
in a different hand. The word is ginesthoi (gin-ES-tho), which means "let
it be done."[35] This is what the official authorizing the decree would write in
order to place his or her stamp of approval on it (the text of the decree itself
would have been written by a scribe). Since the year is 33 B.C. and Cleopatra, as the queen, was the only person who would authorize such a decree,
the handwriting should be hers.

Received: Year 19 = 4, Mecheir 26

We[36] have assented to Publius Canidius and to his heirs that they
may export yearly ten thousand artabas of wheat and that they may
import five thousand Coan jars of wine without paying any tax to
anyone or incurring any other expense at all.[37] In addition, we have
assented that all of the acreage he has throughout the region will be
tax-exempt in that he will owe nothing to the government and nothing
to the private accounts of us or of our children in any way at any time;
also that tenant farmers are exempt and not responsible for making
any payments to anyone, not even contributions to the assessments
done occasionally in the districts or paying civil or military expenses;
also that the yoked animals for the sowing and reaping of wheat as
well as the boats for its transport are exempt and not liable and free
from use as couriers. Therefore, let it be written to those to whom it
pertains, so that they may know and carry out the decree.

Let it be done.

---

34. Indeed, it was alleged in Rome that Canidius had been bribed to support Cleopatra
(Syme 1967, 280).

35. On the form *ginesthoi*, a phonological variant of *ginestho* present in *koine* Greek of
the Ptolemaic period, see Teodorsson 1977, 163–68, 235.

36. The "royal we."

37. An artaba was an Egyptian unit of dry measure equivalent to approximately three
pecks. Coan: from the island of Cos.

PART TWO

Reception

8

Good Woman or Bad?

FROM THE MIDDLE AGES ON, portrayals of Cleopatra take her character to even greater extremes than the ancient sources do. As each age reinvents Cleopatra, the queen becomes a canvas onto which authors and artists project images of women and power. In the Middle Ages and Renaissance, we can experience disparate conceptions of Cleopatra's essential nature. For Boccaccio she is the epitome of vice, but for Chaucer she becomes a martyr of love as he applies to Cleopatra the contemporary concept of courtly love between a knight and his lady.

8.1. Giovanni Boccaccio, *On Famous Women,*[1] Preface (excerpt), "Cleopatra, Queen of Egypt" (1362, Latin, prose)

Renaissance humanist Giovanni Boccaccio grew up in Florence, Italy, where he was a student of Petrarch. Before writing On Famous Women *in 1361–62, he had written on illustrious men. In his preface he gives his reasons for composing such a work.*

Preface (excerpt)

Long ago, some ancient authors wrote anthologies concerning illustrious men; in our time, the prominent man and outstanding

---

1. *De Mulieribus Claris.*

poet, my teacher Petrarch, is writing a work of even broader scope and more careful composition; and rightly so: for those who devoted all their enthusiasm, resources, blood, and spirit—when circumstances demanded—to outdo others in memorable deeds certainly deserve to have their names passed down forever in lasting memory. I am surprised, however, that women are so little mentioned by writers of this genre that they receive no remembrance in any work dedicated exclusively to them, even though it is clear from longer historical works that certain women have done some things both forcefully and courageously.

If men must be celebrated when they accomplish great things with the strength they have been given, how much more must women be praised (since, after all, almost all of them naturally have an innate softness, a weak body, and a slow intellect) if they display a masculine mind and, with considerable intelligence and outstanding courage, both dare and achieve things extremely difficult even for men?

Therefore, lest these women be cheated of what they are owed, I was inspired to tell the stories of those women who are still memorable in a single work to honor their achievements. I also add to these some of the many women who are famous for their daring, mental strength, diligence, innate gifts, or for the favor or disfavor fortune has shown them. I also include a few who, although they are not worthy of renown for something they did, motivated great deeds.

I do not want it to seem strange to readers if they find Medea,[2] Flora,[3] Sempronia,[4] and others of this type whose characters were strong but ruinous, mentioned in the same work with Penelope,[5] Lucretia,[6] and Sulpicia,[7] the most chaste matrons. For my aim is not to understand the term *famous* so strictly that it always applies to virtue, but rather to take it in a broader sense—with the agreement of my readers—and to consider those women famous whom I recognize as objects of fascination the world over for any sort of deed. I remember

2. Medea killed her own children to get revenge on Jason.
3. Flora was the Italian goddess of flowering plants. Her festival, the Floralia, included obscene dramatic performances.
4. Sempronia was a woman who supported Catiline in his efforts to overthrow the Roman government.
5. Penelope was the wife of Odysseus, who faithfully awaited his return from Troy.
6. Lucretia killed herself after being raped in order to avoid setting the example for Roman women that involuntary adultery was excusable.
7. Sulpicia was a female Roman poet who wrote love elegies during the Augustan period.

often reading about the mutinous Gracchi,[8] devious Hannibal,[9] disloyal Jugurtha,[10] Sulla and Marius with their fellow citizens' blood on their hands,[11] Crassus who was both rich and greedy,[12] and other such men among the Leonidases,[13] the Scipios,[14] the Catos,[15] and the Fabricii,[16] all noble men.

Truly, to elevate with praise actions worthy of remembrance and sometimes to bury under rebukes unspeakable transgressions will not only motivate honorable people to seek glory, but also tighten the reins to some extent on wicked individuals and keep them from evil deeds. In addition, this strategy seems to have restored to my work the charm some of the women's shameful behavior cost it. Therefore, I was inspired to add to some of the tales some elegant enticements to virtue as well as some goads for the avoidance and abhorrence of crimes. And so let it be that sacred benefit will covertly enter the reader's mind along with pleasure in the stories.

Cleopatra, Queen of Egypt

Cleopatra was an Egyptian woman, known the world over. Although she came to power through a long line of kings going back to Ptolemy the Macedonian, son of Lagus, and she was the daughter of Ptolemy Dionysius[17] or, as some say, of King Mineus, nevertheless, she gained her kingdom through crime. She was truly notable for almost nothing, except her ancestry and her beauty; rather, she was known throughout the world for her greed, cruelty, and excess.

---

8. The Gracchi attempted to pass revolutionary reforms and were assassinated as a result of the ensuing controversy.
9. Hannibal was the Carthaginian general in the Second Punic War. He invaded Italy and caused great damage before his defeat.
10. Jugurtha was the king of Numidia; he was conquered by the Romans.
11. Sulla and Marius were Roman generals involved in civil conflicts during the Republic.
12. Crassus was a wealthy man and a member of the First Triumvirate.
13. Leonidas was a Spartan king who fought to the death to defend Thermopylae against the Persians.
14. The family of the Scipios produced a number of illustrious men, including generals Scipio Africanus and Scipio Aemilianus.
15. Cato the Elder and Cato the Younger were both Roman politicians with the reputation for uncompromising fairness.
16. Fabricius was a senator during the Republic about whom many accounts of his incorruptibility circulated.
17. Ptolemy XII Auletes, also known as Neos Dionysus, the "New Dionysus."

Let us take up the story at the beginning of her reign when, some say, Dionysius or Mineus, being very friendly with the Roman people, was nearing the end of his life, in the first consulship of Julius Caesar,[18] he made a will indicating that, after his death, the elder of his sons, whom some sources call Lysanias, after marrying Cleopatra, the elder of his two daughters, should rule together with her. This instruction was carried out because, among the Egyptians, it was common to observe the shameful practice of only excluding mothers and daughters from marriages. Next, Cleopatra, seized with a desire to rule, allegedly poisoned (there were no eyewitnesses) the innocent boy of fifteen, her brother and husband, and took the kingdom for herself.

The sources agree that when Pompey the Great had occupied almost all of Asia with his army, he went to Egypt and replaced Cleopatra's surviving brother and made him king of Egypt. Cleopatra, angry over this, took up arms against her brother. This was the state of affairs when Pompey, driven out of Thessaly, was slain on the Egyptian shore by the boy whom he had installed as king. Caesar, arriving after Pompey, found the two waging war among themselves.

When he had commanded them to come before him in order to plead their case—I will pass over young Ptolemy—Cleopatra, having great confidence in herself, appeared dressed in her royal attire and was sure the kingdom would be hers if she could seduce the man who had vanquished the world. Since she was very beautiful and could captivate almost anyone she wished with her sparkling eyes and conversational skills, she attracted the lecherous ruler to her bed without much effort. For many nights, while Alexandria was in tumult, and, as is commonly accepted, she conceived with him a son, whom she later named Caesarion, after his father.

At length, the young Ptolemy, set free by Caesar, attacked his liberator on the urging of his supporters and, at the Delta, confronted Mithradates of Pergamum, who was coming to support Caesar. There, he was defeated by Caesar, who, anticipating his arrival, had come by another route. Ptolemy tried to flee in a small boat, which sank under the weight of those rushing on board. When peace was thus made and the Alexandrians surrendered, Caesar was about to attack Pharnaces, the king of Pontus, who had supported Pompey. He

18. 59 B.C.

presented to Cleopatra, as a kind of reward for the nights he had spent with her and for remaining loyal to him, the kingdom of Egypt, for there was nothing else she desired. He took her sister Arsinoe with him lest, now that Cleopatra was the ruler, there be any revolts against him.

Thus, Cleopatra, who had gained her kingdom with a double crime, now devoted herself to pleasure, becoming, as it were, the whore of the eastern kings. Desirous of gold and jewels, she not only used her arts to strip her lovers of these things, but it is also said that she stripped the temples and shrines of the Egyptians of vases, statues, and the rest of their hoard.

Then, after Caesar was slain and Brutus and Cassius conquered, she presented herself to Antony as he was on his way to Syria. She easily captivated this depraved man with her beauty and her flirtatious eyes and so enslaved the wretch to her love that she, who had killed her brother with poison, made him kill her sister Arsinoe, in order to remove a threat to her power. The crime was committed in the Temple of Diana at Ephesus, where the unlucky girl had fled, seeking sanctuary. It was as if Cleopatra were receiving a sacrifice from her lover: the first fruits of their adultery.

And since the evil woman knew Antony's character, she was not afraid to request from him the kingdoms of Syria and Arabia. Although it seemed to him truly excessive and highly improper, nevertheless to fulfill the wishes of his beloved, he gave her small shares of both and, in addition, all the cities which were located on the Syrian coast between Eleutherus River and the Egyptian border, except Sidon and Tyre.

When she had received these places, she followed Antony to the Euphrates as he campaigned against the Armenians or, as some prefer, against the Parthians. When she returned to Egypt through Syria, she was entertained extravagantly by Herod, who was the son of Antipater and the king of the Jews at that time. She did not blush to urge him, through intermediaries, to sleep with her, saying that, if he agreed, she would take as a reward the kingdom of Judea, which he, with Antony's help, had recovered not long before.

But Herod knew what she was up to and, out of respect for Antony, not only refused, but even would have killed her with his sword to free Antony from such a famously unchaste woman, had his friends not opposed it. Cleopatra, her true mission foiled, acted as if she wanted to give him a contract for the income from Jericho, where balsam was native. Later, she brought this plant to Egyptian Babylon, where it still grows today. Then, after accepting lavish gifts from Herod, she returned to Egypt.

Next, when summoned, she met Antony as he returned after fleeing from the Parthians. By treachery, Antony had captured the Armenian king Artavasdes, son of the late Tigranes, along with his children and satraps.[19] He had plundered great hoards of treasure and was dragging the king bound in silver chains. In order to entice the acquisitive Cleopatra into his embrace, he womanishly cast the captive king with all his royal adornments as well as the spoils into her arms as she arrived. The covetous woman, pleased with the gift, embraced her eager lover so appreciatively that he divorced Octavia, the sister of Octavian, and, with all his passion, joined Cleopatra to himself as his wife.

I will not mention the Arabian ointments, fragrant smoke of Sabea, and intoxication that characterized this glutton as he continuously feasted on lavish banquets. Then he asked Cleopatra, as if he wished to further adorn her banquets, what splendor could be added to their daily banquets. The roguish woman replied that she would, if he wished, spend ten million sesterces on one dinner. Although Antony believed that it could not be done, nevertheless he was eager to see and to enjoy it, so they made a wager and elected Lucius Plancus to judge.[20]

On the following day, when the feast did not surpass the usual food, and Antony laughed at her claims, Cleopatra ordered her servants to bring in the final course. They had been advised ahead of time and brought her a single glass of very strong vinegar. At once, Cleopatra, taking a priceless pearl from one of her ears (she was wearing it there as an ornament in the eastern fashion), she dissolved it in vinegar and, when it had melted away, drank it. When she put her hands on the other one, which was of equal value and worn in her other ear, about to do the same thing, without delay Lucius Plancus declared that Antony was beaten and, because Cleopatra had won, the second pearl was saved. Afterward, this pearl was cut in half and brought to the Pantheon in Rome, where it was

19. Provincial governors.
20. See selection *4.10.*

placed on the ears of the statue of Venus. For a long time after that, it offered visitors evidence of half of Cleopatra's dinner.

But when the greed of this insatiable woman for kingdoms grew daily, in order to gather everything into one, she asked Antony, who was inebriated and perhaps just rising from an outstanding feast, for the Roman Empire, as if it were in Antony's power to grant it. Because he was not in his right mind and did not consider his strength or that of the Romans, he promised he would grant it.

Good God, the stupidity of the one promising this was no less than the temerity of the one asking for it! How generous a man! He gave up an empire sought for so many centuries, with such difficulty, with such bloodshed and the death of so many noble men, and of so many peoples as well, with so many outstanding achievements, with so many wars, to a woman who asked for it, no differently than he might grant possession of a single little house, without a second thought.

But then what? Already, because of the divorce of Octavia, the seeds of war seemed to have been sown between Octavian and Antony. As a result, it happened that, when troops had assembled on both sides, they went to war.

But Antony and Cleopatra went to Epirus, their fleet adorned with gold and with purple sails. There, they met the enemy, initiated a land battle, and retreated in defeat, after which Antony's men returned to their ships and sailed to Actium to try their luck in a sea battle. Octavian met them with his son-in-law Agrippa and, with their large fleet, they attacked with amazing boldness. Once undertaken, the battle was fiercely fought, and for quite a while the outcome was uncertain and hung in the balance. At last, when Antony's men seemed to be surrendering, haughty Cleopatra, first out of all of them, took flight with the golden ship on which she sailed and with sixty other ships. At once, Antony, lowering the insignia on his flagship, followed her. When they reached Egypt, they vainly distributed their forces for the defense of the kingdom, after sending the children they had had together to the Red Sea.

For Octavian the victor pursued them and diminished their strength by winning many battles. When they made a late request for peace, it was denied. Antony was hopeless, as some sources say, and, entering the royal mausoleum, committed suicide with his sword.

After Alexandria was captured, Cleopatra vainly tried to use the old charms, with which she had bewitched Caesar and Antony, to enthrall the young Octavian as well. She, in anger at his daring to take her alive for his triumphal procession and despairing of freedom, dressed herself in her royal garb and followed her Antony. Positioning herself next to him, she opened the veins of her arms, and, resolved to die, placed poisonous snakes on the wounds. Some say these snakes bring death with sleep. And so, relaxed in sleep, the unfortunate woman ended her greed, her licentiousness, and her life, although Octavian tried to revive her, if he could, summoning Psylli to care for her poisoned wounds.

There are others, however, who say that she died earlier and in a different manner. They say that Antony, while preparing for the Battle of Actium, feared that he was not pleasing Cleopatra. Therefore, he refrained from consuming either food or drink unless it had been tasted. When Cleopatra noticed this, in order to prove her loyalty to him, she had the flowers, with which she had, on the previous day, decorated their crowns, dipped in poison before she placed them on her head. She engaged Antony in playful conversation and, as the merriment increased, she suggested that they drink their crowns. After the flowers had been dipped in the cup, Antony was just about to drink when Cleopatra stopped him with her hand, saying, "My dear Antony, I am that Cleopatra whom you consider suspect, to judge from your new and unaccustomed use of tasters; because of this, if I could have allowed you to drink, I had the opportunity and the motive to kill you." When at length Antony understood the trick, after she explained it, he had her imprisoned and forced her to drain the cup from which she had prevented him from drinking. They say that she died thus.

The former account is more common. I would add that Octavian commanded that the mausoleum Antony and Cleopatra began be completed and that they be simultaneously entombed there together.

8.2. Geoffrey Chaucer, *The Legend of Good Women,* Prologue 475–97, 548–79, "The Legend of Cleopatra, Martyr, Queen of Egypt" (1386, Middle English, verse)

From *Chaucer: The Legend of Good Women,* ed. W. W. Skeat (Oxford: Clarendon Press, 1889).

By the later Middle Ages, collecting tales about women had become a recognized genre. The term legend *(literally, that which must be read), was used specifically to describe accounts of saints' lives. Chaucer draws on these traditions and on sources including Plutarch and Boccaccio, in crafting his "Legend of Cleopatra." In addition, he was influenced by medieval ideas of courtly love: the notions that love makes a man a better knight and that love can be seen almost as a kind of religion. In* The Legend of Good Women, *Chaucer collects tales of female "martyrs of love" from classical mythology and history. In the prologue, he frames his creative context as one of necessity and penance.*

Prologue 475–97, 548–79

Chaucer describes a dream in which the God of Love is angry with him for his portrayals of women in his previous writings. Alcestis,[21] one of the martyrs of love, intercedes on Chaucer's behalf.

And she answerde, "lat be[22] thyn arguinge;	475
For Love ne wol nat countrepleted[23] be	
In right ne wrong; and lerne that of me!	
Thou hast thy grace, and hold thee right ther-to.	
Now wol I seyn what penance thou shalt do	
For thy trespas, and understond hit here:	480
Thou shalt, whyl that thou livest, yeer by yere,	
The moste party[24] of thy tyme spende	
In making of a glorious Legende	
Of Gode Wommen, maidenes and wyves,	
That weren trewe in lovinge al hir lyves;	485
And telle of false men that hem bitrayen,	
That al hir lyf ne doon nat but assayen[25]	
How many wommen they may doon a shame;	
For in your world that is now holde[26] a game.	
And thogh thee lyke[27] nat a lover be,	490

---

21. Alcestis gave her own life as a substitute for that of her husband, Admetus.
22. stop
23. pleaded against
24. portion
25. try
26. considered
27. it pleases

Spek wel of love; this penance yive[28] I thee.
And to the god of love I shal so preye,
That he shal charge his servants, by any weye,
To forthren[29] thee, and wel thy labour quyte;[30]
Go now thy wey, this penance is but lyte.   495
And whan this book is maad, yive hit the quene
On my behalfe, at Eltham, or at Shene."[31]

The God of Love then gives Chaucer his instructions for composing the
Legend of Good Women.

"But now I charge thee, upon thy lyf,
That in thy Legend thou make of[32] this wyf,[33]
Whan thou hast other smale[34] y-mad before;   550
And fare now wel, I charge thee no more.
But er[35] I go, thus muche I wol thee telle,
Ne shal no trewe lover come in helle.
Thise other ladies sitting here arowe[36]
Ben[37] in thy balade, if thou canst hem knowe,   555
And in thy bokes alle thou shalt hem fynde;
Have hem now in thy Legend alle in mynde,
I mene of hem that been in thy knowinge.
For heer ben twenty thousand mo[38] sittinge
Than thou knowest, that been good wommen alle   560
And trewe of love, for aught that may befalle;
Make the metres of hem as thee leste.[39]
I mot gon hoom,[40] the sonne draweth weste,
To Paradys, with al this companye;

28. give
29. help
30. reward
31. Eltham and Sheen were palaces; their mention indicates that the queen was Anne
of Bohemia, the first queen of Richard II.
32. mention
33. I.e., Alcestis.
34. brief
35. before
36. in a row
37. are
38. more
39. as it pleases you
40. must go home

And serve alwey the fresshe dayesye.   565
At Cleopatre I wol that thou beginne;
And so forth; and my love so shalt thou winne.
For lat[41] see now what man that lover be,
Wol doon so strong a peyne for love as she.
I wot[42] wel that thou mayest nat al hit ryme,   570
That swiche lovers diden in hir tyme;
It were to[43] long to reden and to here;
Suffyceth me, thou make in this manere,
That thou reherce of al hir lyf the grete,[44]
After thise olde auctours listen to trete.   575
For who-so[45] shal so many a storie telle,
Sey shortly, or he shal to longe dwelle."
And with that word my bokes[46] gan[47] I take,
And right thus on my Legend gan I make.

The Legend of Cleopatra, Martyr, Queen of Egypt

After the deeth of Tholomee[48] the king,   580
That al Egipte hadde in his governing,
Regned his quene Cleopataras;
Til on a tyme befel ther swiche a cas,[49]
That out of Rome was sent a senatour,
For to conqueren regnes[50] and honour   585
Unto the toun of Rome, as was usaunce,[51]
To have the world unto her obeisaunce;
And, sooth to seye, Antonius was his name.
So fil[52] hit,[53] as Fortune him oghte[54] a shame

41. let's
42. know
43. too
44. substance (as opposed to the details)
45. whoever
46. books
47. began
48. Ptolemy XIV.
49. event
50. kingdoms
51. custom
52. happened
53. it
54. owed

Whan he was fallen in prosperitee,   590
Rebel unto the toun of Rome is he.
And over al this, the suster of Cesar,[55]
He lafte[56] hir falsly, er that she was war,[57]
And wolde algates[58] han another wyf;
For whiche he took with Rome and Cesar stryf.   595
Natheles, for-sooth, this ilke[59] senatour
Was a ful worthy gentil werreyour,[60]
And of his deeth hit was ful greet damage.[61]
But love had broght this man in swiche a rage,
And him so narwe[62] bounden in his las,[63]   600
Al for the love of Cleopataras,
That al the world he sette at no value.
Him thoughte,[64] nas to him no thing so due
As Cleopatras for to love and serve;
Him roghte[65] nat in armes for to sterve[66]   605
In the defence of hir, and of hir right.
This noble quene eek[67] lovede so this knight,
Through his desert, and for his chivalrye;
As certeinly, but if[68] that bokes lye,
He was, of persone[69] and of gentilesse,   610
And of discrecioun and hardinesse,
Worthy to any wight[70] that liven may.
And she was fair as is the rose in May.
And, for to maken shortly is the beste,
She wex[71] his wyf, and hadde him as hir leste.[72]   615

55. I.e., Octavia.
56. left
57. without her knowing
58. always
59. same
60. warrior
61. loss
62. tightly
63. snare
64. it seemed to him
65. he cared
66. die
67. likewise
68. unless
69. appearance
70. person
71. became
72. as it pleased her

The wedding and the feste to devyse,[73]
To me, that have y-take swiche empryse
Of so many a story for to make,
Hit were to long, lest that I sholde slake[74]
Of thing that bereth[75] more effect and charge;   620
For men may overlade a ship or barge;
And forthy[76] to theffect than wol I skippe,
And al the remenant,[77] I wol lete hit slippe.
Octovian, that wood[78] was of this dede,
Shoop[79] him an ost[80] on Antony to lede   625
Al-outerly[81] for his destruccioun,
With stoute Romains, cruel as leoun;
To ship they wente, and thus I let hem saile.
Antonius was war,[82] and wol nat faile
To meten with thise Romains, if he may;   630
Took eek[83] his reed,[84] and bothe, upon a day,
His wyf and he, and al his ost, forth wente
To shippe anoon, no lenger they ne stente;[85]
And in the see hit happed hem to mete—
Up goth the trompe—and for to shoute and shete,[86]   635
And peynen hem to sette on with the sonne.
With grisly soun out goth the grete gone,[87]
And heterly they hurtlen[88] al at ones,
And fro the top doun cometh the grete stones.
In goth the grapenel[89] so ful of crokes[90]   640

73. relate
74. slight
75. possesses
76. therefore
77. rest
78. enraged
79. prepared
80. army
81. utterly
82. knew it
83. also
84. counsel
85. declared
86. shoot
87. gun, missile
88. ram
89. grappling hook
90. barbs

Among the ropes, and the shering[91] hokes.
In with the polax[92] presseth he and he;
Behynd the mast beginneth he to flee,
And out agayn, and dryveth him over borde;
He stingeth him upon his speres orde;[93]   645
He rent the sail with hokes lyke a sythe;
He bringeth the cuppe, and biddeth hem be blythe;
He poureth pesen[94] upon the hacches slider;[95]
With pottes ful of lym they goon to-gider;
And thus the longe day in fight they spende   650
Til, at the laste, as every thing hath ende,
Anthony is shent,[96] and put him to the flighte,
And al his folk to-go,[97] that best go mighte.[98]
Fleeth eek the queen, with al her purpre sail,
For strokes, which that wente as thikke as hail;   655
No wonder was, she mighte hit nat endure.
And whan that Anthony saw that aventure,[99]
"Allas!" quod he, "the day that I was born!
My worshipe[100] in this day thus have I lorn!"[101]
And for dispeyr out of his witte he sterte,[102]   660
And roof[103] him-self anoon through-out the herte
Er that he ferther wente out of the place.
His wyf, that coude of Cesar have no grace,
To Egipte is fled, for drede and for distresse;
But herkneth, ye that speke of kyndenesse.   665
Ye men, that falsly sweren many an oth
That ye wol dye, if that your love be wroth,

91. cutting
92. Poleax, a tool that combined an ax, a pike, and a serrated hammer (Skeat 1889 *ad*, 641).
93. point
94. peas
95. slippery
96. ruined
97. scattered
98. each in the way he could best go
99. state of affairs
100. honor
101. lost
102. jumped
103. stabbed

Heer may ye seen of women whiche a trouthe!
This woful Cleopatre hath mad swich routhe[104]
That ther nis[105] tonge noon that may hit telle. 670
But on the morwe[106] she wol no lenger dwelle,
But made hir subtil[107] werkmen make a shryne[108]
Of alle the rubies and the stones fyne
In al Egipte that she coude espye;
And putte ful the shryne of spycerye, 675
And leet the cors embaume;[109] and forth she fette
This dede cors, and in the shryne hit shette.[110]
And next the shryne a pit than doth she grave;[111]
And alle the serpents that she mighte have,
She putte hem in that grave, and thus she seyde: 680
"Now, love, to whom my sorweful herte obeyde
So ferforthly[112] that, fro that blisful houre
That I yow swor to been al frely youre,
I mene yow, Antonius my knight!
That never waking, in the day or night, 685
Ye nere[113] out of myn hertes remembraunce
For wele or wo, for carole or for daunce;
And in my-self this covenant made I tho,
That, right swich as ye felten, wele or wo,
As ferforth as hit in my power lay, 690
Unreprovable unto my wyfhood ay,[114]
The same wolde I felen, lyf or deeth.
And thilke[115] covenant, whyl me lasteth breeth,
I wol fulfille, and that shal wel be sene;
Was never unto hir love a trewer quene." 695

104. pity
105. is not
106. morrow
107. skilled
108. mausoleum
109. caused the body to be embalmed
110. shut
111. dug
112. far forth
113. were not
114. too
115. the same

And with that word, naked, with ful good herte,
Among the serpents in the pit she sterte,
And ther she chees[116] to han hir buryinge.
Anoon the neddres[117] gonne hir[118] for to stinge,
And she hir deeth receyveth, with good chere,   700
For love of Antony, that was her so dere:—
And this is storial[119] sooth,[120] hit is no fable.
Now, er I fynde a man thus trewe and stable,
And wol for love his deeth so frely take,
I pray god lat our hedes never ake!   705

116. chose
117. adders
118. to her
119. historical
120. truly

9

The World Well Lost?

SHAKESPEARE AND DRYDEN BOTH question the Augustan version of Cleopatra's story in which she represents a corrupting, eastern way of life and the Romans, whom Antony betrays, stand for courage and virtue. As is evident in these accounts, the erotic aspects of Antony and Cleopatra's story supersede the political dimension of their relationship.

9.1. William Shakespeare, *Antony and Cleopatra* (excerpts) (1600–1612, English, verse)

Shakespeare's primary source for Antony and Cleopatra was Thomas North's 1579 translation of Plutarch's Life of Antony. *Shakespeare's last tragedy,* Antony and Cleopatra *contains elements of comedy and romance as well as more traditional tragic themes.*

Act I, Scene I, Lines 1–40

Alexandria. A room in Cleopatra's palace.
[*Enter Demetrius and Philo.*][1]

From *The Works of William Shakespeare*, vol. 12, ed. R. G. White (Boston: Little, Brown and Co., 1861).

1. Demetrius and Philo: Romans living at the Alexandrian court. Philo has lived in Alexandria for some time, while Demetrius is a more recent arrival. Philo presents Antony and Cleopatra to Demetrius.

PHILO. Nay, but this dotage of our general's
O'erflows the measure: those his goodly eyes,
That o'er the files and musters of the war
Have glow'd like plated Mars, now bend, now turn,
The office and devotion of their view   5
Upon a tawny front: his captain's heart,
Which in the scuffles of great fights hath burst
The buckles on his breast, reneags all temper,
And is become the bellows and the fan
To cool a gipsy's² lust. Look where they come: 10
[*Flourish.*³ *Enter Antony and Cleopatra, with their trains;*⁴ *Eunuchs fanning her.*]
Take but good note, and you shall see in him
The triple pillar of the world transform'd
Into a strumpet's Fool: behold and see.
CLEOPATRA. If it be love indeed, tell me how much.
ANTONY. There's beggary in the love that can be reckon'd.   15
CLEOPATRA. I'll set a bourn how far to be belov'd.
ANTONY. Then must thou needs find out new Heaven, new
    Earth.
[*Enter an Attendant.*]
ATTENDANT. News, my good lord, from Rome.
ANTONY. Grates me: the sum.
CLEOPATRA. Nay, hear them, Antony:
Fulvia perchance is angry; or, who knows   20
If the scarce-bearded Caesar⁶ have not sent
His powerful mandate to you, "Do this, or this;
Take in that kingdom, and enfranchise that;
Perform 't, or else we damn thee."
ANTONY. How, my love!
CLEOPATRA. Perchance,—nay, and most like,—   25
You must not stay here longer, your dismission
Is come from Caesar; therefore hear it, Antony.—

2. Gypsies were thought to have come from Egypt.
3. Fanfare.
4. I.e., their various attendants.
5. Boundary.
6. Octavian.

Where's Fulvia's process? Caesar's, I would say?—Both?—
Call in the messengers.—As I am Egypt's queen,
Thou blushest, Antony; and that blood of thine   30
Is Caesar's homager:[7] else so thy cheek pays shame
When shrill-tongu'd Fulvia scolds.—The messengers!
ANTONY. Let Rome in Tyber melt, and the wide arch
Of the rang'd empire fall! Here is my space.
Kingdoms are clay: our dungy earth alike   35
Feeds beast as man: the nobleness of life
Is to do thus; when such a mutual pair
[Embracing]
And such a twain can do 't, in which I bind,
On pain of punishment, the world to wit[8]
We stand up peerless.
CLEOPATRA. Excellent falsehood!   40

At a banquet aboard Sextus Pompey's ship, Octavian, Antony, and their companions discuss Egypt.

Act II, Scene VII, Lines 20–56

On board Pompey's galley, lying near Misenum.
[A sennet sounded.[9] Enter Caesar, Antony, Lepidus, Pompey, Agrippa,
Mecaenas, Enobarbus, Menas, with other captains.]
ANTONY. *[To Caesar]* Thus do they, sir: they take the flow
        o' th' Nile   20
By certain scales i' th' pyramid; they know,
By the height, the lowness, or the mean, if dearth
Or foison,[10] follow: the higher Nilus swells,
The more it promises: as it ebbs, the seedsman
Upon the slime and ooze scatters his grain,   25
And shortly comes to harvest.
LEPIDUS. You have strange serpents there.
ANTONY. Aye, Lepidus.
LEPIDUS. Your serpent of Egypt is bred, now, of your mud by
        the operation of your sun: so is your crocodile.   31

7. Tenant.
8. Acknowledge.
9. Fanfare.
10. Plenty.

ANTONY. They are so.

POMPEY. Sit,—and some wine!—A health to Lepidus!

LEPIDUS. I am not so well as I should be, but I'll ne'er out.   36

ENOBARBUS. Not till you have slept; I fear me you'll be in[11]
    till then.

LEPIDUS. Nay, certainly, I have heard, the Ptolemies'
pyramises[12] are very goodly things; without contradiction,
    I have heard that.   41

MENAS. [*Aside*] Pompey, a word.

POMPEY. [*Aside*] Say in mine ear: what is 't?

MENAS. [*Aside*] Forsake thy seat, I do beseech thee, captain,
And hear me speak a word.

POMPEY. [*Aside*] Forbear me till anon.—
This wine for Lepidus!   45

LEPIDUS. What manner o' thing is your crocodile?

ANTONY. It is shap'd, sir, like itself; and it is as broad
as it hath breadth: it is just so high as it is,
and moves with its own organs; it lives by that which
nourisheth it; and the elements once out of it,
it transmigrates.

LEPIDUS. What colour is it of?   52

ANTONY. Of its own colour too.

LEPIDUS. 'Tis a strange serpent.

ANTONY. 'Tis so. And the tears of it are wet.[13]

CAESAR. Will this description satisfy him?

Antony blames Cleopatra for the loss at Actium, but then forgives her.

Act III, Scene XI, Lines 51–74

Alexandria. A room in the palace.

ANTONY. O, whither hast thou led me, Egypt? See,
How I convey my shame out of thine eyes
By looking back what I have left behind
'Stroy'd in dishonor.

CLEOPATRA. O my lord, my lord,

---

    11. I.e., drunk.
    12. Pyramids.
    13. This is a reference to the belief, common in Shakespeare's time, that crocodiles
wept while devouring their prey.

Forgive my fearful sails! I little thought 55
You would have follow'd.
ANTONY. Egypt, thou knew'st too well,
My heart was to thy rudder tied by th' strings,[14]
And thou should'st tow me after: o'er my spirit
Thy full supremacy thou knew'st, and that
Thy beck might from the bidding of the gods 60
Command me.
CLEOPATRA. O, my pardon!
ANTONY. Now I must
To the young man send humble treaties, dodge
And palter in the shifts of lowness, who
With half the bulk o' the world play'd as I pleas'd,
Making and marring fortunes. You did know 65
How much you were my conqueror; and that
My sword, made weak by my affection, would
Obey it on all cause.
CLEOPATRA. Pardon, pardon!
ANTONY. Fall not a tear, I say; one of them rates
All that is won and lost. Give me a kiss; 70
Even this repays me.—We sent our schoolmaster;
Is he come back?—Love, I am full of lead.—
Some wine, within there, and our viands!—Fortune knows
We scorn her most when most she offers blows.
[*Exeunt.*]

Cleopatra decides to take refuge in her mausoleum and send word to Antony that she has died.

Act IV, Scene XI, Lines 1–10

Alexandria. A room in the palace.
[*Enter Cleopatra, Charmian, Iras, and Mardian.*]
CLEOPATRA. Help me, my women! O, he is more mad
Than Telamon for his shield;[15] the boar of Thessaly
Was never so emboss'd.[16]

14. I.e., heartstrings.
15. Ajax, son of Telamon, became enraged after not receiving the shield of Achilles after the Trojan War.
16. The wild boar that the goddess Diana sent to wreak havoc on Calydon.

CHARMIAN. To th' monument!
There lock yourself, and send him word you are dead.
The soul and body rive not more in parting   5
Than greatness going off.
CLEOPATRA. To th' monument!
Mardian, go tell him I have slain myself;
Say, that the last I spoke was "Antony,"
And word it, prythee, piteously. Hence,
Mardian, And bring me how he takes my death.—
To th' monument!   10
[*Exeunt.*]

Upon hearing that Cleopatra is dead, Antony resolves to die.

Act IV, Scene XII, Lines 1–54

The same. Another room.
[*Enter Antony and Eros.*]
ANTONY. Eros, thou yet behold'st me?
EROS. Ay, noble lord.
ANTONY. Sometime we see a cloud that's dragonish;
A vapor, sometime, like a bear, or lion,
A tower'd citadel, a pendent rock,
A forked mountain, or blue promontory   5
With trees upon't, that nod unto the world,
And mock our eyes with air: thou hast seen these signs;
They are black vesper's pageants.
EROS. Ay, my lord.
ANTONY. That, which is now a horse, even with a thought,
The rack dislimns,[17] and makes it indistinct,   10
As water is in water.
EROS. It does, my lord.
ANTONY. My good knave, Eros, now thy captain is
Even such a body: here I am Antony,
Yet cannot hold this visible shape, my knave.
I made these wars for Egypt, and the queen,   15
Whose heart, I thought I had, for she had mine,

17. Eradicate.

Which, whilst it was mine, had annex'd unto 't
A million more, now lost; she, Eros, has
Pack'd cards with Caesar, and false-play'd my glory
Unto an enemy's triumph.—   20
Nay, weep not, gentle Eros; there is left us
Ourselves to end ourselves.—
[*Enter Mardian.*[18]]
O! thy vile lady!
She has robb'd me of my sword.
MARDIAN. No, Antony;
My mistress lov'd thee, and her fortunes mingled
With thine entirely.
ANTONY. Hence, saucy eunuch: peace!   25
She hath betray'd me, and shall die the death.
MARDIAN. Death of one person can be paid but once,
And that she has discharg'd: what thou would'st do,
Is done unto thy hand: the last she spake
Was "Antony! most noble Antony!"   30
Then, in the mid'st a tearing groan did break
The name of Antony; it was divided
Between her heart and lips. She render'd life,
Thy name so buried in her.
ANTONY. Dead, then?
MARDIAN. Dead.
ANTONY. Unarm, Eros: the long day's task is done,
And we must sleep.—That thou depart'st hence safe,   36
Does pay thy labor richly; go.—
[*Exit Mardian.*]
Off, pluck off:—
The seven-fold shield of Ajax cannot keep
The battery from my heart. O, cleave, my sides!
Heart, once be stronger than thy continent,   40
Crack thy frail case!—Apace, Eros, apace.—
No more a soldier:—bruised pieces, go;
You have been nobly borne.—From me awhile.—
[*Exit Eros.*]

18. A eunuch.

I will o'ertake thee, Cleopatra, and
Weep for my pardon. So it must be, for now   45
All length is torture: since the torch is out,
Lie down, and stray no farther. Now all labour
Mars what it does; yea, very force entangles
Itself with strength: seal then, and all is done.—
Eros!—I come, my queen:—Eros!—Stay for me: 50
Where souls do couch on flowers,[19] we'll hand in hand,
And with our sprightly port make the ghosts gaze:
Dido and her Aeneas shall want troops,
And all the haunt be ours. Come,—Eros! Eros!

Cleopatra devises to commit suicide.

Act V, Scene II, Lines 207–331

Alexandria. A room in the monument.
CLEOPATRA. Now, Iras, what think'st thou?
Thou, an Egyptian puppet, shalt be shewn
In Rome, as well as I, mechanic slaves
With greasy aprons, rules, and hammers, shall   210
Uplift us to the view: in their thick breaths,
Rank of gross diet, shall be encouded,
And forc'd to drink their vapour.
IRAS. The gods forbid!
CLEOPATRA. Nay, 'tis most certain, Iras. Saucy lictors[20]
Will catch at us, like strumpets; and scald rhymers   215
Ballad us out o' tune: the quick comedians
Extemporally will stage us, and present
Our Alexandrian revels; Antony
Shall be brought drunken forth, and I shall see
Some squeaking Cleopatra boy my greatness   220
I' th' posture of a whore.[21]
IRAS. O, the good gods!
CLEOPATRA. Nay, that is certain.

19. The Elysian Fields, the part of the Underworld reserved for heroes.
20. Attendants of a Roman consul.
21. I.e., a boy would portray her. Perhaps Shakespeare means to draw attention to the fact that Cleopatra was played by a boy on his stage.

IRAS. I'll never see it; for, I am sure, my nails
Are stronger than mine eyes.
CLEOPATRA. Why, that's the way
To fool their preparation, and to conquer   225
Their most absurd intents.—
[*Enter Charmian.*]
Now, Charmian?—
Shew me, my women, like a queen:—go fetch
My best attires;—I am again for Cydnus,
To meet Mark Antony. Sirrah, Iras, go.—
Now, noble Charmian, we'll dispatch indeed;   230
And, when thou hast done this chare, I'll give thee leave
To play till dooms-day.—Bring our crown and all.
Wherefore's this noise?
[*Exit Iras. A noise within.*]
[*Enter one of the guard.*]
GUARD. Here is a rural fellow
That will not be deni'd your Highness' presence:
He brings you figs.   235
CLEOPATRA. Let him come in. What poor an instrument
[*Exit Guardsman.*]
May do a noble deed! he brings me liberty.
My resolution's plac'd, and I have nothing
Of woman in me: now from head to foot
I am marble-constant; now the fleeting moon   240
No planet is of mine.
[*Enter Guard, with a Clown bringing in a basket.*]
GUARD. This is the man.
CLEOPATRA. Avoid, and leave him.
[*Exit Guard.*]
Hast thou the pretty worm[22] of Nilus there,
That kills and pains not?   244
CLOWN. Truly, I have him; but I would not be the party
that should desire you to touch him, for his biting is immortal:
those that do die of it do seldom or never recover.   248

22. Snake.

CLEOPATRA. Remember'st thou any that have died on 't?

CLOWN. Very many, men and women too. I heard of one of them no longer than yesterday: a very honest woman, but something given to lie,—as a woman should not do, but in the way of honesty;—how she died of the biting of it, what pain she felt.—Truly, she makes a very good report o' the worm; but he that will

believe all that they say, shall never be saved by half that they do. But this is most fallible, the worm's an odd worm.

CLEOPATRA. Get thee hence: farewell.   260

CLOWN. I wish you all joy of the worm.

CLEOPATRA. Farewell.

[*Clown sets down the basket.*]

CLOWN. You must think this, look you, that the worm will   305
do his kind.

CLEOPATRA. Ay, ay; farewell.   265

CLOWN. Look you, the worm is not to be trusted but in the keeping of wise people; for, indeed, there is no goodness in the worm.

CLEOPATRA. Take thou no care: it shall be heeded.

CLOWN. Very good. Give it nothing, I pray you, for it is
not worth the feeding.   271

CLEOPATRA. Will it eat me?

CLOWN. You must not think I am so simple, but I know the Devil himself will not eat a woman: I know that a woman is a dish for the gods, if the Devil dress her not; but, truly, these same whoreson devils do the gods great harm in their women, for in every ten that they make, the devils mar five.

CLEOPATRA. Well, get thee gone: farewell.   280

CLOWN. Yes, forsooth; I wish you joy o' the worm.

[*Exit.*]

[*Enter Iras with a robe, crown, & cup.*]

CLEOPATRA. Give me my robe, put on my crown; I have
Immortal longings in me. Now no more
The juice of Egypt's grape shall moist this lip.—   285
Yare, yare, good Iras; quick.—Methinks I hear
Antony call: I see him rouse himself

To praise my noble act; I hear him mock
The luck of Caesar, which the gods give men
To excuse their after wrath. Husband, I come: 290
Now to that name my courage prove my title!
I am fire, and air; my other elements
I give to baser life.—So,—have you done?
Come then, and take the last warmth of my lips.
Farewell, kind Charmian:—Iras, long farewell.   295
[*Kisses them. Iras falls and dies.*]
Have I the aspic[23] in my lips? Dost fall?
If thou and nature can so gently part,
The stroke of death is as a lover's pinch,
Which hurts, and is desired. Dost thou lie still?
If thus thou vanishest, thou tell'st the world   300
It is not worth leave-taking.
CHARMIAN. Dissolve, thick cloud; and rain, that I may say,
The gods themselves do weep!
CLEOPATRA. This proves me base:
If she first meet the curled Antony,
He'll make demand of her, and spend that kiss   305
Which is my heaven to have. Come, thou
mortal wretch,
[*To the asp, which she applies to her breast*]
With thy sharp teeth this knot intrinsicate[24]
Of life at once untie: poor venomous fool,
Be angry, and dispatch. O, could'st thou speak,
That I might hear thee call great Caesar ass   310
Unpolicied!
CHARMIAN. O eastern star!
CLEOPATRA. Peace, peace!
Dost thou not see my baby at my breast,
That sucks the nurse asleep?
CHARMIAN. O, break! O, break!
CLEOPATRA. As sweet as balm, as soft as air, as gentle.—

23. Asp.
24. Intricate.

O Antony!—Nay, I will take thee too.—   315
[*Applying another asp to her arm.*]
What should I stay—
[*Falls on a bed and dies.*]
CHARMIAN. In this wild world?—So, fare thee well.—
Now boast thee, death, in thy possession lies
A lass unparallel'd.—Downy windows, close;
And golden Phoebus never be beheld   320
Of eyes again so royal! Your crown's awry;
I'll mend it, and then play—
[*Enter the Guard, rushing in.*]
FIRST GUARD. Where is the Queen?
CHARMIAN. Speak softly, wake her not.
FIRST GUARD. Caesar hath sent—
CHARMIAN. Too slow a messenger.
[*Applies the asp.*]
O, come; apace; dispatch: I partly feel thee.   325
FIRST GUARD. Approach, ho! All's not well: Caesar's beguil'd.
SECOND GUARD. There's Dolabella sent from Caesar: call him.
FIRST GUARD. What work is here?—Charmian, is this well
   done?
CHARMIAN. It is well done, and fitting for a princess
Descended of so many royal kings.   330
Ah, soldier!
[*Dies.*]

9.2. John Dryden, *All for Love; or, the World Well Lost* (excerpts) (1678, English, verse)

The play All For Love *takes as its subject the final days of Antony and Cleopatra in Alexandria. John Dryden, living at a time when many were skeptical of religious ideals, creates many characters notable for their flaws and lack of heroism. Dryden himself invites comparison of his work to that of Shakespeare, but he was no stranger to the ancient sources, as he notes in his preface. In addition to the authors he cites there, Vergil may have been a significant influence on Dryden's portrayal of Cleopatra. After*

From *All for Love and the Spanish Friar by John Dryden,* ed. W. Strunk, Jr. (Boston: D. C. Heath and Co., 1911).

writing All for Love, *Dryden published a translation of Vergil's* Aeneid. *Indeed, Dryden's Cleopatra owes some of her characterization to Dido as well as to the ancient historical sources and to Shakespeare.*

Preface (excerpt)

The death of *Anthony* and *Cleopatra* is a subject which has been treated by the greatest wits of our nation, after Shakespeare; and by all so variously, that their example has given me the confidence to try myself in this bow of *Ulysses* amongst the crowd of sutors, and, withal, to take my own measures in aiming at the mark. I doubt not but the same motive has prevailed with all of us in this attempt; I mean the excellency of the moral: For the chief persons represented were famous patterns of unlawful love; and their end accordingly was unfortunate. All reasonable men have long since concluded, that the heroe of the poem ought not to be a character of perfect virtue, for then he could not without injustice be made unhappy; nor yet altogether wicked, because he could not then be pitied: I have therefore steer'd the middle course; and have drawn the character of Anthony as favourably as *Plutarch, Appian,* and *Dion Cassius* wou'd give me leave; the like I have observ'd in Cleopatra. That which is wanting to work up the pity to a greater heighth, was not afforded me by the story; for the crimes of love which they both committed, were not occasion'd by any necessity, or fatal ignorance, but were wholly voluntary; since our passions are, or ought to be, within our power. The fabrick of the play is regular enough as to the inferior parts of it; and the unities of time, place and action, more exactly observ'd, than, perhaps, the English theater requires. Particularly, the action is so much one that it is the only of the kind without episode or underplot; every scene in the tragedy conducing to the main design, and every act concluding with a turn of it. The greatest error in the contrivance seems to be in the person of *Octavia*; for, though I might use the priviledge of a poet, to introduce her into *Alexandria*, yet I had not enough consider'd, that the compassion she mov'd to herself and children was destructive to that which I reserved for *Anthony* and *Cleopatra*; whose mutual love being founded upon vice, must lessen the favor of the audience to them, when virtue and innocence were oppress'd by it. And, though I justified Anthony in some measure, by making *Octavia's* departure to proceed wholly from her self, yet the force of the first machine still remain'd; and the dividing of pity, like the cutting of a river into many channels, abated the strength of the natural stream.

Antony enters in despair over the defeat at Actium.

Act I, Scene I (excerpt)

[*Enter Antony, walking with a disturb'd motion before he speaks*].
ANTONY. They tell me, 'tis my birth-day, and I'll keep it
With double pomp of sadness.
'Tis what the day deserves, which gave me breath.   205
Why was I rais'd the meteor of the world,
Hung in the skies, and blazing as I travel'd,
Till all my fires were spent; and then cast downward,
To be trod out by Caesar?
VENTIDIUS.[25] [*aside*]. On my soul;
'Tis mournful, wondrous mournful!
ANTONY. Count thy gains.   210
Now, Antony, wouldst thou be born for this?
Glutton of fortune, thy devouring youth
Has starv'd thy wanting age.
VENTIDIUS. [*aside*]. How sorrow shakes him!
So, now the tempest tears him up by th' roots,
And on the ground extends the noble ruin.   215
ANTONY [*Having thrown himself down*].
Lie there, thou shadow of an emperor;
The place thou pressest on thy mother earth
Is all thy empire now: now it contains thee:
Some few dayes hence, and then 'twill be too large,
When thou'rt contracted in thy narrow urn,   220
Shrunk to a few cold ashes; then Octavia
(For Cleopatra will not live to see it),
Octavia then will have thee all her own,
And bear thee in her widow'd hand to Caesar;
Caesar will weep, the crocodile will weep,   225

25. One of Antony's generals.

To see his rival of the universe
Lye still and peaceful there. I'll think no more on't.

Act II, Scene I (excerpts)

[*Enter Cleopatra, Iras,*[26] *and Alexas*[27]].
CLEOPATRA. What shall I do, or whither shall I turn?
Ventidius has o'rcome, and he will go.
ALEXAS. He goes to fight for you.
CLEOPATRA. Then he wou'd see me, ere he went to fight;
Flatter me not; if once he goes, he's lost,   5
And all my hopes destroy'd.
ALEXAS. Does this weak passion
Become a mighty queen?
CLEOPATRA. I am no queen:
Is this to be a queen, to be besieg'd
By yon insulting Roman, and to wait
Each hour the victor's chain? These ills are small: 10
For Antony is lost, and I can mourn
For nothing else but him. Now come, Octavius,
I have no more to lose; prepare thy bands;
I'm fit to be a captive; Antony
Has taught my mind the fortune of a slave.   15
IRAS. Call reason to assist you.
CLEOPATRA. I have none.
And none would have; my love's a noble madness,
Which shows the cause deserv'd it. Moderate sorrow
Fits vulgar love, and for a vulgar man;
But I have lov'd with such transcendent passion,   20
I soar'd, at first, quite out of reasons view,
And now am lost above it. No, I'm proud
'Tis thus; would Antony could see me now!
Think you he would not sigh? Though he must leave me,
Sure he would sigh; for he is noble-natur'd,   25
And bears a tender heart: I know him well.
Ah, no, I know him not; I knew him once,

26. One of Cleopatra's maids.
27. Cleopatra's eunuch.

But now 'tis past.

. . . .

Charmion brings news from Antony.

CLEOPATRA. Did he then weep? And was I worth a tear?
If what thou hast to say be not as pleasing,   70
Tell me no more, but let me dye contented.
CHARMION. He bid me say, he knew himself so well,
He could deny you nothing, if he saw you;
And therefore—
CLEOPATRA. Thou would'st say, he wou'd not see me?
CHARMION. And therefore beg'd you not to use a power,   75
Which he could ill resist; yet he should ever
Respect you as he ought.
CLEOPATRA. Is that a word
For Antony to use to Cleopatra?
O that faint word, respect! how I disdain it!
Disdain myself, for loving after it!   80
He should have kept that word for cold Octavia;
Respect is for a wife; am I that thing,
That dull, insipid lump, without desires,
And without pow'r to give 'em?

Octavia arrives in Alexandria to plead her case with Antony.

Act III, Scene I (excerpts)

[*Re-enter Ventidius, with Octavia, leading Antony's two little daughters*].
. . . .
OCTAVIA. Thus long I have attended for my welcome;
Which, as a stranger, sure I might expect.
Who am I?
ANTONY. Caesar's sister.
OCTAVIA. That's unkind.   255
Had I been nothing more than Caesar's sister,
Know, I had still remain'd in Caesar's camp:
But your Octavia, your much injur'd wife,
Tho' banish'd from your bed, driv'n from your house,

In spight of Caesar's sister, still is yours.   260
'Tis true, I have a heart disdains your coldness,
And prompts me not to seek what you should offer,
But a wife's virtue still surmounts that pride;
I come to claim you as my own; to show
My duty first; to ask, nay beg, your kindness: 265
Your hand, my lord; 'tis mine, and I will have it. [*Taking
    his hand*].
VENTIDIUS. Do, take it; thou deserv'st it.
DOLABELLA.[28] On my soul,
And so she does: she's neither too submissive,
Nor yet too haughty; but so just a mean
Shows, as it ought, a wife and Roman too.   270

. . . .

OCTAVIA. My hard fortune
Subjects me still to your unkind mistakes.   290
But the conditions I have brought are such
You need not blush to take, I love your honour,
Because 'tis mine; it never shall be said,
Octavia's husband was her brother's slave.
Sir, you are free; free, ev'n from her you loath;   295
For, tho' my brother bargains for your love,
Makes me the price and cement of your peace,
I have a soul like yours; I cannot take
Your love as alms, nor beg what I deserve.
I'll tell my brother we are reconcil'd;   300
He shall draw back his troops, and you shall march
To rule the East; I may be dropt at Athens;
No matter where, I never will complain,
But only keep the barren name of wife,
And rid you of the trouble.   305

. . . .

ANTONY. Octavia, I have heard you, and must praise
The greatness of your soul;
But cannot yield to what you have propos'd: 315

28. Antony's friend and close associate.

For I can ne'er be conquer'd but by love;
And you do all for duty. You would free me,
And would be dropt at Athens; was't not so?
OCTAVIA. It was, my lord.
ANTONY. Then I must be oblig'd
To one who loves me not; who to her self,   320
May call me thankless and ungrateful man:—
I'll not endure it; no.
VENTIDIUS. [*aside*]. I am glad it pinches there.
OCTAVIA. Would you triumph o'er poor Octavia's virtue?
That pride was all I had to bear me up;   325
That you might think you ow'd me for your life,
And ow'd it to my duty, not my love.
I have been injur'd, and my haughty soul
Could brook but ill the man who slights my bed.
ANTONY. Therefore you love me not.
OCTAVIA. Therefore, my lord,   330
I should not love you.
ANTONY. Therefore you wou'd leave me?
OCTAVIA. And therefore I should leave you—if I could.
DOLABELLA. Her souls too great, after such injuries,
To say she loves; and yet she lets you see it.
Her modesty and silence plead her cause.   335
ANTONY. O Dolabella, which way shall I turn?
I find a secret yielding in my soul;
But Cleopatra, who would die with me,
Must she be left? Pity pleads for Octavia;
But does it not plead more for Cleopatra?   340
VENTIDIUS. Justice and pity both plead for Octavia;
For Cleopatra, neither.
One would be ruin'd with you; but she first
Had ruin'd you: The other, you have ruin'd,
And yet she would preserve you.   345
In everything their merits are unequal.
ANTONY. O my distracted soul!
OCTAVIA. Sweet Heav'n compose it!—
Come, come, my lord, if I can pardon you,
Methinks you should accept it. Look on these;

Are they not yours? or stand they thus neglected, 350
As they are mine? Go to him, children, go;
Kneel to him, take him by the hand, speak to him;
For you may speak, and he may own you too,
Without a blush; and so he cannot all
His children: go, I say, and pull him to me, 355
And pull him to yourselves, from that bad woman.
You, Agrippina, hang upon his arms;
And you, Antonia, clasp about his waste:
If he will shake you off, if he will dash you
Against the pavement, you must bear it, children; 360
For you are mine, and I was born to suffer.
[*Here the Children go to him, etc.*].
VENTIDIUS. Was ever sight so moving?—Emperor!
dolabella. Friend!
OCTAVIA. Husband!
BOTH CHILDREN. Father!
ANTONY. I am vanquish'd: take me,
Octavia; take me, children; share me all. [*Embracing them*].
I've been a thriftless debtor to your loves, 365
And run out much, in riot, from your stock;
But all shall be amended.
OCTAVIA. O blest hour!
dolabella. O happy change!

Antony then changes his mind.

Act IV, Scene I (excerpt)

[*Enter Antony and Dolabella*].
DOLABELLA. Why would you shift it from yourself on me?
Can you not tell her, you must part?
ANTONY. I cannot.
I could pull out an eye and bid it go,
And t'other should not weep. Oh Dolabella,
How many deaths are in this word, "Depart"! 5
I dare not trust my tongue to tell her so:
One look of hers would thaw me into tears,
And I should melt, till I were lost agen.

The deaths of Antony and Cleopatra.

Act V, Scene I (excerpts)

CLEOPATRA. Too long, ye heavens, you have been cruel to me: 370
Now show your mended faith, and give me back
His fleeting life!
ANTONY. It will not be, my love;
I keep my soul by force.
Say but, thou art not false.
CLEOPATRA. 'Tis now too late
To say I'm true: I'll prove it, and die with you.   375
Unknown to me, Alexas feign'd my death,
Which, when I knew, I hasted to prevent
This fatal consequence. My fleet betray'd
Both you and me.

. . . .

ANTONY. But grieve not, while thou stayest,
My last disastrous times;
Think we have had a clear and glorious day,
And Heav'n did kindly to delay the storm,   390
Just till our close of ev'ning. Ten years love,
And not a moment lost, but all improv'd
To th'utmost joys,—what ages have we liv'd?
And now to die each others; and so dying,
While hand in hand we walk in groves below,   395
Whole troops of lovers ghosts shall flock about us,
And all the train be ours.
CLEOPATRA. Your words are like the notes of dying swans,
Too sweet to last. Were there so many hours
For your unkindness, and not one for love?   400
ANTONY. No, not a minute.—This one kiss—more worth
Than all I leave to Caesar.
[*Dies*].
CLEOPATRA. O tell me so again,
And take ten thousand kisses for that word.
My lord, my lord! speak, if you yet have being;   405
Sign to me, if you cannot speak; or cast
One look! Do anything that shows you live.

IRAS. He's gone too far to hear you;
And this you see, a lump of sensless clay,
The leavings of a soul.
CHARMION. Remember, madam,   410
He charg'd you not to grieve.
CLEOPATRA. And I'll obey him.
I have not lov'd a Roman, not to know
What should become his wife; his wife, my Charmion!
For 'tis to that high title I aspire;
And now I'll not die less. Let dull Octavia   415
Survive, to mourn him dead; My nobler fate
Shall knit our spousals with a tie too strong
For Roman laws to break.
IRAS. Will you then die?
CLEOPATRA. Why shou'dst thou make that question?
IRAS. Caesar is merciful.
CLEOPATRA. Let him be so   420
To those who want his mercy; My poor lord
Made no such cov'nant with him, to spare me
When he was dead. Yield me to Caesar's pride?
What! to be led in triumph through the streets,
A spectacle to base plebeian eyes;   425
While some dejected friend of Antony's,
Close in a corner, shakes his head, and mutters
A secret curse on her who ruin'd him!
I'll none of that.
CHARMION. Whatever you resolve,
I'll follow, even to death.
IRAS. I only feared   430
For you; but more shou'd fear to live without you.
CLEOPATRA. Why, now, 'tis as it shou'd be. Quick, my friends,
Dispatch; ere this, the town's in Caesar's hands:
My lord looks down concern'd, and fears my stay,
Lest I should be surprised;   435
Keep him not waiting for his love too long.
You, Charmion, bring my crown and richest jewels;
With 'em, the wreath of victory I made
(Vain augury!) for him, who now lies dead;

You, Iras, bring the cure of all our ills.   440
IRAS. The aspicks, madam?[29]
CLEOPATRA. Must I bid you twice?
[*Exit Charmion and Iras*].
'Tis sweet to die, when they wou'd force life on me,
To rush into the dark aboad of death,
And seize him first; if he be like my love,
He is not frightful, sure.   445
We're now alone, in secresie and silence;
And is not this like lovers? I may kiss
These pale, cold lips; Octavia does not see me;
And, oh! 'tis better far to have him thus,
Than see him in her arms.—O, welcome, welcome!   450
[*Enter Charmion and Iras*].
CHARMION. What must be done?
CLEOPATRA. Short ceremony, friends;
But yet it must be decent. First, this laurel
Shall crown my hero's head; he fell not basely,
Nor left his shield behind him.—Only thou
Cou'dst triumph o'er thy self; and thou alone   455
Wert worthy so to triumph.
CHARMION. To what end
These ensigns of your pomp and royalty?
CLEOPATRA. Dull, that thou art! why 'tis to meet my love;
As when I saw him first, on Cydnos bank,
All sparkling, like a goddess: so adorned,   460
I'll find him once again; my second spousals
Shall match my first in glory. Haste, haste, both,
And dress the bride of Antony.
CHARMION. 'Tis done.
CLEOPATRA. Now seat me by my lord. I claim this place;
For I must conquer Caesar too, like him,   465
And win my share o'th' world.—Hail, you dear relicks
Of my immortal love!
O let no impious hand remove you hence:

29. Asps.

But rest for ever here! Let Egypt give
His death that peace, which it deny'd his life.— 470
Reach me the casket.
IRAS. Underneath the fruit
The aspick lies.
CLEOPATRA. [*Putting aside the leaves*]. Welcom, thou kind deceiver!
Thou best of thieves; who, with an easie key,
Dost open life, and, unperceiv'd by us,
Ev'n steal us from ourselves; discharging so 475
Death's dreadful office, better than himself;
Touching our limbs so gently into slumber,
That Death stands by, deceiv'd by his own image,
And thinks himself but Sleep.
SERAPION. [*Within*]. The queen, where is she?
The town is yielded, Caesar's at the gates. 480
CLEOPATRA. He comes too late t'invade the rights of death.
Haste, bare my arm, and rouze the serpent's fury.
[*Holds out her arm, and draws it back*].
Coward flesh,
Wou'dst thou conspire with Caesar to betray me,
As thou wert none of mine? I'll force thee to't, 485
And not be sent by him,
But bring, my self, my soul to Antony.
[*Turns aside, and then shows her arm bloody*].
Take hence; the work is done.
SERAPION. [*Within*]. Break ope the door,
And guard the traitor well.
CHARMION. The next is ours.
IRAS. Now, Charmion, to be worthy 490
Of our great queen and mistress.
[*They apply the aspics*].
CLEOPATRA. Already, death, I feel thee in my veins:
I go with such a will to find my lord,
That we shall quickly meet.
A heavy numbness creeps through every limb, 495
And now 'tis at my head: My eye-lids fall,
And my dear love is vanquish'd in a mist.

Where shall I find him, where? O turn me to him,
And lay me on his breast!—Caesar, thy worst;
Now part us, if thou canst.
[*Dies*].
[*Iras sinks down at her feet, and dies; Charmion stands behind her chair,
as dressing her head*].
[*Enter Serapion, two Priests, Alexas bound, Egyptians*].
TWO PRIESTS. Behold, Serapion,   500
What havoc death has made!
SERAPION. 'Twas what I fear'd.—
Charmion, is this well done?
CHARMION. Yes, 'tis well done, and like a queen, the last
Of her great race; I follow her.
[*Sinks down: dies*].
ALEXAS. 'Tis true,
She has done well: much better thus to die,   505
Than live to make a holy-day in Rome.
SERAPION. See how the lovers sit in state together,
As they were giving laws to half mankind!
Th'impression of a smile, left in her face,
Shows she dy'd pleas'd with him for whom she liv'd,   510
And went to charm him in another world.
Caesar's just entring: grief has now no leisure.
Secure that villain, as our pledge of safety,
To grace th'imperial triumph.—Sleep, blest pair,
Secure from humane chance, long ages out,   515
While all the storms of fate fly o'er your tomb;
And fame to late posterity shall tell,
No lovers liv'd so great, or died so well.
[*Exeunt*].

10

Women's Voices

WOMEN WROTE BOTH OF the accounts of Cleopatra that follow. Not surprisingly, issues of gender and women's roles are prominent in both. In *Villette*, Charlotte Brontë dramatically juxtaposes Cleopatra with contemporary women. In Sarah Fielding's *The Lives of Cleopatra and Octavia*, however, the two title characters themselves represent two extremes of female experience.

10.1. Sarah Fielding, *The Lives of Cleopatra and Octavia* (excerpts) (1757, English, prose)
Sarah Fielding imagines Cleopatra and Octavia in the underworld after their deaths, where each gives an account of her life. As the author's introduction reveals, the tales have a moral purpose. It is telling, however, that Cleopatra's story is four times the length of Octavia's.

Introduction (excerpt)

Thus the famous Amours of *Anthony* and *Cleopatra*, having a true Foundation, will more effectually impress the fatal Consequences of

From S. Fielding, *The Lives of Cleopatra and Octavia by the Author of David Simple* (London: Printed for the Author and Sold by Andrew Millar, in the Strand; R. and J. Dodsley, in Pall-Mall; and J. Leake, at Bath, 1757).

a mad intoxicated Lover, and a false insinuating Woman, than may be expected from the most admired or accomplished Novels; and the Distresses of a virtuous *Octavia* will excite a more lasting Sensibility of Pity or Relentment, than can be indulged from the most pathetic Descriptions of Romance. For in the latter the Reader seldom so far forgets himself, as not to recollect that the Characters are imaginary and feigned; whereas the former, like true Mirrours, reflect the real Images of our Persons.

These superior Advantages of real Characters induced the Author of the Lives of *Cleopatra* and *Octavia* to select the most interesting Parts of their Histories for the Entertainment of the Public. But as the modern Relish for Works of Imagination would almost tempt her to despair of Approbation, without some Mixture of Romance, she has, in Complaisance to this Taste, introduced the Lives of these Ladies, as supposed to have been delivered by themselves in the Shades below. By which Method the Reader may at least expect a more impartial, distinct, and exact Narrative of their several Adventures, and of the Motives they were influenced by: unless he is so inveterately prejudiced in Disfavour of the Fair-sex, as to presume, with the ill-natured Satyrist, That a Woman is not to be credited, any more than trusted, tho' dead.

The Author begs to Leave to account for her Interview with those Heroines, as *Homer, Virgil, Aristophanes, Lucan,* and others, have on the like Occasion, through the Assistance of an Eastern Sorcerer or Magician, who conveyed her to the gloomy Realms of *Pluto* and by his Interest at Court, prevailed on that grand Monarch to command those celebrated Shades to give her a faithful Detail of their Lives, during their Abode on Earth. There was no disputing his Orders; and the only Shadow the imperious Queen of *Egypt* retained of her former Royalty, was, the Permission granted her to take Place of *Octavia,* in the Recital of her Story, which she did in the following Manner.

The Life of Cleopatra (excerpt)

But now, at the Approach of my last Hours, I could not avoid reflecting on my past Life; and found, upon the whole, that the Indulgence of my Ambition, and the cultivating in myself the Spirit of Pride and Vanity, had produced far more Misery than Happiness. How indeed can it be otherwise? when instead of restraining, we give a loose to Passions, which, like a Dropsy, increase by Indulgence, are too greedy to be satisfied, prey on our Hearts, and raise in us a Perplexity more painful than any Misfortune that can attend or befal us. To be for ever pursuing what we can never attain (which is constantly the Case of ungovernable Passions), is the State of all others most to be deplored.

When in *Anthony's* Triumph over the King of *Armenia,* I was placed on a Throne, and the Procession ended at my Feet, instead of the Statue of *Jupiter,*[1] even whilst I was so much the Object of the public Envy, I was more grieved at observing that the Prisoners who opened their Eyes, saw I was not a real Goddess, and would not bow down before me, than I was pleased with the most extravagant Honours paid me by the deluded and enamoured Triumvir. For when my Mind was tortured by Excess of Passion, and all within was Tempest and Confusion, what Tranquility or Happiness could I possibly enjoy? But it was now too late to change this dismal Situation; and my last Minutes rolled on in the same Tumult, which had run through all the Hours of my Life preceding *Anthony's* Death. Caesar's Power, the Triumph of *Livia* and *Octavia,* with my own approaching Fate, crouded my Mind with such various and bitter Reflections, as almost hurried me to Distraction; and at last, had I not had Art enough to impose on myself, as I had on others, and fancy that I despised Life, because I fixed my Thoughts on other Objects, Death would have appeared to me in its most frightful Terrors. But I was somewhat flattered in presuming I should attain Glory by dying with *Anthony;* and by robbing *Livia* and *Octavia* (the one, my Rival with *Anthony;* the other, in the Universe), of their Exultation over me; and that as I could neither allure nor conquer, yet that I should deceive the great and powerful *Caesar.* Thus I breathed my last, sadly imposing on myself, and fell a wretched Sacrifice to that Treachery and Ambition, wherein I had so long placed my chief Delight; and of whose fatal Consequences I shall be, to all future Ages, a perpetual and disgraceful Monument.

1. A triumphal procession in Rome ended at the temple of Jupiter on the Capitoline.

The Life of Octavia (excerpts)

As soon as I could compose my Thoughts after his[2] Departure, I employed myself wholly in the Care of his Children, as well as those he had by *Fulvia,* as my own. The unfortunate Children, who had lost their Mother, were the objects of my Compassion; and the Love I bore their Father, extended to them, as his Offspring. Nor did the News I had heard of *Cleopatra,* abate my Care, or irritate my Revenge to gratify itself on their helpless Innocence. To confess the Truth, Revenge was not much in my Disposition; and I now experienced the Falsehood of the Assertion, that Love may be turned into Hatred, and that Hatred be heightened in Proportion to the Degree of the Love it succeeds. Love indeed, when it is only the Consequence of Pride gratified, will vanish as soon as that Pride is piqued; and will surrender up its Place to Aversion; which is the more natural and more general Consequence of unbounded Pride. But as Love was my predominant Passion, it was built on the Gratification of no other; and therefore its Disappointment, whatever it made me suffer, did not burst out into Rage. This I am certain of, that I did not hate *Anthony.* For though from this Time forward he treated me with the utmost Scorn and Neglect, yet I could with Pleasure hear of his Prosperity, and was concerned at his Ruin; notwithstanding his mad Passion for *Cleopatra* was the Occasion of it.

At length did I receive the Reward of conscious Virtue; for, applauded by the *Romans,* valued by their Emperor, gratefully treated by my Children, and with a Mind steady, serene, and calm, I sunk in Peace, and resigned my Breath, without any Remorse to embitter, or One Thought of Terror to disturb, my last and departing Moments.

10.2. Charlotte Brontë, *Villette,* Chapter XIX, "The Cleopatra" (excerpt) (1853, English, prose)

In the nineteenth-century British novel Villette, *we see Cleopatra portrayed by a female author and described through the eyes of a female character,*

From C. Brontë, *Villette. By Currer Bell, Author of "Jane Eyre," "Shirley," "The Professor," Etc. Etc.* A New Edition (London: Smith, Elder and Co., 15, Waterloo Place, 1873).
   2. Antony's.

Lucy Snow, who encounters a portrait of Cleopatra. From Lucy's descrip-
tion, the painting seems to be of a familiar type: Cleopatra reclining, semi-
nude; it is Lucy's interpretation that creates a distinctive Cleopatra from
this image.

One day, at a quiet early hour, I found myself nearly alone in a
certain gallery, wherein one particular picture of portentous size, set
up in the best light, having a cordon of protection stretched before
it, and a cushioned bench duly set in front for the accommodation of
worshipping connoisseurs, who, having gazed themselves off their
feet, might be fain to complete the business sitting: this picture, I
say, seemed to consider itself the queen of the collection.

It represented a woman, considerably larger, I thought, than the life.
I calculated that this lady, put into a scale of magnitude suitable for the
reception of a commodity of bulk, would infallibly turn from fourteen
to sixteen stone. She was, indeed, extremely well fed: very much
butcher's meat—to say nothing of bread, vegetables, and liquids—must
she have consumed to attain that breadth and height, that wealth of
muscle, that affluence of flesh. She lay half-reclined on a couch: why, it
would be difficult to say; broad daylight blazed round her; she
appeared in hearty health, strong enough to do the work of two plain
cooks; she could not plead a weak spine; she ought to have been
standing, or at least sitting bolt upright. She had no business to lounge
away the noon on a sofa. She ought likewise to have worn decent
garments; a gown covering her properly, which was not the case: out
of abundance of material—seven-and-twenty yards, I should say, of
drapery—she managed to make inefficient raiment. Then, for the
wretched untidiness surrounding her, there could be no excuse. Pots
and pans—perhaps I ought to say vases and goblets—were rolled
here and there on the foreground; a perfect rubbish of flowers was
mixed amongst them, and an absurd and disorderly mass of curtain
upholstery smothered the couch and cumbered the floor. On referring
to the catalogue, I found that this notable production bore name
"Cleopatra."

Well, I was sitting wondering at it (as the bench was there, I
thought I might as well take advantage of its accommodation), and
thinking that while some of the details—as roses, gold cups, jewels,
etc., were very prettily painted, it was on the whole an enormous

piece of claptrap; the room, almost vacant when I entered, began to fill. Scarcely noticing this circumstance (as, indeed, it did not matter to me) I retained my seat; rather to rest myself than with a view to studying this huge, dark-complexioned gipsy-queen; of whom, indeed, I soon tired, and betook myself for refreshment to the contemplation of some exquisite little pictures of still life: wild flowers, wild-fruit, mossy woodnests, casketing eggs that looked like pearls seen through clear green sea-water; all hung modestly beneath that coarse and preposterous canvass.

Suddenly a light tap visited my shoulder. Starting, turning, I met a face bent to encounter mine; a frowning, almost a shocked face it was.

"Que faites vous ici?"[3] said a voice.

"Mais, monsieur, je m'amuse."[4]

"Vous vous amusez! et à quoi, s'il vous plait? Mais d'abord, faites-moi le plaisir de vous lever; prenez mon bras, et allons de l'autre côté."[5]

I did precisely as I was bid. M Paul Emanuel (it was he) returned from Rome, and now a travelled man, was not likely to be less tolerant of insubordination now, than before this added distinction laurelled his temples.

"Permit me to conduct you to your party," said he, as we crossed the room.

"I have no party."

"You are not alone?"

"Yes, monsieur."

"Did you come here unaccompanied?"

"No, monsieur. Dr. Bretton brought me here."

"Dr. Bretton and Madame his mother, of course?"

"No; only Dr. Bretton."

"And he told you to look at *that* picture?"

"By no means; I found it out for myself."

M Paul's hair was shorn close as raven down, or I think it would have bristled on his head. Beginning now to perceive his drift, I had a certain pleasure in keeping cool, and working him up.

3. "What are you doing here?" (French).
4. "But, sir, I'm having fun."
5. "You're having fun! Doing what, if you please? But first, allow me the pleasure of helping you up; take my arm, and then the other side."

"Astounding insular audacity!" cried the Professor. "Singulières femmes que ces Anglaises!"[6]

"What is the matter, monsieur?"

"Matter! How dare you, a young person, sit coolly down, with the self-possession of a *garçon*, and look at *that* picture?"

"It is a very ugly picture, but I cannot at all see why I should not look at it."

"Bon! bon! Speak no more of it. But you ought not to be here alone."

"If, however, I have no society—no *party*, as you say? And then, what does it signify whether I am alone, or accompanied? nobody meddles with me."

"Taisez-vous, et asseyez-vous là—là!"[7] Setting down a chair with emphasis in a particularly dull corner, before a series of most specially dreary "cadres."

"Mais, monsieur."

"Mais, mademoiselle, asseyez-vous, et ne bougez pas—entendez-vous? jusqu'à ce qu'on vienne vous chercher, ou que je vous donne la permission."[8]

"Quel triste coin!"[9] cried I, "et quelles laids tableaux!"[10]

And "laids," indeed, they were; being a set of four, denominated in the catalogue "La vie d'une femme."[11] They were painted rather in a remarkable style—flat, dead, pale, and formal. The first represented a "Jeune Fille,"[12] coming out of a church-door, a missal in her hand, her dress very prim, her eyes cast down, her mouth pursed up—the image of a most villainous little precocious she-hypocrite. The second, a "Mariée"[13] with a long white veil, kneeling, at prie-dieu in her chamber, holding her hands plastered together, finger to finger, and showing the whites of her eyes in a most exasperating manner. The third, a "Jeune Mère,"[14] hanging disconsolate over a clayey and puffy

6. "Peculiar women, these English."
7. "Hush, and sit down here, here!"
8. "But Miss, sit down and don't budge, do you hear? Until someone comes to find you, or until I give you permission."
9. "What a sad corner!"
10. "And what ugly pictures!"
11. "The life of a woman."
12. "Young girl."
13. "Bride."
14. "Young mother."

baby with a face like an unwholesome full moon. The fourth, a "Veuve,"[15] being a black woman, holding by the hand a black little girl, and the twain studiously surveying an elegant French monument, set up in a corner of some Père la Chaise.[16] All these four "Anges"[17] were grim and grey as burglars, and cold and vapid as ghosts. What women to live with! insincere, ill-humoured, bloodless, brainless nonentities! As bad in their way as the indolent gypsy-giantess, the Cleopatra, in hers.

15. "Widow."
16. A cemetery in Paris, the site of a monastery founded by Louis XIV. The monastery's first superior was Père la Chaise, the king's favorite confessor, who died in 1709.
17. "Angels."

11

Egyptomania

EGYPTOMANIA, A FASCINATION WITH all things Egyptian, peaked following the Napoleonic invasion of Egypt in 1798, although interest in Egypt's exoticism existed even in the Augustan period. Napoleon brought with him to Egypt many scholars, surveyors, and draftsmen to record the monuments. The result of this work was the twenty-one-volume *Description of Egypt*, published from 1809 to 1829. This work made Egypt available to Europeans for research and also captured their imagination, spurring the creation of everything from Egyptian-style home furnishings to poetry.

11.1. Percy Bysshe Shelley, "Ozymandias" (1817, English, verse)

The Napoleonic exploration of Egypt brought to light many artifacts and monuments and also created a fascination with Egyptian antiquities. Shelley takes his inspiration both from these explorations and from the historian Diodorus Siculus. Diodorus, writing in the first century B.C., describes a statue of Usermaatra Ramesses II, whom he refers to by the Hellenized form of the pharaoh's first name, Osymandyas. He quotes the inscription found on the statue: "I am Osymandyas, king of kings. If anyone wishes to know how great I am and where I lie, let him surpass one of my works."[1]

From *The Complete Poetical Works of Percy Bysshe Shelley: The Text Carefully Revised with Notes and a Memoir in Three Volumes,* vol. 3, ed. W. M. Rosetti (London: John Slark, 12 Busby Place, Camden Road N.W., 1885).
    1. Diodorus Siculus 1.47.4.

I met a traveller from an antique land   1
Who said: "Two vast and trunkless legs of stone
Stand in the desert. Near them, on the sand,
Half sunk, a shattered visage lies, whose frown
And wrinkled lip, and sneer of cold command   5
Tell that its sculptor well those passions read
Which yet survive, stamped on these lifeless things,
The hand that mocked them and the heart that fed.
And on the pedestal these words appear:
`My name is Ozymandias, king of kings: 10
Look on my works, ye mighty, and despair!'
Nothing beside remains. Round the decay
Of that colossal wreck, boundless and bare
The lone and level sands stretch far away."

11.2. Arthur O'Shaughnessy, *An Epic of Women*, "Cleopatra I" (1870, English, verse)

British poet and naturalist Arthur O'Shaughnessy's "Cleopatra I" is the first of two poems about Cleopatra included in his collection of lyric poems, An Epic of Women. *In the work's first poem, "Creation," he describes woman as God made her.*

He feasted her with ease and idle food   65
    Of gods, and taught her lusts to fill the whole
Of life; withal He gave her nothing good,
    And left her as He made her—without soul.

And lo, when he had held her for a season
    In His own pleasure-palaces above,   70
He gave her unto man; this is the reason
    She is so fair to see, so false to love.

Cleopatra

I.

She made a feast for great Marc Antony: 1
    Her galley was arrayed in gold and light;

From A. W. E. O'Shaughnessy, *Epic of Women and Other Poems* (London: John Camden Hotten, Piccadilly, 1871).

That evening, in the purple sea and sky,
　　It shone green-golden like a chrysolite.[2]

She was reclined upon a Tyrian couch   5
　　Of crimson wools: out of her loosened vest
Set on one shoulder with a serpent brooch
　　Fell one arm white and half her foamy breast.

And, with the breath of many a fanning plume,
　　That wonder of her hair that was like wine—   10
Of mingled fires and purples that consume,
　　Moved all its mystery of threads most fine—

Moved like some threaded instrument that thrills,
　　Played on with unseen kisses in the air
Weaving a music from it, working spells   15
　　We feel and know not of—so moved her hair:

And under saffron canopies all bright
　　With clash of lights, e'en to the amber prow,
Crept like enchantments subtle passing sight,
　　Fragrance and siren music soft and slow.   20

Amid the thousand viands of the feast,
　　And Nile fruits piled in panniers, where they vied
With palm-tree dates and melons of the East,
　　She waited for Marc Antony and sighed.

—Where tarries he?—What gift doth he invent   25
　　For costly greeting?—How with look or smile,
Out of love treasures not already spent
　　Prepares he now her fondness to beguile?

—But lo, he came between the whiles she sighed;
　　Scarce the wave murmurs troubling,—lo, most dear,   30
His galley, with the oars all softly plied,
　　Warned her with music distant, and drew near.

And on that night—for present,—he did bring
　　A pearl; and gave it her with kissing sweet:

2. A gemstone; also known as periodot, it was believed to promote foresight and protect
against evil and was prized by the pharaohs.

"Would half the Roman empires were this thing,"   35
    He said, "that I might lay them at your feet."

Fairly then moved the magic all arrayed
    About that fragrant feast; in every part
The soft Egyptian spells did lend their aid
    To work some strange enamouring of the heart.   40

It was her whim to show him on that night
    All she was queen of; like a perfect dream,
Wherein there should be gathered in one sight
    The gold of many lives, as it might seem

Spent and lived through at once,—so she made pass   45
    A splendid pageantry of all her East
Beauteous and captive,—so she did amass
    The riches of each land in that one feast.

More jewelries than one could name or know,
    Set in a thousand trinkets or in crowns   50
Each one a sovereignty, in a glittering row
    Numbered the suppliant lands and all her thrones.

And fairest handmaidens in gracious rank,
    Their captive arms enchained with links of gold,
Knelt and poured forth the purple wine she drank,   55
    Or served her there in postures manifold.

And beaded women of a yellow Ind
    Stood at the couch, with bended hand to ply
Great silver feathered fans wherein the wind
    Gat all the choicest fumes of Araby.   60

There in the midst, of shape uncouth and hard,
    Juggled his arts some Ethiopian churl;
Changing fierce natures of the spotted pard
    Or serpents of the Nile that creep and curl.

And many a minstrelsy of voice and string,   65
    Twining sweet sounds like tendrils delicate,
Seemed to ensnare the moments—seemed to cling
    Upon their pleasure all interminate.

But now at length she made them serve her wine
    In the most precious goblet,—wine that shed   70
Great fragrance, in a goblet fair with shine
    Of jewels: so they poured the wine out red:

And lo, to mark that more than any feast
    And honour Antony,—or for mere pride
To do so proud a vanity, at least   75
    The proudest, vainest, woman ever tried—

She took the unmatched pearl, and, taking, laughed;
    And when they served her now that wine of worth
She cast it gleaming in; then with the draught
    Mingling she drank it in their midst with mirth.   80

And all that while upon the ocean high,
    The golden galley, heavy in its light,
Ruled the hoarse sea-sounds with its revelry—
    Changing afar the purples of the night!

12

Fatal Cleopatra

Lucy Hughes-Hallett has observed that Cleopatra's cruelty and her sexuality merge in the Romantic period.[1] The catalyst for the creation of Cleopatra as a femme fatale was a long-neglected anecdote from the fourth century A.D.

12.1. Alexander Pushkin, *Egyptian Nights*, "Cleopatra" (1825, Russian, prose and verse), translated by Alla Gaydukova

Alexander Pushkin revived a little-known anecdote about one of Cleopatra's pastimes. The fourth century A.D. historian Sextus Aurelius Victor is the only ancient source for this story. As he puts it, Cleopatra was "so lustful that she often prostituted herself, and so beautiful that many men bought a night with her at the price of their lives."[2] The tale may be no more than stock invective, however; Diodorus Siculus relates the same anecdote about the Babylonian queen Semiramis. In Egyptian Nights, *an unfinished work in prose and verse, one of the characters, an Italian poet, shows off his talent for improvisation by composing poems on topics his audience provides. One of these topics is "Cleopatra and her lovers."*

"Gentlemen," he said, speaking to the public, "the lot gave me Cleopatra and her lovers as the subject of the improvisation. I kindly

---

1. Hughes-Hallett 1991, 225.
2. Sextus Aurelius Victor, *De Viris Illustribus Urbis Romae* 86.2.

ask the person, who chose this theme, to explain to me her thought: about which lover is the subject here, perché la grande regina aveva molto . . ."[3]

With these words many men started laughing loudly. The Improviser was a bit confused.

"I would wish to know," he continued, "to what historical characteristic did the person who chose this theme hint at. . . . I would be very grateful, if it would please her to explain herself."

No one was in a hurry to answer. Some ladies turned their glances on a plain young woman, who wrote down the theme because of the command of her mother. The poor girl noticed that unfavorable attention and was so embarrassed, that tears hung on her eyelashes, . . . Charskiy could not bear this and, turning to the Improviser, told him in Italian:

"The theme was suggested by me. I meant the testimony of Aurelius Victor, who writes that Cleopatra would give death as a price for her love, and that admirers were found whom this condition did not scare and who did not turn away. . . . It seems to me, however, that the subject is a bit difficult . . . perhaps, you would choose another one? . . ."

But the improviser was already feeling the approach of the god. . . . He gave a signal to the musicians to play. . . . His face became dreadfully pale, he shook as if with fever; his eyes were lit up by a wondrous fire; with his hand he lifted his black hair, with a handkerchief he wiped his high brow, that was covered with the drops of sweat . . . and suddenly he stepped forward, crossed his hands on his chest . . . the music fell silent . . . the improvisation began.

> The palace shone. The chorus of singers
> Thundered with the sound of flutes and lyres.
> The Queen with voice and look
> Enlivened her fancy feast;
> The hearts race to her throne,
> But suddenly, above the golden chalice
> She pondered and down
> She sank with her marvelous forehead . . .
>
> And the fancy feast is as if asleep.
> The guests are mute, the chorus silent.

3. "Because the Great Queen had many" (Italian).

But yet again she raises her brow
And with a clear sight she speaks:
"Does the bliss for you exist in my love?
That happiness you might buy . . .
Listen carefully to me: I can equality
Restore between us.
Who will begin the passionate bargain?
My love I'm selling;
Say, who between you will buy,
With the price of your life, a night with me?"—

She said—and all are gripped with horror,
And hearts trembled with passion . . .
She absorbs the embarrassing murmurs
With cold haughtiness of her face,
And her contemptuous eye roams over
The circle of her admirers . . .
Suddenly from the crowd one comes out,
And after him two others.
Brave is their step; their eyes are clear;
She rises towards them;
It happened: three nights are bought.
And her bed of death calls them.

—"I swear, O mother of passion,
I will serve you in unheard ways,
On the couch of passionate sins
I will come as a common slave.
So look, powerful Cytherean,
And you, the underground kings,
O gods of ferocious Hades;
I swear to the morning sunrise
The wishes of my lords
I will tire with voluptuous passion
And with all secrets of kisses
And with wondrous nakedness those wishes I will quench.
But as soon as with a morning purple
The eternal Aurora will shine forth,
I swear: under the deadly axe
The heads of these lucky ones will fall."

Blessed by the lot,
Now from the fateful urn
Before the statuesque guests
They pick the order one by one.
And the first—Flavius, a brave warrior,
In Roman legions growing grey;
He could not bear from his wife
The look of high contempt;
He took the call of pleasure,
Like he took in times of war
The call of a fierce battlefield.
After him came Criton, a young philosopher,
Born in groves of Epicurus,
Criton, the admirer and singer of
The Graces, the Cytherean goddess,[4] and Love.
Pleasant to the hearts and eyes,
Like a vernal color barely developed,
The last lover his name to ages
Did not betray. His smooth cheek
Was softly shadowed with the first sign of a beard;
The rapture gleamed in his eyes;
The inexperienced strength of passion
Boiled in his young heart . . .
And stopped the sad eye of
The proud Queen on him.

12.2. Algernon Swinburne, "Cleopatra" (1866, English, verse)

Swinburne, a British poet of the Victorian age, was part of "a revolution in poetry and morals."[5] *Cleopatra, of course, provided a perfect subject for one interested in themes of eroticism and cruelty. His "Cleopatra" appeared in* The Cornhill Magazine, *a literary periodical first published in London in 1860.*[6] *An engraving by Frederick Sandys (fig. 7), showing Cleopatra dipping long strands of pearls into a cup, accompanied Swinburne's poem.*

From A. Swinburne, "Cleopatra," *The Cornhill Magazine*, vol. 14, July–December (London: Smith, Elder and Co., 65, Cornhill, 1866).
   4. Venus.
   5. Thomas 1979, 1.
   6. Eddy 1970, 1.

The image most likely refers to the story recounted by Pliny the Elder that Cleopatra won a bet with Antony by disintegrating a pearl in vinegar and drinking the resulting solution (see selection 4.10).

Swinburne's poem, like Pushkin's "Cleopatra" (selection 12.1), treats the story in which Cleopatra prostitutes herself, provided that men pay with their lives. While the poem and the illustration depict different episodes from Cleopatra's life, there are thematic connections between the two, and the image of pearls also provides continuity. The lines from Hayman's "Fall of Anttony" that Swinburne uses as an epigraph may imply that Swinburne saw Antony's fate as similar to the price these men paid.

Cleopatra

"Her beauty might outface the jealous hours,
turn shame to love and pain to a tender sleep,
And the strong nerve of hate to sloth and tears;
Make spring rebellious in the sides of frost,
Thrust out lank winter with hot August growths,
Compel sweet blood into the husks of death,
And from strange beasts enforce harsh courtesy."
                    T. Hayman, "Fall of Antony," 1655

I.

Her mouth is fragrant as a vine,
    A vine with birds in all its boughs;
Serpent and scarab for a sign
    Between the beauty of her brows
And the amorous deep lids divine.

II.

Her great curled hair makes luminous
    Her cheeks, her lifted throat and chin.
Shall she not have the hearts of us
    To shatter, and the loves therein
To shed between her fingers thus?

III.

Small ruined broken strays of light,
    Pearl after pearl she shreds them through

CLEOPATRA

Fig. 7. "Cleopatra," engraving by Frederick Sandys. *The Cornhill Magazine*, London, 1866.

Her long sweet sleepy fingers, white
    As any pearl's heart veined with blue,
And soft as dew on a soft night.

IV.

As if the very eyes of love
    Shone through her shutting lids, and stole
The slow looks of a snake or dove;
    As if her lids absorbed the whole
Of love, her soul the soul thereof.

V.

Lost, all the lordly pearls that were
    Wrung from the sea's heart, from the green
Coasts of the Indian gulf-river;
    Lost, all the loves of the world—so keen
Towards this queen for love of her.

VI.

You see against her throat the small
    Sharp glittering shadows of them shake;
And through her hair the imperial
    Curled likeness of the river snake,
Whose bite shall make an end of all.[7]

VII.

Through the scales sheathing him like wings,
    Through hieroglyphs of gold and gem,
The strong sense of her beauty stings,
    Like a keen pulse of love in them,
A running flame through all his rings.

VIII.

Under those low large lids of hers
    She hath the histories of all time;

---

7. Cf. the drawing of Cleopatra by Michelangelo, in which the coils of Cleopatra's hair merge with the sinuous body of the asp (see Walker and Higgs 2001, 354–56). Swinburne elsewhere describes it as "a meeting of serpents which recognise and embrace . . . almost as though this match for death were a monstrous love-match . . . so closely do the snake and the queen of snakes caress and cling. . . . For what indeed is lovelier or more luxuriously loving than a strong and graceful snake of the nobler kind?" ("Notes on Designs of the Old Masters in Florence," *Fortnightly Review* [July 1868], quoted in Praz 1970, 250–51).

The fruit of foliage-stricken years;
   The old seasons with their heavy chime
That leaves its rhyme in the world's ears.

IX.

She sees the heart of death made bare,
   The ravelled riddle of the skies,
The faces faded that were fair,
   The mouths made speechless that were wise,
The hollow eyes and dusty hair;

X.

The shape and shadow of mystic things,
   Things that fate fashions or forbids;
The staff of time-forgotten kings
   Whose name falls off the Pyramids,
Their coffin-lids and grave-clothings.

XI.

Dank dregs, the scum of pool or clod,
   God-spawn of lizard-footed clans,
And those dog-headed hulks that trod
   Swart necks of the old Egyptians,
Raw draughts of man's beginning God;

XII.

The poised hawk, quivering ere he smote,
   With plume-like gems on breast and back;
The asps and water-worms afloat
   Between the rush-flowers moist and slack;
The cat's warm black bright rising throat.

XIII.

The purple days of drouth expand
   Like a scroll opened out again;
The molten heaven drier than sand,
   The hot red heaven without rain,
Sheds iron pain on the empty land.

XIV.

All Egypt aches in the sun's sight;
   The lips of men are harsh for drouth,

The fierce air leaves their cheeks burnt white,
    Charred by the bitter blowing south,
Whose dusty mouth is sharp to bite.

XV.

All this she dreams of, and her eyes
    Are wrought after the sense hereof.
There is no heart in her for sighs;
    The face of her is more than love—
A name above the Ptolemies.

XVI.

Her great grave beauty covers her
    As that sleek spoil beneath her feet
Clothed once the anointed soothsayer;
    The hallowing is gone forth from it
Now, made unmeet for priests to wear.

XVII.

She treads on gods and god-like things,
    On fate and fear and life and death,
On hate that cleaves and love that clings,
    All that is brought forth of man's breath
And perisheth with what it brings.

XVIII.

She holds her future close, her lips
    Hold fast the face of things to be;
Actium, and sound of war that dips
    Down the blown valleys of the sea,
Far sails that flee, and storms of ships;

XIX.

The laughing red sweet mouth of wine
    At ending of life's festival;
That spice of cerecloths,[8] and the fine
    White bitter dust funereal
Sprinkled on all things for a sign;

---

8. Wax-coated cloth used to wrap corpses.

XX.

His face, who was and was not he,
    In whom, alive, her life abode;
The end, when she gained heart to see
    Those ways of death wherein she trod,
Goddess by god, with Antony.

Cleopatra in Arabic

[handwritten: She]

[handwritten: FIND SNAKES]

TO THE EGYPTIANS CLEOPATRA has been a national heroine, this tradition emphasizing her erudition, shrewdness, and beneficence. Many works of scholarship were attributed to Cleopatra, as were many heroic feats, including her bringing about the death of Octavian.

13.1. John, Bishop of Nikiu, *The Chronicle* 67.1–11 (ca. A.D. 690, Greek,[1] prose), translated by R. H. Charles[2]

As its title suggests, The Chronicle *records facts in chronological order. John, the bishop of Nikiu, a province in Egypt, describes a Cleopatra who worked tirelessly in the interests of her people.*

[handwritten: Egyptian View]

[handwritten: Pride]

[handwritten: She stood up to Rome]

And queen Cleopatra went down from Palestine into Egypt in order to make her royal residence there. And when she came to the city Farmâ she gave battle to the Egyptians and overcame them. (2) And next she came to Alexandria, and reigned there. And she was great in herself ~~and in her achievements~~ (in) courage and strength. There was none of the kings who preceded her who wrought such achievements as she. (3) And she built in the confines of Alexandria

[handwritten: Positive figure]

[handwritten: Exemplary Queen]

---

1. This work exists only in an Ethiopic translation. The translator reveals that the work was originally written in Greek but that the Ethiopic translation, done in 1602, is based on an Arabic translation of the original (Charles 1982, v–vi; published by the APA-Philo Press, Amsterdam, Netherlands [ISBN 90 6022 3039]).
2. Ibid., 50.

a great (and) magnificent palace, and all that saw it admired, there was not the like in all the world. (4) And she built it on an island in the quarter of the north to the west of the city of Alexandria, outside the city and at a distance of four stadia. (5) And she raised a dike against the waters of the sea with stones and earth, and made the place of the waters over which they voyaged formerly in ships into dry land, and she made it passable on foot. (6) And this stupendous and difficult achievement she wrought through the advice of a wise man named Dexiphanes, who made the sea into dry land that there might be a means of passage on foot. (7) And next she constructed a canal to the sea, and she brought water from the river Gihon and conducted it into the city. And by this means she brought it about that ships could approach and enter the city and by this means there was great abundance. (8) Now the city was formerly without access to water, but she brought all the water it required (lit. made it full of water) so that ships could sail thereon, and by this means fish became abundant in the city. (9) And she executed all these works in vigilant care for the well-being of the city. And before she died she executed many noble works and (created) important institutions. And this woman, the most illustrious and wise amongst women, died in the fourteenth year of the reign of Caesar Augustus. (10) Thereupon the inhabitants of Alexandria and of (lower) Egypt and upper Egypt submitted to the emperors of Rome, who set over them prefects and generals. (11) And Augustus reigned fifty-six years and six months.

13.2. Al-Mas'udi, *Prairies of Gold* (excerpt) (10th c. A.D., Arabic, prose), translated by Camilo Gomez-Rivas

*That Arab historian al-Mas'udi has little interest in the Romans is partic-
ularly clear in this passage. In what is perhaps the boldest revision of the
Cleopatra story, al-Mas'udi has Octavian (Augustus) die soon after he
discovers that Cleopatra has committed suicide.*

Ptolemy [XII Auletes, king of Egypt] was succeeded by his daughter, Cleopatra. Her reign lasted twenty-two years. She was wise, tried her hand at philosophy and was a close companion to wise men. She has works, both bearing her name and ascribed to her, of medicine, magic, and science, known by those versed in medicine. This queen was the last of the Greek kings, so that [with her death] their reign ended, their era was forgotten, the vestiges of their civilization were obliterated, and their sciences, except for what remained in the hands of their wise men, disappeared.

There is a curious report regarding the death of this queen, [namely] her suicide. She had a husband by the name of Antony, with whom she shared the rule of Macedonia, a country of Egypt comprising Alexandria and other cities.

Augustus, the second of the Roman kings, the first to be named Caesar, and thus, the originator of the line of Caesars, struck out toward Antony and Cleopatra in hostility. (We will discuss Augustus' story in the chapter concerning the kings of Rome, after this section). Augustus thus fought wars in Syria and Egypt against Cleopatra and her husband Antony, resulting in Antony's death and leaving Cleopatra with no means of keeping Augustus, king of the Romans, from possessing Egypt.

Augustus aimed to capture Cleopatra by means of a ruse, for he had knowledge of her wisdom and wanted to learn from her—as one of the last Greek sages. Afterwards, [according to his plan] he would torture and kill her. He wrote to Cleopatra, but she knew his [real] intentions and of the harm done to her by the murder of her husband and soldiers. She therefore sent for a [kind of] serpent that exists between the Hijaz and Egypt. It is of the species of serpents that watches a person until it is able to see one of that person's limbs. It then springs, like the wind, across a distance of many cubits, and it does not pass by that limb before delivering its venom, which afflicts the victim unawares due to the swiftness of the ensuing death. People are then left under the illusion that [the victim] has died a sudden death from natural causes.

I personally have seen one species of this serpent in the water, in the country of Khurasan, in the rural district of al-Ahwaz, coming from Basra on the way to Fars, in a place known as Khan Mardawayh, between the city of Dawraq and the countries of Basyan and al-Fundum. They are hand-length serpents, known there by the name of *fitriyah*, and they have two heads. [One of these serpents] will be in the sand, under the earth, until it feels [the presence] of a person or other living creature. It then rushes from its place a distance of many cubits and strikes with one of its heads at any spot on that creature, whose life instantly ceases.

This queen, Cleopatra, therefore sent for and was brought a serpent of the kind described above, found in the regions of Hijaz. When the day came in which she knew Augustus would enter the palace of her queen-ship, Cleopatra ordered one of her maids—who desired her own destruction before Cleopatra's and that no torment touch her after [her queen's departure]—to bring her hand to the vessel holding the serpent. She touched it and instantly went still. The queen sat on her royal throne and put her crown on her head, dressed in her royal finery. She laid out all sorts of aromatic plants, flowers, fruits and perfumes—all the marvelous aromatic herbs that can be gathered in Egypt and others which we have described in detail—in her court, before her throne.

She delegated what needed to be delegated of her affairs and disbanded her courtiers who became distracted from their queen as their enemy was already upon them. Augustus had entered the house of their kingdom before Cleopatra had brought her hand to the glass vessel with the serpent. But then she brought her hand to it, the serpent delivered its venom and she dried up at once. The serpent slithered out of its vessel but found no stone [to hide under] or way out [of the court] due to the perfection of its ornamental stone, marble, and varnish.

The serpent thus went into the ornamental plants as Augustus entered [the palace] until he came to the court and saw Cleopatra sitting with the crown on her head. He did not doubt that she could speak so he approached her. Then it became clear to him that she was dead.

He was amazed, as were his companions, by the aromatic plants, and he put his hand on every sort. He touched and savored the smell of each. Augustus did not know what the reason of Cleopatra's death had been and lamented what had slipped away from him with her death. And, as he was taking in the plants and their aromas, the serpent sprung on him and shot him with its poison. Instantly, the right side of Augustus' body dried up. His right eye and ear left him. He was astounded by Cleopatra's actions, her suicide—choosing death over a life of shame—and by how she had laid him a snare by putting the serpent in the plants.

He expressed all of this in verse in the language of the Romans, describing what had befallen him and telling her story. He stayed alive for one day, after what befell him as we have described above, and died. Had the serpent not unloaded its venom on the maid and then on Cleopatra, Augustus would have died instantly, not granting him the time [to tell] the poem so well known by the Romans, which they recite in their mourning, with which they eulogize their kings and dead, and maybe even recall in their songs, it is so well known.

In our previous writings we have told of the lives of the Greek kings, their stories and wars, distant travels in countries, the reports of their wise men, the ideas and beliefs they produced, the teachings of their philosophers, and much beside that concerning their secrets and strange stories.

What one counting their kings and what the people of knowledge agree upon is that the number of the Greek kings was fourteen, the last of which was the queen, and that the entire number of the years of their reign, the stretch of their days and the duration of their power, was three hundred and one years.

And every king who reigned over the Greeks after Alexander son of Philip was named Ptolemy, that name being the most common name for their kings, much as is the case of the kings of Fars, who are named Chrosroes, and the kings of Rome, Caesar, the kings of Yemen, Tobba, the kings of Abyssinia, Nujashi, and the kings of the Zanj, Flimi.

In what has preceded of our book, we have discussed the general and most widely known classification of the kings of the world, their characteristics and names. Below and after this section, we will discuss again and in general kings and kingdoms, in the section when it is appropriate, God willing, may He be exalted and He alone grants success.

13.3. Ahmad Shawqi, *The Death of Cleopatra*[3] (1929, Arabic, prose) (excerpts), translated by Camilo Gomez-Rivas

Shawqi was an Egyptian playwright who saw Cleopatra as a national heroine for Egypt. In describing her exploits, he imagines motives and strategies for Cleopatra that support his pro-Egyptian perspective. For Shawqi the conflict between Egypt and an imperialistic European power such as Rome had particular resonance. In 1922 Britain had granted

---

3. *Masra' Kliyubatra.*

Egypt independence, but it nevertheless continued to exercise a great deal of influence on the country. Shawqi himself went into exile after coming into conflict with British authorities following World War I.[4]

Act I (excerpt)

[*Cleopatra enters; behind her is her son Caesarion, between her two maids, Shramiyun and Haylana. Behind them is Anshu, the queen's jester and the palace eunuch.*]

THE QUEEN. Greetings to the secretaries of the office and to their senior secretary in rank.

ZAYNUN [*the palace secretary*]. The peace of the heavens in her glory upon the exalted lady of the crown. I would wish for two heads, not one. When she touches the earth, the most important of men bow one head to the glory of her faculties, and lower another to the glory of her beauty.

[*Haba, Dayun, and Lisyas turn to each other anxiously.*]

ANSHU [*the jester*] [*to the two maids and Caesarion*]. Or would a head with two faces free him from two heads? For sometimes he is Egyptian and sometimes Greek. In the court of Julius and Antony, Roman. And when he meets the eunuch of the palace, Nubian or Sudanese.

[*Anubis the priest enters from a door opposite.*]

THE QUEEN. Priest of the reign, peace. May we be not without your blessings. Pray for me and don't forget my little ones in your prayers.

ANUBIS. Queen of the Nile, chaste greetings to you. Isis has kept your crown and extended your life.

THE QUEEN. Look at my son Caesarion who receives your gifts.

THE PRIEST [*to himself*]. Isis, how do I pray for the son of Julius Caesar? His father is lofty but Pharaoh is loftier and greater.

[*He hears a call from outside the palace and a group chants the hymn to the recent victory in Actium.*]

THE QUEEN [*frowning*]. Priest of the reign, sirs. Have you heard the ring of the voices in the corners of my palace?

ANUBIS. They are the subjects of my queen.

THE QUEEN. I wish I knew whether for good they gather, or evil?

SHARMIYUN. The crowds, oh queen, come in waves to the shore in joy and good tidings. They are gladdened by what you met at

---

4. Hughes-Hallett 1991, 297.

Actium, gaining the upper hand over the enemy in triumph. They don't speak or celebrate but that good news has come to the city.

THE QUEEN. Oh the falsehood of men! What they spread is a lie, what they tell is clear, by my life. What victory did I meet so that the tongues of people take up praising and thanking me? Something sweet has got the better of the mouth of honesty. If only we had some of the trimmings. But tomorrow my nation will know the truth, for nothing is secret to the people.

SHARMIYUN. Lady of the crown, that favor was mine alone and that deception mine. There was much talk and speculation by people not knowing concerning your return yesterday. So I spread what I spread about the victory, and I made every hut and palace hear. I feared what the crowds would do regarding you, and I was afraid of hostility against you. So forgive my insolence. Accept my excuse though my many faults tire.

THE QUEEN. Sharmiyun, calm down, for you are nothing but an angel made of devoutness and tenderness. You are my loyal servant. It's as if I were of a family of misfortunes, and the faithful servant of the family were brought closer in bad times and good ones. Listen now how my misfortune came to pass and see my patience in my afflictions. Gentlemen, listen to the news of the war, of the killing and of my matters therein, of my storming of the waves while the sea raged and the ships flowed with blood on it. A legendary day, the kind that happens once in an age, was coming between Antony and Octavius. Every one who owned a sail took to preparations for war and for evil. There you saw nothing but swift-sailing ships from front and back reeling and escaping, and ships chasing ships as eagles chases one another. It seemed that the smoke in the air formed wings of the dark night spreading. The roar of the wind in the abyss was sound of thunder and roar of lion. And in the water you saw the shape of a bed for the drowned and the contour of tomb maliciously cleaning the wounds of those who weakened and despaired of life. I was in my ship between my soldiers weighing the war and the situation in my mind. I said Rome has burst apart, half of the people in enmity of the other. Its two heroes split the navy and the army kindling uproar on sea and land. When conflict comes between shepherds, they teach fugitive wolves to venture. So I pondered my situation at length, and I planned something bright and sweet. I perceived that if

Rome disappeared from the sea, no one would rule it but me. I was in a storm, I lowered my sails and my warships withdrew behind me. I was rid of the war and of the capture and destruction that might have followed the ships. I forgot my love and the support of Antony, so that I betrayed him. God knows I abandoned my love, the father of my boy, my help and treasure, who lost the throne and sacrificed in my path a thousand and one tracts of land. What is surprising is that at the highest, I was daughter and queen of Egypt.

Act II (excerpt)

ROMAN COMMANDER [*whispering to his companions*]. Did you not see the princess? Indeed she is intoxicated, stumbling in her shamelessness.
ANOTHER [Roman]. And did you look at the enraptured one [Antony], how he ran after her and was swept into her current?
ANOTHER [*to his companions, whereupon Arus, loyal servant of Antony, and Olympus hear*]. And look at Arus in his wavering how he refuses the call of his birth.
OLYMPUS [*mocking*] [to Arus]. Arus, whose today and tomorrow is filled with the young hero, whose Indian sword is clamorous with war. And heroes lust after the superiority of their power. His blind dedication to his lord frightens me, relinquishing his self, his nation and his birth. He dotes like a dog in his affection. The dog is shackled behind his lookout. And shackled he guards his house.
ARUS. This joking, doctor, is heavyhearted. Be cautioned, and then some, of repeating it. Were it not for the banquet and the wine and the reverence for the princess of the Sa'id Valley and her House, I would bite out the tip of your uvula, for its excess recklessness for the heroes.

Act III (excerpt)

[*Antony sees a figure appear and asks Arus, astonished.*]
ANTONY. Arus!
ARUS. My lord.
ANTONY. Do you see what I see?
ARUS. That is Olympus quickening his pace.
ANTONY. I wonder where to and where from?
ARUS. There he comes toward us. He approaches.
[*Enter Olympus.*]

OLYMPUS. Hail Caesar.

ANTONY. Antony rather, none other. Or say rather "the pursued fugitive." None of you dupe me in strength or weakness, deception in friendship is enough.

olympus. My lord.

ANTONY. Today I am no one's lord. Octavius is master and I am servant. You passed by the palace, so how are its people? Does Olympus have any news of Cleopatra? Speak frankly, son. Say she has been disloyal, that she has renewed the empire of passion with the third Caesar. She did to me, needful during the uproar, what the enemy did not. Her navy took refuge in its anchors. Her army threw down its weapons and saved itself.

OLYMPUS. My lord, forgive me.

ANTONY. Speak. Fear not. I see sorrow in you.

OLYMPUS. My lord, be hesitant and slow to cast aspersions, for from doubt come accusations and harm. In spite of your great chivalry, you have charged with treachery the most dear one who has served.

ANTONY. What are you saying?

OLYMPUS. Cleopatra has killed herself this morning with a stab of a dagger to the chest.

ANTONY. Oh to the heavens! Killed herself? Where and why? How and when?

OLYMPUS. I went by the palace this morning and found it in disarray and ill spirits. A desolate emptiness appeared to my eyes, with wailing here and there.

ANTONY. Killed herself! Oh the news! And the severity of fate! Indeed matters progressed from one momentous event to another. She never was disloyal. It was only I who was disloyal to her, and you were ashamed by their words, "she killed herself and he didn't!" Go, Olympus, and leave me and the grief and sorrows. For doctors have no eyes to see the wounds of the heart.

[*Exit Olympus.*]

After a long monologue and a dialogue with Arus, Arus and Antony commit suicide in grief by stabbing themselves. Before dying, Antony is brought before Cleopatra and Olympus's treachery is revealed.

14

Afrocentric Cleopatra

CLEOPATRA'S ANCESTRY WAS ESSENTIALLY Macedonian Greek. She was a descendant of Ptolemy I, a general in Alexander the Great's army and the founder of the Ptolemaic dynasty in Egypt. The tradition that Cleopatra was of African descent has at its origin two points of uncertainty in Cleopatra's family tree. The identities of her mother and paternal grandmother are not known with certainty, and there has been speculation that one or both of these ancestors were members of Egypt's native population. To judge from the ancient sources, Cleopatra considered herself culturally a Ptolemy. Nonetheless, the debate, often framed in terms of skin color, has been an enduring one, becoming especially prominent in the second half of the twentieth century.

Afrocentrism aims to reclaim lost African achievements and to recognize Africa as the true source of European culture, on the grounds that the elements of that culture were stolen from Egypt. As the following passages illustrate, Cleopatra figures prominently in the debate.

14.1. Joel Augustus Rogers, "Cleopatra: Exemplar of Feminine Fascination Throughout the Ages (69–30 B.C.)"[1] (excerpt) (1946, English, prose) *After WWII*

1. Rogers 1996, 122–23.

In his description of Cleopatra's dramatic arrival in Julius Caesar's quarters concealed in a carpet, Rogers gives a detailed physical description of the queen, in which she has clearly African features. In the references for his chapter on Cleopatra, he offers as evidence for this portrayal Shakespeare's description of Cleopatra as "tawny."[2] He adds: "Robert Ripley, who says he has proof of all his facts, calls Cleopatra 'fat and black.' (Believe It or Not, p. 83, 6th printing. 1934)."[3]

When she reached Alexandria, Caesar, who had arrived with a large army, ordered both Cleopatra and Ptolemy to yield. Ptolemy obeyed; Cleopatra thought the matter over. She had heard much of Caesar. He was undoubtedly a very great man but to her and her people Rome was a land of barbarians. Still she could use him to further her ambitions. He had an army.

She decided to call on him. But how to do so? He had made his headquarters in a palace on the Lochias Promontory. To reach this she would have to pass through her brother's lines, and Photion,[4] his general, would made a bloody finish of her if he caught her. Then an idea occurred to her. Calling a trusted slave, she bade him wrap her in a silken covering, place a magnificent carpet over that, wrap the whole in an ordinary covering, and take it as a present to Caesar.

Caesar received the bearer with his usual politeness but with ordinary interest. Since his arrival he had been deluged with presents—vases, statues, and hundreds of objects for which he had no use. He bade the slaves undo the bundle. Then he gasped as the silken covering stirred and a laughing brown-skinned girl with crinkly hair and voluptuous figure, nude to the waist, stood before him.

In her eyes was a gleam that made him forget his fifty-four years. When, to crown all, she addressed him in flawless Latin a voice full of music, instinct told him that into his surfeited life had come at last the one woman. He ordered his attendants from the room and from then on began to leave the gayest of lives with her.

14.2. John Henrik Clarke, "African Warrior Queens"[5] (excerpt) (1984, English, prose)

2. See Shakespeare, *Antony and Cleopatra*, Act I, Scene I (selection *9.1*).
3. Rogers 1996, 129–30.
4. Pothinus.
5. Clarke 1987, 126–28.

Clarke includes Cleopatra in his catalog of African warrior queens and emphasizes her identity as a black woman, providing as an illustration the modern painting Cleopatra *by Earl Sweeney and citing Pierre Louys's 1896 novel* Aphrodite, *in which Louys claims that Cleopatra's mother was a Nubian woman.*

More nonsense has been written about Cleopatra than about any other African queen, mainly because it has been the desire of many writers to paint her white. She was not a white woman. She was not a Greek. Let us dispose of this matter before explaining the more important aspects of her life. Until the emergence of the doctrine of white superiority, Cleopatra was generally pictured as a distinctly African woman, dark in color. Shakespeare in the opening line of *Antony and Cleopatra* calls her "tawny." In his day, mulattos were called "tawny Moors." The word "Moor" came into the European languages meaning black or blac-kamoor. In the *Book of Acts,* Cleopatra describes herself as "black."[6]

Born in 69 B.C., Cleopatra came to the throne that she shared with her brother, Ptolemy XIII, when she was 18 years old. Egypt, now a Roman protectorate, was beset with internal strife and intrigue. Cleopatra aligned herself with Julius Caesar, who reinforced her power. Their political and sexual relationship was a maneuver to save Egypt from the worst aspects of Roman domination. After Julius Caesar was murdered, Cleopatra, still in her early twenties, met Mark Antony and a love affair, strongly motivated by politics, began.

Her effect on Mark Antony was profound. This noble Roman turned traitor to his own people when he attempted to save the country of this fascinating black queen from Roman domination. After Antony's death, the victor, Octavius, assumed full control of Egypt, and Cleopatra, now without a protector or champion, committed suicide.

Contrary to popular belief, Cleopatra did not commit suicide over the loss of Mark Antony. Her great love was Egypt. She was a shrewd politician and an Egyptian nationalist. She committed suicide when she lost control of Egypt.

After Cleopatra's death, Egypt became a Roman colony and the harsher aspects of Roman rule settled over Egypt and the Middle East.

---

6. The book of Acts does not mention Cleopatra.

To the south, in the lands untouched by Rome, new proud civilizations were rising. And in the centuries that followed, black women once again began to play major roles in the theatre of history.

14.3. C. W. King, *Antique Gems and Rings*[7] (excerpt) (1872, English, prose)

In a discussion of the classification of cameos, Cambridge University art historian C. W. King discusses the reasons behind a trend in Renaissance representations of Cleopatra on cameos.

The same age[8] was, a little later, extremely fruitful in heads of *negroes,* and also of *negresses,* the latter often in the character of Cleopatra holding to her breast the asp. There is reason to believe that some of the latter are intended to commemorate the renowned black concubine of Clement VII, the mother of Alessandro dei Medici. Such heads are never found antique. Another reason, besides the celebrity of the sable beauty, that prompted the Florentine school to produce such swarms of miniature Ethiopians, was their discovery of the secret of staining black one of the layers of the common agate-onyx, and obtaining thus the contrast, so great a desideratum in this style.

14.4. Shelley P. Haley, "Black Feminist Thought and Classics: Re-membering, Re-claiming, Re-empowering"[9] (excerpt) (1993, English, prose)

In an autobiographical response to the question of Cleopatra's ethnicity, self-identified Black feminist classicist Shelley Haley raises the crucial question, "What do we mean by 'black'?" when speaking of Cleopatra.

. . . in my second year at Howard, I found myself teaching "Women in the Ancient World." As I look back at the syllabus now, it was not particularly feminist; it was a classics survey, Homer, the tragedians, Livy, Vergil, with a few women thrown in. The feminist

---

7. King 1872, vol. 1, 326.
8. I.e., the Renaissance.
9. Haley 1993, 28–30. The parenthetical references in this selection are Haley's. Notes to the remainder of this selection include Haley's notes (identified as such) as well as my own. In notes that contain both Haley's and my own material, each section of the note is preceded by an identification of its source.

literature I assigned was not particularly current or radical.[10] I didn't relate to it personally but found places for it in my course. The only women in Africa I dealt with were Dido and Cleopatra, but I didn't regard them as Black, or African.

It was Cleopatra who haunted me. In a "Women in the Ancient World" class, we were studying Cleopatra and Octavian's propaganda against her. Ray, a Black male student, asked me to cover again the arguments identifying Cleoaptra as a Greek. I sighed and presented all the evidence. I pulled out the *Cambridge Ancient History* (*CAH*), and we pored over the genealogy. I brought in the research of my colleague Frank Snowden (1970). We reviewed other secondary sources: Volkmann (1958), Grant (1972, 1982), and Lindsay (1971). Ray, very politely but intently, repeated the question my grandmother had posed years before:[11] "But Professor Haley, who wrote those books?" I was going through it all again (growing somewhat irate), when I stared at the *CAH* genealogy and saw—for the first time—question marks where Cleopatra's grandmother should be. As I stared, I heard Ray, again politely, say, "I understand, Professor Haley. You believe what you say is true, but you have bought a lie." The other students in the class were divided; some agreed with Ray, some with me, others were totally indifferent. I was shaken; what did those question marks mean? Why didn't all the students see the evidence as I did? What did they know that I didn't? In buying the lie, had I sold out my race?

At that point, I confronted Cleopatra, and I discovered that my Black students and indeed my grandmother read her on a different level. For them and for me, although I suppressed her, Cleopatra was the lost and found window where we could "claim an identity they taught us to despise" (Cliff 1988: 61). I had disliked discussing Cleopatra; I had been uncomfortable and ill at ease. Why? I began to see and am still arriving at seeing that Cleopatra is the crystallization of the tension between my yearning to fit in among classicists and my identity politics. I clouded this tension by professing that the Ptolemies of the first century B.C.e. were Greco-Egyptian. To me,

10. [Haley's note] Looking at a syllabus from that time I see listed Bullough (1978), de Beauvoir (1974), Putnam (1910), Rogers (1966), and Slater (1968).

11. "'Remember, no matter what you learn in school, Cleopatra was black.'" (Haley 1993, 27).

"Egyptian", "Greco-Egyptian," "Greek," "Roman" had been cultural designations. I refused, rather self-righteously, I admit, to colorize the question as my grandmother had done, along with my students, and, most recently, *Newsweek* ("Was Cleopatra Black": September 23, 1991). What I resisted was the fact that my culture is colorized: Black literature, Black music, Black art, Black feminism. Gradually, by reading my history and Black feminist thought, I perceived that Cleopatra was a signifier on two levels.[12] She gives voice to our "anxiety about cultural disinheritance" (Sadoff 1990: 205), and she represents the contemporary Black woman's double history of oppression and survival.

In the Black oral tradition, Cleopatra becomes a symbolic construction voicing our Black African heritage so long suppressed by racism and the ideology of miscegenation. When we say, in general, that the ancient Egyptians were Black and, more specifically, that Cleopatra was Black, we claim them as part of a culture and history that has known oppression and triumph, exploitation and survival. Cleopatra reacted to the phenomenon of oppression and exploitation as a Black woman would. Hence we embrace her as sister; she is Black. Alice Walker (1989: 267) employs a similar symbolic construction with Medusa. Here, Medusa's decapitation by Perseus represents the rape and cultural suppression of Africa by Europeans.

My grandmother and students were also reading Cleopatra on the level of their experience with miscegenation and the law of miscegenation (Saks 1988). We had been told that if we have one Black ancestor, then we are Black. Films and plays have reinforced this idea. Our family histories and photographs proved this to us. My grandmother was white, had straight black hair, and the nose of her Onondagan grandmother, but she was "colored." Even as a "Greco-Egyptian," Cleopatra was a product of miscegenation.[13] How is she not Black? My grandmother and students were being logical; they were applying to Cleopatra the social decoding typically applied to them.

12. [Haley's note] My ideas were formed by reading Cooper (1892), DuBois collected by Huggins (1986), King (1988), Collins (1990), Moses (1990), hooks (1981), Walker (1983), Hull, Scott, and Smith (1982), and Terrell (1940).
13. [Haley's note] The *Cambridge Ancient History* genealogy has "by a concubine" where Cleopatra's grandmother should be; the Greeks took Egyptian and Ethiopian women as mistresses. See Pomeroy (1990: 55); cf. Cameron (1990). I think it is safe to say that Cleopatra had Black ancestors.

It seemed to me that the Cleopatra I studied as the "true Cleopatra" was a construction of classical scholars and the Greek and Roman authors they consulted.[14] In this particular case, they were willing— eager—to erase the Black ancestor and claim the beautiful Cleopatra for Europe. Like the biracial family cited earlier,[15] classics has kept Cleopatra's Africanity and Blackness a secret and questionable. Many African-Americans did the same for themselves. My family claimed the West Indies as our point of origin. Shame arising from internalized racism never let us go further back until the rise of the Black pride movement. Sadoff's (1990) analysis and critique of misreading led me to apply this theory to classics and Cleopatra.[16] Classicists and historians have misread Cleopatra as a way of furthering ideas of racial purity and hegemony. Martin Bernal's work (1987) on the demise of ancient Egypt in classical scholarship brought him to the conclusion that we classicists still work within racist paradigms.[17]

I applied the same critique to the ancient evidence; I began to wonder how the Romans and the Greeks misread Cleopatra. I did research on foreign women and their image in Roman history and literature. Here Cleopatra was the archetype of the temptress and she was transformed into other characters: Dido in poetry and Sophoniba in historiography.[18] The Romans misread these women as exempla of the temptress who distracted men from their "manliness," *virtus*. As strong queens of African kingdoms, they also constituted a grave threat to the Roman concept of empire. Black feminists, especially

14. [Haley's note] The construction by scholars and filmmakers struck me as I viewed Pascal's 1945 film version of G. B. Shaw's *Caesar and Cleopatra,* starring Vivien Leigh. The dialogue intends for us to take Cleopatra as darker than the Roman Caesar, but the visual presence of a very White and European Vivien Leigh contradicts the dialogue. [Jones's note] See selection *15.1.*

15. A biracial couple who kept their marriage and children a secret (*New York Times,* December 2, 1991, p. 1).

16. [Haley's note] The theoretical standpoint I take here has been articulated by Bloom (1973), Gilbert and Gubar (1979), and Sadoff (1990). My use is unusual in that I am applying it to history and historiography rather than literature.

17. [Haley's note] This conclusion is one of the most important and overlooked of his work. The American Philological Association Panel (1989) and the subsequent special issue (1989) of *Arethusa,* "The Challenge of Black Athena," concentrate on rather esoteric points of research and interpretation. Lefkowitz (1992) trivializes the ramifications of this conclusion. [Jones's note] See also Lefkowitz and Rogers 1996 and Lefkowitz 1996, both of which treat the Black Athena controversy in greater depth.

18. [Haley's note] See Haley (1989, 1990). [Jones's note] Sophoniba was a Numidian queen who took poison to avoid being taken captive by the Romans.

King (1988) and Collins (1990), discuss in their work the controlling image of the jezebel/seductress and its impact on the perception and treatment of Black women. Palmer (1983) analyzes the symbolism of Black women in America as sexual enticers who could overthrow reason and social order. She relates this to the virgin/whore dualism in cultural imagery for White women, in existence at least since classical Greece (Palmer 1983: 157).

15

Modern Cleopatras

THE CLEOPATRAS IN THIS chapter are themselves receptions of the post-antique tradition of Cleopatra. The authors of the selections that follow respond as much to other Cleopatras created out of the historical tradition as they do to the historical tradition itself.

15.1. George Bernard Shaw, *Caesar and Cleopatra* (excerpts) (1898, English, prose)

Shaw's Caesar and Cleopatra *is both a polemic against Shakespeare's glorification of immorality through his sympathetic portrayal of the love between Antony and Cleopatra and a frustration of audience expectations and potential comparisons to Shakespeare. By portraying Cleopatra as a child, Shaw reacts against the common tendency to focus on Cleopatra as a lover. Instead, Shaw comments, through his drama, on the politics of his day. In 1884 he played a role in the foundation of the Fabian Society, a socialist group that led to the establishment of the Labour Party. The Fabian Society aimed to transform society not through revolution, but through "permeation," the attempt to convert politically influential people to their way of thinking.[1] Thus, one of the primary themes in* Caesar and

The prologue, from B. Shaw, *Three Plays for Puritans: The Devil's Disciple, Caesar and Cleopatra, and Captain Brassbound's Conversion* (London: Constable and Co., 1931). Act I, from B. Shaw, *Caesar and Cleopatra: A Page of History* (New York: Brentano's, 1906).

1. Weintraub 1987, 30.

Cleopatra is that of old versus new: Pompey the soldier represents the old Roman society and Caesar the clever politician represents the new.

Prologue

[*In the doorway of the temple of Ra in Memphis. Deep gloom. An august personage with a hawk's head is mysteriously visible by his own light in the darkness within the temple. He surveys the modern audience with great contempt; and finally speaks the following words to them.*]

Peace! Be silent and hearken unto me, ye quaint little islanders. Give ear, ye men with white paper on your breasts and nothing written thereon (to signify the innocence of your minds). Hear me, ye women who adorn yourselves alluringly and conceal your thoughts from your men, leading them to believe that ye deem them wondrous strong and masterful whilst in truth ye hold them in your hearts as children without judgment. Look upon my hawk's head; and know that I am Ra, who was once in Egypt a mighty god. Ye cannot kneel nor prostrate yourselves; for ye are packed, in rows without freedom to move, obstructing one another's vision; neither do any of ye regard it as seemly to do ought until ye see all the rest do so too; wherefore it commonly happens that in great emergencies ye do nothing though each telleth his fellow that something must be done. I ask you not for worship, but for silence. Let not your men speak nor your women cough; for I am come to draw you back two thousand years over the graves of sixty generations. Ye poor posterity, think not that ye are the first. Other fools before ye have seen the sun rise and set, and the moon change her shape and her hour. As they were so ye are; and yet not so great; for the pyramids my people built stand to this day; whilst the dust heaps on which ye slave, and which ye call empires, scatter in the wind even as ye pile your dead sons' bodies on them to make yet more dust.

Hearken to me then, oh ye compulsorily educated ones. Know that even as there is an old England and a new, and ye stand perplexed between the twain; so in the days when I was worshipped was there an old Rome and a new, and men standing perplexed between them. And the old Rome was poor and little, and greedy and fierce, and evil in many ways; but because its mind was little and its work was simple, it knew its own mind and did its own work; and the gods pitied it and helped it and strengthened it and shielded it; for the gods are patient with littleness. Then the old Rome, like the beggar on horseback, presumed on the favor of the gods, and said, "Lo! there is neither riches nor greatness in our littleness: the road to riches and greatness is through robbery of the poor and slaughter of the weak." So they robbed their own poor until they became great masters of that art, and knew by what laws it could be made to appear seemly and honest. And when they had squeezed their own poor dry, they robbed the poor of other lands, and added those lands to Rome until there came a new Rome, rich and huge. And I, Ra, laughed; for the minds of the Romans remained the same size whilst their dominion spread over the earth.

Now mark me, that ye may understand what ye are presently to see. Whilst the Romans still stood between the old Rome and the new, there arose among them a mighty soldier: Pompey the Great. And the way of the soldier is the way of death; but the way of the gods is the way of life; and so it comes that a god at the end of his way is wise and a soldier at the end of his way is a fool. So Pompey held by the old Rome, in which only soldiers could become great; but the gods turned to the new Rome, in which any man with wit enough could become what he would. And Pompey's friend Julius Caesar was on the side of the gods; for he saw that Rome had passed beyond the control of the little old Romans. This Caesar was a great talker and a politician: he bought men with words and with gold, even as ye are bought. And when they would not be satisfied with words and gold, and demanded also the glories of war, Caesar in his middle age turned his hand to that trade; and they that were against him when he sought their welfare, bowed down before him when he became a slayer and a conqueror; for such is the nature of you mortals. And as for Pompey, the gods grew tired of his triumphs and his airs of being himself a god; for he talked of law and duty and other matters that concerned not a mere human worm. And the gods smiled on Caesar; for he lived the life they had given him boldly, and was not forever rebuking us for our indecent ways of creation, and hiding our handiwork as a shameful thing. Ye know well what I mean; for this is one of your own sins.

And thus it fell out between the old Rome and the new, that Caesar said, "Unless I break the law of old Rome, I cannot take my share in ruling her; and the gift of ruling that the gods gave me will perish without fruit." But Pompey said, "The law is above all; and if thou break it thou shalt die." Then said Caesar, "I will break it: kill me who can." And he broke it. And Pompey went for him, as ye say, with a great army to slay him and uphold the old Rome. So Caesar fled across the Adriatic sea; for the high gods had a lesson to teach him, which lesson they shall also teach you in due time if ye continue to forget them and to worship that cad among gods, Mammon.[2] Therefore before they raised Caesar to be master of the world, they were minded to throw him down into the dust, even beneath the feet of Pompey, and blacken his face before the nations. And Pompey they raised higher than ever, he and his laws and his high mind that aped the gods, so that his fall might be the more terrible. And Pompey followed Caesar, and overcame him with all the majesty of old Rome, and stood over him and over the whole world even as ye stand over it with your fleet that covers thirty miles of the sea. And when Caesar was brought down to utter nothingness, he made a last stand to die honorably, and did not despair; for he said, "Against me there is Pompey, and the old Rome, and the law and the legions: all all against me; but high above these are the gods; and Pompey is a fool." And the gods laughed and approved; and on the field of Pharsalia the impossible came to pass; the blood and iron ye pin your faith on fell before the spirit of man; for the spirit of man is the will of the gods; and Pompey's power crumbled in his hand, even as the power of imperial Spain crumbled when it was set against your fathers in the days when England was little, and knew her own mind, and had a mind to know instead of a circulation of newspapers. Wherefore look to it, lest some little people whom ye would enslave rise up and become in the hand of God the scourge of your boastings and your injustices and your lusts and stupidities.

And now, would ye know the end of Pompey, or will ye sleep while a god speaks? Heed my words well; for Pompey went where ye have gone, even to Egypt, where there was a Roman occupation even as there was but now a British one. And Caesar pursued Pompey to Egypt: a Roman fleeing, and a Roman pursuing: dog eating dog. And the Egyptians said, "Lo: these Romans which have lent money

2. Ammon.

to our kings and levied a distraint upon us with their arms, call for ever upon us to be loyal to them by betraying our own country to them. But now behold two Romes! Pompey's Rome and Caesar's Rome! To which of the twain shall we pretend to be loyal?" So they turned in their perplexity to a soldier that had once served Pompey, and that knew the ways of Rome and was full of her lusts. And they said to him, "Lo: in thy country dog eats dog; and both dogs are coming to eat us: what counsel hast thou to give us?" And this soldier, whose name was Lucius Septimius, and whom ye shall presently see before ye, replied, "Ye shall diligently consider which is the bigger dog of the two; and ye shall kill the other dog for his sake and thereby earn his favor." And the Egyptians said, "Thy counsel is expedient; but if we kill a man outside the law we set ourselves in the place of the gods; and this we dare not do. But thou, being a Roman, art accustomed to this kind of killing; for thou hast imperial instincts. Wilt thou therefore kill the lesser dog for us?" And he said, "I will; for I have made my home in Egypt; and I desire consideration and influence among you." And they said, "We knew well thou wouldst not do it for nothing: thou shalt have thy reward." Now when Pompey came, he came alone in a little galley, putting his trust in the law and the constitution. And it was plain to the people of Egypt that Pompey was now but a very small dog. So when he set his foot on the shore he was greeted by his old comrade Lucius Septimius, who welcomed him with one hand and with the other smote off his head, and kept it as it were a pickled cabbage to make a present to Caesar. And mankind shuddered; but the gods laughed; for Septimius was but a knife that Pompey had sharpened; and when it turned against his own throat they said that Pompey had better have made Septimius a ploughman than so brave and readyhanded a slayer. Therefore again I bid you beware, ye who would all be Pompeys if ye dared; for war is a wolf that may come to your own door.

Are ye impatient with me? Do ye crave for a story of an unchaste woman? Hath the name of Cleopatra tempted ye hither? Ye foolish ones; Cleopatra is as yet but a child that is whipped by her nurse. And what I am about to shew you for the good of your souls is how Caesar, seeking Pompey in Egypt, found Cleopatra; and how he received that present of a pickled cabbage that was once the head of Pompey; and what things happened between the old Caesar and the

child queen before he left Egypt and battled his way back to Rome
to be slain there as Pompey was slain, by men in whom the spirit of
Pompey still lived. All this ye shall see; and ye shall marvel, after
your ignorant manner, that men twenty centuries ago were already
just such as you, and spoke and lived as ye speak and live, no worse
and no better, no wiser and no sillier. And the two thousand years
that have past are to me, the god Ra, but a moment; nor is this day
any other than the day in which Caesar set foot in the land of my
people. And now I leave you; for ye are a dull folk, and instruction is
wasted on you; and I had not spoken so much but that it is in the
nature of a god to struggle for ever with the dust and the darkness,
and to drag from them, by the force of his longing for the divine,
more life and more light. Settle ye therefore in your seats and keep
silent; for ye are about to hear a man speak, and a great man he was,
as ye count greatness. And fear not that I shall speak to you again: the
rest of the story must ye learn from them that lived it. Farewell; and
do not presume to applaud me. [*The temple vanishes in utter darkness.*]

Act I

[*Dead silence. Suspense. Then the blackness and stillness breaks softly into
silver mist and strange airs as the windswept harp of Memnon plays at the
dawning of the moon. It rises full over the desert; and a vast horizon comes
into relief, broken by a huge shape which soon reveals itself in the spreading
radiance as a Sphinx pedestalled on the sands. The light still clears, until the
upraised eyes of the image are distinguished looking straight forward and
upward in infinite fearless vigil, and a mass of color between its great paws
defines itself as a heap of red poppies on which a girl lies motionless, her silken
vest heaving gently and regularly with the breathing of a dreamless sleeper,
and her braided hair glittering in a shaft of moonlight like a bird's wing.*

*Suddenly there comes from afar a vaguely fearful sound (it might be
the bellow of a Minotaur softened by great distance) and Memnon's music
stops. Silence: then a few faint high-ringing trumpet notes. Then silence
again. Then a man comes from the south with stealing steps, ravished by
the mystery of the night, all wonder, and halts, lost in contemplation, opposite
the left flank of the Sphinx, whose bosom, with its burden, is hidden from
him by its massive shoulder.*]

THE MAN. Hail, Sphinx: salutation from Julius Caesar! I have wandered
in many lands, seeking the lost regions from which my birth into this

world exiled me, and the company of creatures such as I myself. I have found flocks and pastures, men and cities, but no other Caesar, no air native to me, no man kindred to me, none who can do my day's deed, and think my night's thought. In the little world yonder, Sphinx, my place is as high as yours in this great desert; only I wander, and you sit still; I conquer, and you endure; I work and wonder, you watch and wait; I look up and am dazzled, look down and am darkened, look round and am puzzled, whilst your eyes never turn from looking out—out of the world—to the lost region—the home from which we have strayed. Sphinx, you and I, strangers to the race of men, are no strangers to one another: have I not been conscious of you and of this place since I was born? Rome is a madman's dream: this is my Reality. These starry lamps of yours I have seen from afar in Gaul, in Britain, in Spain, in Thessaly, signalling great secrets to some eternal sentinel below, whose post I never could find. And here at last is their sentinel—an image of the constant and immortal part of my life, silent, full of thoughts, alone in the silver desert. Sphinx, Sphinx: I have climbed mountains at night to hear in the distance the stealthy footfall of the winds that chase your sands in forbidden play—our invisible children, O Sphinx, laughing in whispers. My way hither was the way of destiny; for I am he of whose genius you are the symbol: part brute, part woman, and part god—nothing of man in me at all. Have I read your riddle, Sphinx?

THE GIRL [*who has wakened, and peeped cautiously from her nest to see who is speaking.*] Old gentleman.

CAESAR [*starting violently, and clutching his sword.*] Immortal gods!

THE GIRL. Old gentleman: dont run away.

CAESAR [*stupefied.*] "Old gentleman: dont run away!!!" This! to Julius Caesar!

THE GIRL [*urgently.*] Old gentleman.

CAESAR. Sphinx: you presume on your centuries. I am younger than you, though your voice is but a girl's voice as yet.

THE GIRL. Climb up here, quickly; or the Romans will come and eat you.

CAESAR [*running forward past the Sphinx's shoulder, and seeing her.*] A child at its breast! a divine child!

THE GIRL. Come up quickly. You must get up at its side and creep round.

CAESAR [*amazed.*] Who are you?

THE GIRL. Cleopatra, Queen of Egypt.

CAESAR. Queen of the Gypsies, you mean.

CLEOPATRA. You must not be disrespectful to me, or the Sphinx will let the Romans eat you. Come up. It is quite cosy here.

CAESAR [*to himself.*] What a dream! What a magnificent dream! Only let me not wake, and I will conquer ten continents to pay for dreaming it out to the end. [*He climbs to the Sphinx's flank, and presently reappears to her on the pedestal, stepping round its right shoulder.*]

CLEOPATRA. Take care. That's right. Now sit down: you may have its other paw. [*She seats herself comfortably on its left paw.*] It is very powerful and will protect us; but [*shivering, and with plaintive loneliness*] it would not take any notice of me or keep me company. I am glad you have come: I was very lonely. Did you happen to see a white cat anywhere?

CAESAR [*sitting slowly down on the right paw in extreme wonderment.*] Have you lost one?

CLEOPATRA. Yes: the sacred white cat: is it not dreadful? I brought him here to sacrifice him to the Sphinx; but when we got a little way from the city a black cat called him, and he jumped out of my arms and ran away to it. Do you think that the black cat can have been my great-great-great-grandmother?

CAESAR [*staring at her.*] Your great-great-great-grandmother! Well, why not? Nothing would surprise me on this night of nights.

CLEOPATRA. I think it must have been. My great-grandmother's great-grandmother was a black kitten of the sacred white cat; and the river Nile made her his seventh wife. That is why my hair is so wavy. And I always want to be let do as I like, no matter whether it is the will of the gods or not: that is because my blood is made with Nile water.

CAESAR. What are you doing here at this time of night? Do you live here?

CLEOPATRA. Of course not: I am the Queen; and I shall live in the palace at Alexandria when I have killed my brother, who drove me out of it. When I am old enough I shall do just what I like. I shall be able to poison the slaves and see them wriggle, and pretend to Ftata-teeta that she is going to be put into the fiery furnace.[3]

CAESAR. Hm! Meanwhile why are you not at home and in bed?

3. Ftatateeta: Cleopatra' nurse.

CLEOPATRA. Because the Romans are coming to eat us all. You are not at home and in bed either.

CAESAR [*with conviction.*] Yes I am. I live in a tent; and I am now in that tent, fast asleep and dreaming. Do you suppose that I believe you are real, you impossible little dream witch?

CLEOPATRA [*giggling and leaning trustfully towards him.*] You are a funny old gentleman. I like you.

CAESAR. Ah, that spoils the dream. Why dont you dream that I am young?

CLEOPATRA. I wish you were; only I think I should be more afraid of you. I like men, especially young men with round strong arms; but I am afraid of them. You are old and rather thin and stringy; but you have a nice voice; and I like to have somebody to talk to, though I think you are a little mad. It is the moon that makes you talk to yourself in that silly way.

CAESAR. What! you heard that, did you? I was saying my prayers to the great Sphinx.

CLEOPATRA. But this isnt the great Sphinx.

CAESAR [*much disappointed, looking up at the statue.*] What!

CLEOPATRA. This is only a dear little kitten of a Sphinx. Why, the great Sphinx is so big that it has a temple between its paws. This is my pet Sphinx. Tell me: do you think the Romans have any sorcerers who could take us away from the Sphinx by magic?

CAESAR. Why? Are you afraid of the Romans?

CLEOPATRA [*very seriously.*] Oh, they would eat us if they caught us. They are barbarians. Their chief is called Julius Caesar. His father was a tiger and his mother a burning mountain; and his nose is like an elephant's trunk. [*Caesar involuntarily rubs his nose.*] They all have long noses, and ivory tusks, and little tails, and seven arms with a hundred arrows in each; and they live on human flesh.

CAESAR. Would you like me to show you a real Roman?

CLEOPATRA [*terrified.*] No. You are frightening me.

CAESAR. No matter: this is only a dream—

CLEOPATRA [*excitedly.*] It is not a dream: it is not a dream. See, see. [*She plucks a pin from her hair and jabs it repeatedly into his arm.*]

CAESAR. Ffff—Stop. [*Wrathfully*] How dare you?

CLEOPATRA [*abashed.*] You said you were dreaming. [*Whimpering*] I only wanted to shew you—

CAESAR [*gently.*] Come, come: dont cry. A queen mustnt cry. [*He rubs his arm, wondering at the reality of the smart.*] Am I awake? [*He strikes his hand against the Sphinx to test its solidity. It feels so real that he begins to be alarmed, and says perplexedly*] Yes, I—[*quite panicstricken*] no: impossible: madness, madness! [*Desperately.*] Back to camp—to camp. [*He rises to spring down from the pedestal.*]

CLEOPATRA [*flinging her arms in terror round him.*] No: you shant leave me. No, no, no: dont go. I'm afraid—afraid of the Romans.

CAESAR [*as the conviction that he is really awake forces itself on him.*] Cleopatra: can you see my face well?

CLEOPATRA. Yes. It is so white in the moonlight.

CAESAR. Are you sure it is the moonlight that makes me look whiter than an Egyptian? [*Grimly*] Do you notice that I have a rather long nose?

CLEOPATRA [*recoiling, paralyzed by a terrible suspicion.*] Oh!

CAESAR. It is a Roman nose, Cleopatra.

CLEOPATRA. Ah! [*With a piercing scream she springs up; darts round the left shoulder of the Sphinx; scrambles down to the sand; and falls on her knees in frantic supplication, shrieking*] Bite him in two, Sphinx: bite him in two. I meant to sacrifice the white cat—I did indeed—I [*Caesar, who has slipped down from the pedestal, touches her on the shoulder*] Ah! [*She buries her head in her arms.*]

CAESAR. Cleopatra: shall I teach you a way to prevent Caesar from eating you?

CLEOPATRA [*clinging to him piteously.*] Oh do, do, do. I will steal Ftatateeta's jewels and give them to you. I will make the river Nile water your lands twice a year.

CAESAR. Peace, peace, my child. Your gods are afraid of the Romans: you see the Sphinx dare not bite me, nor prevent me carrying you off to Julius Caesar.

CLEOPATRA [*in pleading murmurings.*] You wont, you wont. You said you wouldnt.

CAESAR. Caesar never eats women.

CLEOPATRA [*springing up full of hope.*] What!

CAESAR [*impressively.*] But he eats girls [*she relapses*] and cats. Now you are a silly little girl; and you are descended from the black kitten. You are both a girl and a cat.

CLEOPATRA [*trembling.*] And will he eat me?

CAESAR. Yes; unless you make him believe that you are a woman.

CLEOPATRA. Oh, you must get a sorcerer to make a woman of me. Are you a sorcerer?

CAESAR. Perhaps. But it will take a long time; and this very night you must stand face to face with Caesar in the palace of your fathers.

CLEOPATRA. No, no. I darent.

CAESAR. Whatever dread may be in your soul—however terrible Caesar may be to you—you must confront him as a brave woman and a great queen; and you must feel no fear. If your hand shakes: if your voice quavers; then—night and death! [*She moans.*] But if he thinks you worthy to rule, he will set you on the throne by his side and make you the real ruler of Egypt.

CLEOPATRA [*despairingly.*] No: he will find me out: he will find me out.

CAESAR [*rather mournfully.*] He is easily deceived by women. Their eyes dazzle him; and he sees them not as they are, but as he wishes them to appear to him.

After further conversation, Caesar and Cleopatra leave the sphinx and Cleopatra brings Caesar to the palace.

[*The moonlight wanes: the horizon again shows black against the sky, broken only by the fantastic silhouette of the Sphinx. The sky itself vanishes in darkness, from which there is no relief until the gleam of a distant torch falls on great Egyptian pillars supporting the roof of a majestic corridor. At the further end of this corridor a Nubian slave appears carrying the torch. Caesar, still led by Cleopatra, follows him. They come down the corridor, Caesar peering keenly about at the strange architecture, and at the pillar shadows between which, as the passing torch makes them hurry noiselessly backwards, figures of men with wings and hawks' heads, and vast black marble cats, seem to flit in and out of ambush. Further along, the wall turns a corner and makes a spacious transept in which Caesar sees, on his right, a throne, and behind the throne a door. On each side of the throne is a slender pillar with a lamp on it.*]

CAESAR. What place is this?

CLEOPATRA. This is where I sit on the throne when I am allowed to wear my crown and robes. [*The slave holds his torch to shew the throne.*]

CAESAR. Order the slave to light the lamps.

CLEOPATRA [*shyly.*] Do you think I may?

CAESAR. Of course. You are the Queen. [*She hesitates.*] Go on.

CLEOPATRA [*timidly, to the slave.*] Light all the lamps.

FTATATEETA [*suddenly coming from behind the throne.*] Stop. [*The slave stops. She turns sternly to Cleopatra, who quails like a naughty child.*] Who is this you have with you; and how dare you order the lamps to be lighted without my permission? [*Cleopatra is dumb with apprehension.*]

CAESAR. Who is she?

CLEOPATRA. Ftatateeta.

FTATATEETA [*arrogantly.*] Chief nurse to—

CAESAR [*cutting her short.*] I speak to the Queen. Be silent. [*To Cleopatra*] Is this how your servants know their places? Send her away; and do you [*to the slave*] do as the Queen has bidden. [*The slave lights the lamps. Meanwhile Cleopatra stands hesitating, afraid of Ftatateeta.*] You are the Queen: send her away.

CLEOPATRA [*cajoling.*] Ftatateeta, dear: you must go away—just for a little.

CAESAR. You are not commanding her to go away: you are begging her. You are no Queen. You will be eaten. Farewell. [*He turns to go.*]

CLEOPATRA [*Clutching him.*] No, no, no. Dont leave me.

CAESAR. A Roman does not stay with queens who are afraid of their slaves.

CLEOPATRA. I am not afraid. Indeed I am not afraid.

FTATATEETA. We shall see who is afraid here. [*Menacingly*] Cleopatra—

CAESAR. On your knees, woman: am I also a child that you dare trifle with me? [*He points to the floor at Cleopatra's feet. Ftatateeta, half cowed, half savage, hesitates. Caesar calls to the Nubian*] Slave. [*The Nubian comes to him*] Can you cut off a head? [*The Nubian nods and grins ecstatically, showing all his teeth. Caesar takes his sword by the scabbard, ready to offer the hilt to the Nubian, and turns again to Ftatateeta, repeating his gesture.*] Have you remembered yourself, mistress?

[*Ftatateeta, crushed, kneels before Cleopatra, who can hardly believe her eyes.*]

FTATATEETA [*hoarsely.*] O Queen, forget not thy servant in the days of thy greatness.

CLEOPATRA [*blazing with excitement.*] Go. Begone. Go away. [*Ftatateeta rises with stooped head, and moves backwards towards the door. Cleopatra watches her submission eagerly, almost clapping her hands, which are trembling. Suddenly she cries*] Give me something to beat her with.

[*She snatches a snake-skin from the throne and dashes after Ftatateeta, whirling it like a scourge in the air. Caesar makes a bound and manages to catch her and hold her while Ftatateeta escapes.*]

CAESAR. You scratch, kitten, do you?

CLEOPATRA [*breaking from him.*] I will beat somebody. I will beat him. [*She attacks the slave.*] There, there, there! [*The slave flies for his life up the corridor and vanishes. She throws the snake-skin away and jumps on the step of the throne with her arms waving, crying*] I am a real Queen at last—a real, real Queen! Cleopatra the Queen! [*Caesar shakes his head dubiously, the advantage of the change seeming open to question from the point of view of the general welfare of Egypt. She turns and looks at him exultantly. Then she jumps down from the steps, runs to him, and flings her arms round him rapturously, crying*] Oh, I love you for making me a Queen.

CAESAR. But queens love only kings.

CLEOPATRA. I will make all the men I love kings. I will make you a king. I will have many young kings, with round, strong arms; and when I am tired of them I will whip them to death; but you shall always be my king: my nice, kind, wise, good old king.

CAESAR. Oh, my wrinkles, my wrinkles! And my child's heart! You will be the most dangerous of all Caesar's conquests.

CLEOPATRA [*appalled.*] Caesar! I forgot Caesar. [*Anxiously*] You will tell him that I am a Queen, will you not?—a real Queen. Listen! [*stealthily coaxing him*] let us run away and hide until Caesar is gone.

CAESAR. If you fear Caesar, you are no true queen; and though you were to hide beneath a pyramid, he would go straight to it and lift it with one hand. And then-! [*he chops his teeth together.*]

CLEOPATRA [*trembling.*] Oh!

CAESAR. Be afraid if you dare. [*The note of the bucina resounds again in the distance. She moans with fear. Caesar exults in it, exclaiming*] Aha! Caesar approaches the throne of Cleopatra. Come: take your place. [*He takes her hand and leads her to the throne. She is too downcast to speak.*] Ho, there, Teetatota. How do you call your slaves?

CLEOPATRA [*spiritlessly, as she sinks on the throne and cowers there, shaking.*] Clap your hands.

[*He claps his hands. Ftatateeta returns.*]

CAESAR. Bring the Queen's robes, and her crown, and her women; and prepare her.

CLEOPATRA [*eagerly—recovering herself a little.*] Yes, the crown, Ftata-teeta: I shall wear the crown.

FTATATEETA. For whom must the Queen put on her state?

CAESAR. For a citizen of Rome. A king of kings, Totateeta.

[*The Nubian comes running down the hall.*]

NUBIAN. The Romans are in the courtyard. [*He bolts through the door. With a shriek, the women fly after him. Ftatateeta's jaw expresses savage resolution: she does not budge. Cleopatra can hardly restrain herself from following them. Caesar grips her wrist, and looks steadfastly at her. She stands like a martyr.*]

CAESAR. The Queen must face Caesar alone. Answer "So be it."

CLEOPATRA [*white.*] So be it.

CAESAR [*releasing her.*] Good.

[*A tramp and tumult of armed men is heard. Cleopatra's terror increases. The bucina sounds close at hand, followed by a formidable clangor of trumpets. This is too much for Cleopatra: she utters a cry and darts towards the door. Ftatateeta stops her ruthlessly.*]

FTATATEETA. You are my nursling. You have said "So be it"; and if you die for it, you must make the Queen's word good. [*She hands Cleopatra to Caesar, who takes her back, almost beside herself with appre-hension, to the throne.*]

CAESAR. Now, if you quail—! [*He seats himself on the throne.*]

[*She stands on the step, all but unconscious, waiting for death. The Roman soldiers troop in tumultuously through the corridor, headed by their ensign with his eagle, and their bucinator, a burly fellow with his instrument coiled round his body, its brazen bell shaped like the head of a howling wolf. When they reach the transept, they stare in amazement at the throne; dress into ordered rank opposite it; draw their swords and lift them in the air with a shout of* Hail, Caesar. *Cleopatra turns and stares wildly at Caesar; grasps the situation; and, with a great sob of relief, falls into his arms.*]

15.2. Thornton Wilder, *The Ides of March*[4] (excerpt) (1948, English, prose)

In Thornton Wilder's epistolary novel, The Ides of March, *Julius Caesar, Cleopatra, Antony, and others come to life as very human characters*

---

4. Wilder 1948.

*through their imagined correspondence. Wilder vividly paints the Roman
context of Cleopatra's relationship with Caesar: there are references to her
interaction with members of Caesar's family and to the hostility she faced
in Rome (see selection 3.17). Wilder's Cleopatra bears some resemblance to
Shaw's, but she develops as a much more refined and intelligent woman.*

XXXIV Letter and Questionnaire: Cleopatra to Caesar.
[*October 9.*]

My *Deedja*,[5] *Deedja, Deedja—Crocodeedja* is very unhappy-happy,
very happy-unhappy. Happy that she is to see her *Deedja* on the
night of the twelfth, all the night of the twelfth, and unhappy that the
night of the twelfth is a thousand years away. When I am not with
my *Deedja* I sit weeping. I tear my robe to pieces, I wonder why I am
here, why I am not in Egypt, what I am doing in Rome. Everybody
hates me; everybody sends me letters wishing me dead. Cannot my
Deedja come before the twelfth? Oh, *Deedja*, life is short, love is short;
why cannot we see one another? All day and night other people are
seeing my *Deedja*. Do they love him more than I do? Does he love
them more than he loves me? No, no, there is nothing in the world
that I love more than my *Deedja*, my *Deedja* in my arms, my *Deedja*
happy, happy, happy in my arms. Separation is cruel, separation is
waste, separation is meaningless.

But if my *Deedja* wishes it so I weep; I do not understand, but I
weep and wait for the twelfth. But I must write a letter every day.
And oh my *Deedja*, write me a letter every day. I cannot sleep when
night comes after a day when I have had no real letter from you.
Every day there are your presents with five words. I kiss them; I hold
them long; but when there is no real letter with the presents I cannot
love them.

I must write a letter every day to tell my *Deedja* that I love only
him, and think only of him. But there are other tiresome little things
I must ask him, too. Things I must know so that I will be a dignified
guest worthy of his protection. Forgive *Crocodeedja* these little tiresome questions.

1. At my party, at my rout, I go to the lowest step of my throne to
welcome my *Deedja's* wife. Do I also go to the lowest step to meet my

---

5. Cleopatra's pet name for Caesar.

Deedja's aunt? What do I do to welcome the consuls and the consuls' wives?

> [*Caesar's answer*: Hitherto all queens have come to the lowest step. I am changing all that. My wife and my aunt will be with me. You will meet us at the arch. Your throne will not be raised by eight steps, but by one. All other guests you will greet standing before your throne. This arrangement may seem to rob you of the dignity of eight steps, but eight steps are not a dignity for those who must descend them and you would have to descend them to welcome the consuls who are or have been sovereigns. Think this over and you will see that *Deedja* is right.]

2. The Lady Servilia has not replied to my invitation. *Deedja,* you understand that I cannot suffer that. I know ways to enforce her attendance and I must use them.

> [*Caesar's answer*: I do not understand you. The Lady Servilia will be present.]

3. If it's a cold night, I shall not move an inch from my braziers or I shall perish. But where can I get enough braziers for my guests at the water-ballet?

> [*Caesar's answer*: Furnish the ladies of your court with braziers. We Italians are accustomed to the cold and we dress to warm ourselves.]

4. In Egypt royalty does not receive dancers and theater people. I am told that I should invite the actress Cytheris,[6] that she is received by many patricians, and that your nephew or cousin Marc Antony goes nowhere without her. Must I invite her? Indeed, must I invite *him?*—he comes every day to my court; he has very impudent eyes; I am not accustomed to being laughed at.

> [*Caesar's answer*: Yes, and more than invite her: learn to know her. She is the daughter of a carter but there is no woman of the highest aristocracy who could not learn from her what dignity, charm, and deportment are.

---

6. Cytheris was an actress with whom Antony had a love affair. This was considered scandalous, because entertainers were of low social status in Rome.

You will soon discover all the reasons for my admiration of her. In addition I am indebted to her for a personal reason: her long association with my relative Marc Antony has given me, in him, a friend. We men are for the most part what you women make us—and women too; for men cannot remake a woman who is herself ill-made. Marc Antony was and always will be the best athlete and the best-liked athlete in a provincial school. Ten years ago a few moments of sober conversation exhausted him and he would be fretting to balance three tables on his chin. Wars themselves employed but a fraction of his thoughtless energy. Rome lived under the menace of practical jokes which did not stop short of setting fires to entire blocks, to loosing all the boats on the riverside, and to stealing the garments of the Senate. He had no malice; but he had no judgment. All this Cytheris has remade; she has taken nothing away, but has rearranged the elements in a different order. I am surrounded by and hate those reformers who can only establish an order by laws which repress the subject and drain him of his joy and aggression. The Cato and the Brutus envision a state of industrious mice; and in the poverty of their imaginations they charge me with the same thing. Happy would I be if it could be said of me that like Cytheris I could train the unbroken horse without robbing him of the fire in his eye and the delight in his speed. And has not Cytheris had a fair reward? He will go no place without her, and with reason, for he will find no better company.

But I must close. A deputation from Lusitania has been waiting this half hour to protest against my cruelty and injustice. Tell Charmian to put all in readiness for a visitor tonight. He will enter, dressed as a night guard, through the Alexandrian port. Tell Charmian that it will be nearer sunrise than sunset; but as soon as ardor at war with prudence can effect it. Let the great Queen of Egypt, the phoenix of women, sleep; she will be awakened by no ungentle hand. Yes, life is short; separation is insane.]

15.3. Ted Hughes, "Cleopatra to the Asp"[7] (1960, English, verse)

7. Hughes 1960, 60.

British poet Ted Hughes imagines Cleopatra addressing the asp that will cause her death.

The bright mirror I braved: the devil in it   1
Loved me like my soul, my soul:
Now that I seek myself in a serpent
My smile is fatal.

Nile moves in me; my thighs splay   5
Into the squalled Mediterranean;
My brain hides in that Abyssinia
Lost armies foundered towards.

Desert and river unwrinkle again.
Seeming to bring them the waters that make drunk   10
Caesar, Pompey, Antony I drank.
Now let the snake reign.

A half-deity out of Capricorn,[8]
This rigid Augustus mounts
With his rigid sword virginal indeed; and has shorn   15
Summarily the moon-horned river

From my bed. May the moon
Ruin him with virginity! Drink me, now, whole
With coiled Egypt's past; then from my delta
Swim like a fish toward Rome.   20

15.4. Barbara Chase-Riboud, *Portrait of a Nude Woman as Cleopatra,* Preface (excerpts), "III: Cleopatra," "IV: Cleopatra"[9] (1987, English, prose and verse)

The inspiration for African American poet Barbara Chase-Riboud's verse novel, Portrait of a Nude Woman as Cleopatra, *was a Rembrandt drawing of the same title.*[10]

---

8. Octavian's astrological sign.
9. Chase-Riboud 1987, 16–18, 24–25.
10. See Walker and Higgs, eds. 2001, 360–61, for another poem from the collection and a photograph of Chase-Riboud's work of art, *Cleopatra's Marriage Contract III.*

Preface (excerpts)

I considered Cleopatra the exemplar of dramatic action, a narrative pyramid, a poetic Himalayas. Yet later when I recalled that small black and white sketch, nothing indicated either the theatricality, or the heroic, or the historical obligations of her theme. This gave me courage. There was no asp, no Antony, no Roman soldiers, or warring fleets; no eunuchs, or slaves, or ladies in waiting, or imperial architecture. The pen-and-ink drawing showed an ordinary woman, of a certain age, half turned from the spectator, sitting on the side of an unmade bed, nude. Not one of the famous romantic elements of the historical Cleopatra was evident, but she was more real to me than any Cleopatra I had ever seen. The unerring rendering of a beautifully banal woman had seduced me into believing she was indeed *the* Cleopatra. Why? It could have been simply the genius of a masterful sketch. Or had Rembrandt had in mind a full-fledged painting of Cleopatra of which he had put down only a memento? Perhaps the *novel* of the painting had existed in his head all the time. Or had the title of Cleopatra been only an excuse to draw a nude woman? If so, then why did he call her Cleopatra? And why did I believe him? The more I looked at the drawing, the more the woman became Cleopatra. A nude woman had taken on a complex and continuous narrative in which the adventures of two protagonists (one invisible) put into motion and existence a whole world of feelings. The nude woman's destiny had been sealed centuries ago. Culturally she had become an object of memory. Yet the woman I saw was a new woman because the artist who had sketched her, however, casually, knew her as a writer knows his characters: from the inside out, through his own inclinations. Somewhere the man who had drawn her had met up with Cleopatra, knew her very well, through love, pity, or fury.

Thus, as a contemporary poet, I was confronted with a "historical theme," which I had to make at once classical and modern. The woman sitting on the side of a bed *with the loose change of History strung out all over my bed* is also the woman sitting on the side of a bed with the loose change of the subway strung all over *her* bed.

Nevertheless, this is not an "epic" or "storical" poem, but rather a meditation on History as well as poetry in the form of a melologue, that is a recitation, written to be acted by one actor playing all characters, by imitating both the masculine and feminine voice, accompanied by music.

III: Cleopatra

I shall be Venus Genetrix[11] and greet   1
With chaste lips this Dionysus I first saw at fourteen.
I shall trap his quintessential heart and waltz it round
My own gods quivering in unmarked graves.
For so long as one dank breath escapes from Karnak,[12]   5
So long as one brace of bones, churns like rolling dice,
Away from Delphi's oracle,[13] so long as one
Handful of red earth crumbles under the
Saturnine & Equatorial sun of Ethiopia's Pharaohs
I refuse to be eclipsed by Caesar's shadow & Caesar's sex,   10
For, so long as Egypt rests its shaven head
On my Cleopatrian breasts,
Caesar's manhood curled loosely in my hand,
Rome, don't cross me.

IV: Cleopatra

How many pebbles on how many beaches have got   1
Wind of us & how many alabaster whistles and brass
Trumpets have made their announcements?
I suffocate here under the airless dome of so much knowledge.
For after the moon has raced through here,   5
After the asteroids and comets have ricocheted
Back and forth and back across the arc of the century,
Who am I but a Nude Woman?
Caesar knew me when I was but a young thing.
You discovered me filtered through finesse, men, and years,   10
Sailing into your butterfly shaped harbor,
Leaving wet tracks on your purple carpet
To lie between lighted lamps, for like all Africans,
I am afraid of the dark.

11. Venus in her role as mother goddess; Julius Caesar placed a statue of Cleopatra in the temple of Venus Genetrix that he established in his forum.
12. An Egyptian temple complex.
13. The oracle of Apollo.

Maps, Genealogies, and Chronology

Map 1
Alexandria

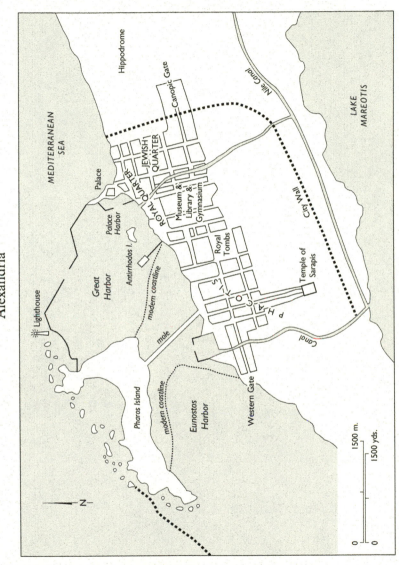

MEDITERRANEAN SEA

Hippodrome

Canopic Gate

Nile Canal

LAKE MAREOTIS

City Wall

Palace

ROYAL QUARTER

JEWISH QUARTER

Museum & Library & Gymnasium

Royal Tombs

Palace Harbor

Antirrhodos I.

modern coastline

Great Harbor

Lighthouse

mole

Pharos Island

modern coastline

Eunostos Harbor

Western Gate

Temple of Sarapis

Canal

N

1500 m.

1500 yds.

0

0

Map 2
The Mediterranean World in the Time of Cleopatra

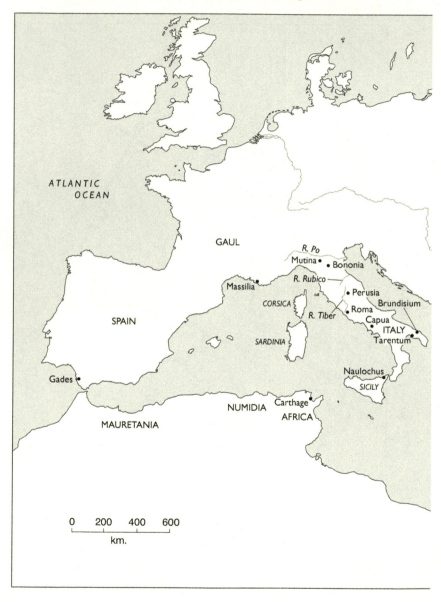

ATLANTIC
OCEAN

GAUL

R. Po

Mutina • • Bononia

SPAIN

Massilia •

R. Rubico —

CORSICA

• Perusia

Brundisium

R. Tiber

• Roma

Capua •

ITALY

SARDINIA

Tarentum

Gades •

Naulochus •

SICILY

NUMIDIA   Carthage •

AFRICA

MAURETANIA

0   200   400   600

km.

N

DACIA

R. Danube

ILLYRICUM

MACEDONIA

BLACK SEA

PONTUS

ARMENIA

CASPIAN
SEA

Dyrrhachium   Philippi
Apollonia   Thessalonica
THESSALY
EPIRUS Phardalus
Actium
Patrae   Athens
ACHAEA
Corcyra

Corinth

CRETE

MEDITERRANEAN SEA

Cyrene

BITHYNIA

ASIA   GALATIA
CAPPADOCIA

Ephesus

CILICIA

CYPRUS

Zela   Nicopolis Carana

Cydnus

Tarsus R.

Antioch
SYRIA

MEDIA
ATROPATENE

PARTHIA
R. Euphrates

Tyre

Jerusalem JUDAEA

Alexandria

Pelusium

EGYPT

R. Nile

RED
SEA

Hermonthis

Genealogical Table 1

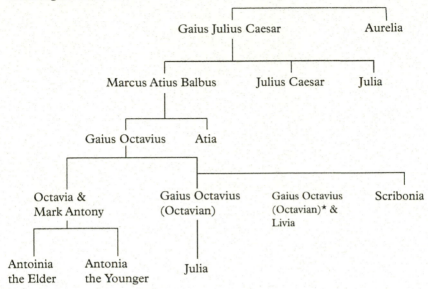

Abbreviated Genealogy of Julius Caesar, Octavian, and Antony

Note: *indicates that the same individual appears elsewhere in the table.*

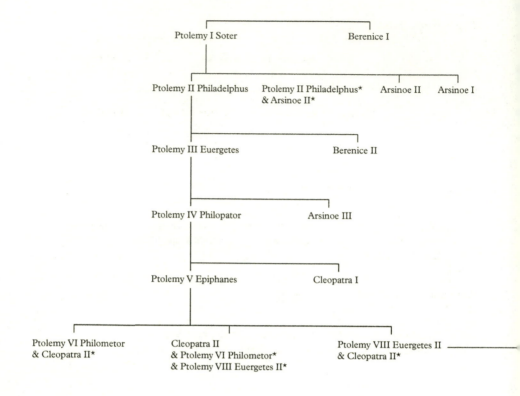

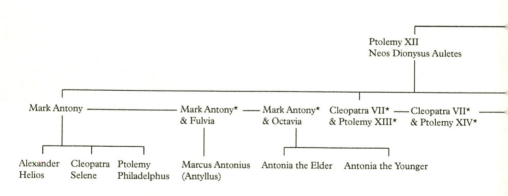

Abbreviated Genealogy of the Ptolemies
Note: *indicates that the same individual appears elsewhere in the table.

Genealogical Table 2

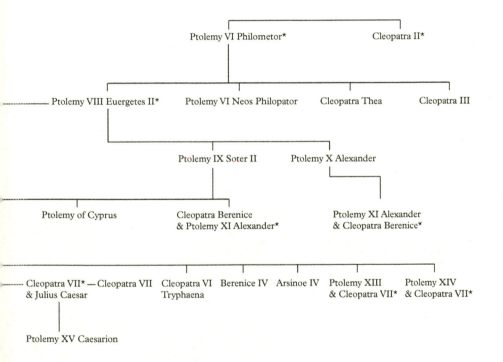

Ptolemy VI Philometor★   Cleopatra II★

——— Ptolemy VIII Euergetes II★   Ptolemy VI Neos Philopator   Cleopatra Thea   Cleopatra III

Ptolemy IX Soter II   Ptolemy X Alexander

Ptolemy of Cyprus   Cleopatra Berenice & Ptolemy XI Alexander★   Ptolemy XI Alexander & Cleopatra Berenice★

Cleopatra VII★ — Cleopatra VII   Cleopatra VI   Berenice IV   Arsinoe IV   Ptolemy XIII   Ptolemy XIV
& Julius Caesar   Tryphaena   & Cleopatra VII★ & Cleopatra VII★

Ptolemy XV Caesarion

Chronological Table

The Death of Alexander the Great to the Death of Cleopatra

B.C.

323   Death of Alexander the Great; Ptolemy I takes control of Egypt

305   Ptolemy I becomes king of Egypt

106   Pompey born

100   Julius Caesar born

83   Mark Antony born

80   Ptolemy XII Auletes becomes king of Egypt

70–69   Cleopatra VII born

70–68   Disappearance of Cleopatra V from the historical record

68–65   Arsinoe IV born

63   Octavian born

61   Ptolemy XIII born

60   First Triumvirate (Julius Caesar, Pompey, and Crassus) formed

59   Ptolemy XIV born; Ptolemy XII recognized as a friend of the Roman people

58   Ptolemy XII flees to Rome; Cleopatra VI and Berenice IV become queens of Egypt

55   Gabinius restores Ptolemy XII to the throne; possible first meeting of Antony and Cleopatra

51   Death of Ptolemy XII; Cleopatra VII and Ptolemy XIII become rulers of Egypt; Cleopatra goes to Hermonthis for installation of Buchis bull

49   Cleopatra exiled to Upper Egypt; war between Pompey and Caesar begins

48   Cleopatra expelled from Egypt; Pompey defeated at Battle of Pharsalus and killed in Egypt; Caesar arrives in Egypt; Alexandrian War begins

47   Ptolemy XIII defeated and drowned; Caesar installs Cleopatra and Ptolemy XIV as rulers of Egypt; Caesarion born

46   Arsinoe IV displayed in Caesar's triumph; Cleopatra and Ptolemy XIV arrive in Rome

44   Caesar assassinated; Ptolemy XIV murdered; Cleopatra and Caesarion become rulers of Egypt

43   Second Triumvirate (Octavian, Antony, and Lepidus) formed

42   Antony and Octavian conquer Brutus and Cassius at Philippi

41   Meeting of Antony and Cleopatra in Tarsus; they winter at Alexandria

40   Antony's Parthian campaign; Battle of Perusia; Treaty of Brundisium; Antony marries Octavia; twins Alexander Helios and Cleopatra Selene born to Antony and Cleopatra

39   Antony and Octavia live in Athens

37   Second Triumvirate renewed for five years; Antony sends Octavia back to Rome

36   Ptolemy Philadelphus born to Antony and Cleopatra

34   Antony invades Armenia and captures the king; Donations of Alexandria

32   Roman consuls and two hundred senators leave Rome to join Antony; Antony divorces Octavia; Octavian publishes Antony's will; Octavian declares war on Cleopatra

31   Battle of Actium

30   Octavian annexes Egypt; suicides of Antony and Cleopatra; execution of Antyllus and Caesarion

Glossary

ACHILLAS. Army commander in Alexandria and advisor to Ptolemy XIII. Along with Pothinus and Theodotus, he conspired to murder Pompey and drive Cleopatra out of Egypt.

ACTIUM. Promontory in northwestern Greece. The Battle of Actium was fought off its coast in 31 B.C. Octavian's fleet, commanded by Agrippa, defeated the forces of Antony and Cleopatra, who fled to Egypt.

AENEAS. Legendary Trojan progenitor of the Romans and of the family of Julius Caesar; hero of Vergil's *Aeneid.*

AGRIPPA (Marcus Vipsanius Agrippa). Ca. 64–12 B.C. He was the right-hand man of Octavian and commanded the Roman fleet at Actium.

AHENOBARBUS, DOMITIUS. Roman consul (32 B.C.) and associate of Antony, he opposed Cleopatra's participation in the Battle of Actium and deserted to Octavian before the battle. He died shortly thereafter of a fever.

ALEXANDER THE GREAT (Alexander III of Macedon). 356–323 B.C. He established the largest empire the world had ever seen. Upon his death the territory was divided among his generals, with Ptolemy I receiving Egypt.

ALEXANDER HELIOS. Son of Cleopatra and Mark Antony, b. 41 B.C. In the Donations of Alexandria, he was named King of the East and West.

ALEXANDRIA. City in Egypt founded by Alexander the Great in 331 B.C. when he conquered Egypt. The Ptolemies made it the capital of their kingdom and Egypt's main Mediterranean port. Its citizens came from all over the Greek world, and it was the major intellectual center of the Hellenistic world.

ALEXANDRIAN WAR. Four-month conflict in 48 B.C. between Julius Caesar's troops and the Greek and Egyptian forces commanded by Achillas. Caesar won but did not annex Egypt, instead installing Cleopatra VII and Ptolemy XIV as rulers.

ANTONY, MARK (Marcus Antonius). 83–30 B.C.. He was a member of the Second Triumvirate with Octavian and Lepidus. In 41 B.C. he met Cleopatra. In 40 B.C. their twin children Alexander Helios and Cleopatra Selene were born. Antony repaired his damaged relationship with Octavian and married Octavia, Octavian's sister. He returned to Cleopatra, however, and in 36 B.C. their third child, Ptolemy Philadelphus, was born. Defeat in the Battle of Actium led to Antony's suicide in 30 B.C.

ANTYLLUS (Marcus Antonius Antyllus). Son of Mark Antony and his wife, Fulvia. He was executed by Octavian in 30 B.C. after the capture of Alexandria.

APOLLO. Also referred to as Phoebus; god of light, music, and rationality. Octavian identified himself with Apollo, in contrast to Antony's identification with Dionysus.

ARSINOE II. Sister and wife of Ptolemy II. Their marriage established the custom of brother-sister marriages in the Ptolemaic dynasty.

ARSINOE IV. Daughter of Ptolemy XII and sister of Cleopatra. Antony had her killed as a favor to Cleopatra.

ASCANIUS. Son of Aeneas. He was also called Iulus, from which the Julian family was said to get its name.

AUGUSTUS. *See* Octavian.

BERENICE II. Wife of Ptolemy III, c. 273–221 B.C. She is best known from Callimachus's and Catullus's poems on the lock of Berenice (*see* selections *1.6* and *1.7*).

BERENICE IV. Daughter of Ptolemy XII and sister of Cleopatra. She ruled with another sister, Cleopatra VI, from 58 to 55 B.C. while their father was exiled from Egypt.

BRUNDISIUM. City in southern Italy. It was the site of the Treaty of Brundisium in 40 B.C., which extended the Second Triumvirate for five years.

BRUTUS (Marcus Junius Brutus). One of the leading conspirators against Julius Caesar. He claimed descent from the Brutus who participated in expelling the kings from Rome in 509 B.C. and, thus, felt compelled to carry on the family legacy of tyrannicide. He and Cassius fought Octavian and Antony at Philippi. After being defeated and deserted by his army, Brutus committed suicide.

BUCHIS. Bull worshipped at Hermonthis as the living soul of the god Amon-Ra. In 51 B.C. a new bull was installed and Cleopatra attended the ceremony.

CAESAR, JULIUS (Gaius Julius Caesar). 100–44 B.C. With Pompey and Crassus he formed the First Triumvirate, but the alliance disintegrated into civil war between Caesar and Pompey. Caesar pursued Pompey to Egypt and, after Pompey's death in 48 B.C., spent several months with Cleopatra in Alexandria. Upon his return to Rome, Caesar celebrated triumphs and held the position of dictator. He was killed by a conspiracy led by Brutus and Cassius.

CAESARION (Ptolemy XV). 47–30 B.C.. He was the eldest son of Cleopatra, who claimed Julius Caesar was his father. In the Donations of Alexandria, he was named King of Kings. In 30 B.C. he was told to escape to India, but he was overtaken and killed on the orders of Octavian.

CASSIUS (Gaius Cassius Longinus). One of the leaders in the conspiracy against Julius Caesar. He participated in the assassination of Caesar and fought Octavian and Antony, who were avenging Caesar's death. He committed suicide after the Battle of Philippi, under the impression that his cause was lost.

CHARMION. One of Cleopatra's maids. Along with Iras, she killed herself with the asp that killed Cleopatra.

CLEOPATRA VII. Last of the Ptolemaic rulers of Egypt. Often referred to simply as Cleopatra, she was the daughter of Ptolemy XII and ruled Egypt from 51 to 30 B.C. She had affairs with Julius Caesar and Mark Antony. Octavian declared war upon her and defeated her in 30 B.C., at which time she committed suicide.

CLEOPATRA SELENE. Daughter of Cleopatra and Mark Antony, b. 41 B.C. In the Donations of Alexandria, she was named Queen of Cyrene.

CRASSUS (Marcus Licinius Crassus). D. 55 B.C. A member of the First Triumvirate with Caesar and Pompey, he was killed in battle against the Parthians.

CRASSUS, CANIDIUS. Commander of Antony's land army, which was captured by Octavian after the Battle of Actium.

DIDO. Legendary queen of Carthage. Her story is told in Vergil's *Aeneid,* in which she detains Aeneas on his journey from Troy to Italy, where he is to found the Roman race.

DIONYSUS. The god of wine, he also presides over the world of the theater. Antony identified himself with Dionysus.

DONATIONS OF ALEXANDRIA. Ceremony in which Mark Antony granted titles and control of territories to Cleopatra and her children.

FULVIA. Wife of Antony. While Antony was in the East, Fulvia and Antony's brother, Lucius Antonius, opposed Octavian. In 41 B.C. they were beseiged by Octavian at Perusia and captured. Fulvia fled to Greece to join Antony, but she was not well received by him and died soon thereafter. Her role in the conflict with Octavian earned her the reputation of a wicked woman.

GABINIUS, AULUS. Roman general who restored Ptolemy XII to the throne in 55 B.C. Mark Antony served as a cavalry commander under him.

GALLUS, CORNELIUS. Poet and associate of Octavian, 70/69–27/26 B.C. He became the first prefect of Egypt but was forced to commit suicide when he exploited his position for his own aggrandizement.

HERACLES/HERCULES. Greek hero from whom Antony claimed descent.

HERMONTHIS. Sacred place in Egypt near Thebes where the Buchis bull was worshipped.

IRAS. One of Cleopatra's maids. Along with Charmion, she killed herself with the asp that also killed Cleopatra.

ISIS. An Egyptian goddess, she was equated with a number of Roman goddesses, including Venus and Demeter, because of her associations with fertility. In myth she is the wife of Osiris and the mother of Horus, bearing Horus after being impregnated by Osiris after his murder by Set. She brings the Nile flood and is capable of bringing about rebirth.

LEPIDUS (Marcus Aemilius Lepidus). Member of the Second Triumvirate along with Octavian and Antony.

OCTAVIA. Sister of Octavian, she married Antony in 40 B.C. This marriage was intended to strengthen the bond between Antony and Octavian, but Antony soon returned to the East, leaving her behind. When Octavian sent her to Antony with reinforcements for his army, Antony forbade her to proceed beyond Athens, and in 32 B.C. he divorced her. Her nobility and loyalty won her wide esteem and sympathy. She died in 11 B.C.

OCTAVIAN. Heir to Julius Caesar, 63 B.C.–A.D. 14. Born Gaius Octavius, he was adopted by his great-uncle, Julius Caesar, his name then becoming Gaius Julius Caesar Octavianus. Scholars refer to him as Octavian during this period, but he often went by the name Caesar. In 27 B.C., when he "restored the republic," he took the title Augustus. After Julius Caesar's death, Octavian avenged Caesar's death by defeating Brutus and Cassius. With Antony and Lepidus, he formed the Second Triumvirate. He declared war on Cleopatra to avoid calling his conflict with Antony a civil war and defeated Antony and Cleopatra in the Battle of Actium.

OMPHALE. Legendary queen of Lydia who enslaved Hercules, making him dress in women's clothing and do women's work.

PERUSIA (modern Perugia). Italian city in which Lucius Antonius and Fulvia barricaded themselves in a conflict with Octavian. Octavian's forces captured and plundered Perusia to defeat Antonius and Fulvia.

PELUSIUM. City at the eastern edge of the Nile Delta. The easiest point of entry to Egypt from the northeast, it was used by Alexander the Great, Antony, and Octavian.

PHAROS. The name of both the island located at the mouth of the harbor of Alexandria and the lighthouse at the entrance to the harbor.

PHARSALUS. City in northern Greece, it was the site of the defeat of Pompey by Julius Caesar in 48 B.C.

PHILIPPI. City in eastern Macedonia, it was the site of the defeat of Brutus and Cassius by Antony and Octavian in 42 B.C.

POMPEY (Gnaeus Pompeius Magnus, also known as Pompey the Great). 106–48 B.C. Pompey was a member of the First Triumvirate with Caesar and Crassus. In the civil war against Caesar, Pompey fled to Egypt, where he was stabbed to death as he landed.

POMPEY, SEXTUS. Son of Pompey the Great, he threatened Octavian's power and was defeated at Naulochos, Sicily.

POTHINUS. Eunuch and advisor to Ptolemy XIV. Along with Achillas and Theodotus, he conspired to murder Pompey and drive Cleopatra out of Egypt.

PROCULEIUS. A member of Octavian's staff, he succeeded in taking Cleopatra prisoner.

PTOLEMY I. General in Alexander the Great's army. After Alexander's death, he took control of Egypt and established the Ptolemaic dynasty.

PTOLEMY XII (called Auletes, "flute player"). He ruled Egypt from 80 to 51 B.C. and was the father of Cleopatra.

PTOLEMY XIII. Younger brother of Cleopatra, 61–47 B.C. He ruled with her from 51 to 47 B.C., when he died in the Alexandrian War.

PTOLEMY XIV. Younger brother of Cleopatra, 59–44 B.C. He ruled with her from 47 to 44 B.C., when Cleopatra had him killed.

PTOLEMY XV. *See* Caesarion.

PTOLEMY PHILADELPHUS. Youngest son of Antony and Cleopatra, b. 36 B.C.

TARSUS. City in Cilicia where Antony met with Cleopatra in 41 B.C. It was at this meeting that they took their famous cruise on the River Cydnus, formed their alliance, and began their love affair.

THEODOTUS. Tutor of Ptolemy XIV, he conspired with Achillas and Pothinus to murder Pompey and drive Cleopatra from Egypt.

TROY. City in Asia Minor defeated by the Greeks in the Trojan War, it was the home of Aeneas.

VENUS. Roman goddess of love. She was the mother of Aeneas and thus ancestor of Julius Caesar (*see* Aeneas; Ascanius).

Selective Cleopatra Filmography

FEATURE FILMS

Cléopâtre (1899)
The first ever Cleopatra movie, a black-and-white silent French horror film (U.S. titles: *Cleopatra's Tomb, Robbing Cleopatra's Tomb*); directed by Georges Méliès.

Cleopatra (1912) 88 min. (also known as *Helen Gardner in Cleopatra*)
Black-and-white silent film starring Helen Gardner as Cleopatra; directed by Charles L. Gaskill.

Cleopatra (1917) 125 min.
Black-and-white silent film based on the novel by Rider Haggard; Theda Bara as Cleopatra; directed by J. Gordon Edwards; no known print exists.

Cleopatra (1934) 100 min.
Black-and-white Hollywood epic starring Claudette Colbert as Cleopatra; directed by Cecil B. DeMille.

Cleobatra (1943)
Black-and-white film in Arabic that tells the Egyptian version of the story of Cleopatra; Amina Rizk as Cleopatra; directed by Ibrahim Lama.

Due Notti con Cleopatra (1953) 78 min.
Italian comedy in color released in the United States in 1964 as *Two Nights with Cleopatra;* Sophia Loren as Cleopatra; directed by Mario Mattoli; based on the story of men who must pay with their lives for a night with Cleopatra.

Cleopatra (1963) 243 min. (director's cut, 320 min.)
Epic film in color starring Elizabeth Taylor as Cleopatra, Richard Burton as Mark Antony, and Rex Harrison as Caesar; directed by Joseph L. Mankiewicz. *Cleopatra* was the most expensive film ever made until *Titanic* in 1997. Life imitated art in the tempestuous relationship between Taylor and Burton.

Cleopatra (1970) 155 min.
Color; an homage to Andy Warhol's cinema set partly in upstate New York; Viva (Auder) as Cleopatra; directed by Michael Auder. Only an uncut copy survives, as Auder never edited the film.

MADE FOR TELEVISION

Cleopatra (1999) 177 min.
Color miniseries (ABC TV) starring Leonor Varela as Cleopatra, Timothy Dalton as Julius Caesar, and Billy Zane as Mark Antony; directed by Franc Roddam.

PLAYS ON FILM

Caesar and Cleopatra (1945) 123 min.
A British production of George Bernard Shaw's play, filmed in color; Vivien Leigh as Cleopatra, Claude Rains as Caesar; directed by Gabriel Pascal.

Antony and Cleopatra (1974) 161 min.
A Royal Shakespeare Company Production of Shakespeare's play, broadcast in color on the BBC; Janet Suzman as Cleopatra, Richard Johnson as Mark Antony; directed by Jon Scoffield.

PARODIES

Carry On Cleo (1964) 92 min.
Comedy by the British Carry On troupe, filmed in color using some sets from Joseph L. Mankiewicz's 1963 film; Amanda Barrie as Cleopatra; directed by Gerald Thomas.

Astérix and Cléopâtre (1968) 72 min.
Animated French comedy in color based on the book of the same title; Micheline Dax as the voice of Cleopatra; directed by René Goscinny, Lee Payzant, and Albert Uderzo.

Astérix & Obélix: Mission Cléopâtre (2002) 107 min.
French comedy in color slated for possible release in the United States by Miramax as *Asterix and Obelix: Mission Cleopatra;* Gerard Depardieu as Obélix, Christian Clavier as Astérix, and Monica Bellucci as Cléopâtre; directed by Alain Chabat, who also plays Jules César.

Bibliography

Bernal, M. 1987. *Black Athena: The Afroasiatic Roots of Classical Civilization.* Vols. 1 and 2, *The Fabrication of Greece, 1785–1985.* New Brunswick, N.J.: Rutgers University Press.

Bloom, H. 1973. *The Anxiety of Influence: A Theory of Poetry.* New York: Oxford University Press.

Brunt, P. A., and J. M. Moore. 1990. *Res Gestae Divi Augusti: The Achievements of the Divine Augustus.* New York: Oxford University Press.

Bullough, V. 1978. *The Subordinate Sex.* Athens: University of Georgia Press.

Cameron, A. 1990. "Two Mistresses of Ptolemy Philadelphus." *Greek, Roman and Byzantine Studies* 31:287–311.

———. 1995. *Callimachus and His Critics.* Princeton, N.J.: Princeton University Press.

Charlesworth, J. H., ed. 1983. *The Old Testament Pseudepigrapha.* Garden City, N.Y.: Darton, Longman and Todd.

Chase-Riboud, B. 1987. *Portrait of a Nude Woman as Cleopatra.* New York: Quill/William Morrow.

Chauveau, M. 2002. *Cleopatra: Beyond the Myth.* Translated by D. Lorton. Ithaca, N.Y.: Cornell University Press.

Clarke, J. H. 1987. "African Warrior Queens." In *Black Women in Antiquity,* edited by I. Van Sertima, 123–34. New Brunswick, N.J.: Transaction Books.

Clausen, W. V. 1995. *A Commentary on Virgil: Eclogues.* New York: Oxford University Press.

Cliff, M. 1988. "A Journey into Speech." *The Graywolf Annual* 5:57–62.

Collins, P. H. 1990. *Black Feminist Thought: Knowledge, Consciousness, and the Politics of Empowerment.* Boston: Unwin Hyman.

Conte, G. B. 1999. *Latin Literature: A History.* Translated by J. B. Solodow. Baltimore: Johns Hopkins University Press.

Cooper, A. J. [1892] 1988. *A Voice from the South.* Reprint, Schomberg Library of Nineteenth Century Black Women Writers, New York: Oxford University Press.

Curl, J. S. 1994. *Egyptomania: The Egyptian Revival, A Recurring Theme in the History of Taste.* New York: St. Martin's Press.

de Beauvoir, S. 1974. *The Second Sex.* New York: Vintage Books.

Degrassi, A., ed. 1963. *Inscriptiones Latinae Liberae Rei Publicae.* Florence, Italy: La Nuova Italia.

Eddy, S. L., Jr. 1970. *The Founding of The Cornhill Magazine.* Ball State Monograph, no. 19, Publications in English, no. 13. Muncie: Ball State University.

Ferguson, J. 1980. *Callimachus.* Boston: Twayne Publishers.

French, R. 1994. *Ancient Natural History: Histories of Nature.* New York: Routledge.

Gilbert, S., and S. Gubar. 1979. *The Madwoman in the Attic: The Woman Writer and the Nineteenth Century Literary Imagination.* New Haven, Conn.: Yale University Press.

Goudchaux, G. W. 2001. "Was Cleopatra Beautiful? The Conflicting Answers of Numismatics." In *Cleopatra of Egypt: From History to Myth,* edited by S. Walker and P. Higgs, 210–14. Princeton, N.J.: Princeton University Press.

Grant, M. 1972. *Cleopatra.* New York: Dorset Press.

———. 1982. *From Alexander to Cleopatra: The Hellenistic World.* New York: Scribners.

Haley, S. P. 1989. "Livy's Sophoniba." *Classica et Mediaevalia* 40:171–81.

———. 1990. "Livy, Passion and Cultural Stereotypes." *Historia* 39:375–81.

———. 1993. "Black Feminist Thought and Classics: Re-membering, Re-claiming, Re-empowering." In *Feminist Theory and the Classics,* edited by N. S. Rabonowitz and A. Richlin, 23–43. New York: Routledge.

hooks, b. 1981. *Ain't I a Woman: Black Women and Feminism.* Boston: South End Press.

Housman, A. E. 1958. *Belli Civilis Libri Decem.* Oxford, England: Blackwell.

Huggins, N. 1986. *W. E. B. DuBois:Writings.* New York: Library of America.

Hughes, T. 1960. *Lupercal.* London: Faber and Faber.

Hughes-Hallet, L. 1991. *Cleopatra: Histories, Dreams, and Distortions.* New York: Harper Perennial.

Hull, G. T., P. B. Scott, and B. Smith, eds. 1982. *All the Women Are White, All the Blacks Are Men, but Some of Us Are Brave: Black Women's Studies.* New York: Feminist Press.

Humbert, J.-M. 1994. *Egyptomania: Egypt in Western Art, 1790–1930.* Ottowa: National Gallery of Canada.

Hutchinson, G. O. 1990. *Hellenistic Poetry.* New York: Clarendon Press.

John, Bishop of Nikiu. 1982. *The Chronicle of John (ca. 690 A.D.), Coptic Bishop of Nikiu, Being a History of Egypt Before and During the Arab Conquest. Translated from Hermann Zotenberg's Edition of the Ethiopic Version, with an Introduction, Critical and Linguistic Notes, and an Index of Names.* Translated by R. H. Charles. Amsterdam, Netherlands: APA-Philo Press.

Jones, A. H. M. 1971. *Augustus.* New York: Norton.

King, C. W. 1872. *Antique Gems and Rings.* London: Bell and Daldy.

King, D. K. 1988. "Multiple Jeopardy, Multiple Consciousness: The Context of a Black Feminist Ideology." *Signs* 14:42–72.

Kühn, C. G. 1821–33. *Medicorum Graecorum Opera Quae Exstant.* Leipzig, Germany: K. Knobloch.

Lefkowitz, M. 1992. "Not Out of Africa." *New Republic,* February 10, 29–35.

———. 1996. *Not Out of Africa: How Afrocentrism Became an Excuse to Teach Myth as History.* New York: Basic Books.

———, and M. B. Fant. 1992. *Women's Life in Greece and Rome: A Source Book in Translation.* Baltimore, Md.: Johns Hopkins University Press.

———, and G. M. Rogers, eds. 1996. *Black Athena Revisited.* Chapel Hill: University of North Carolina Press.

Lindsay, J. 1971. *Cleopatra.* London: Constable.

Mond, R., and O. H. Myers. 1934. *The Bucheum, with Chapters by T. J. Baly, D. B. Harden, J. W. Jackson, D.Sc., G. Mattha, and Alan W. Shorter, and the Hieroglyphic Inscriptions Edited by H. W. Fairman.* 3 vols. London: Egypt Exploration Society.

Moses, W. J. 1990. *The Wings of Ethiopia.* Ames: Iowa State University Press.

Palmer, P. M. 1983. "White Women/Black Women: The Dualism of Female Identity and Experience in the United States." *Feminist Studies* 9:151–70.

Peissel, M. 1984. *The Ants' Gold: The Discovery of the Greek El Dorado in the Himalayas.* London: Harvill Press.

Pfeiffer, R. 1965. *Callimachus.* Oxford: Clarendon Press.

Pomeroy, S. 1990. *Women in Hellenistic Egypt: From Alexander to Cleopatra.* Detroit: Wayne State University Press.

Praz, M. 1970. *The Romantic Agony.* Translated by A. Davidson. New York: Oxford University Press.

Putnam, E. 1910. *The Lady.* New York: Putnam Publishers.

Quinn, K. 1985. *Catullus: The Poems.* New York: St. Martin's Press.

Ramsey, J. T., and A. L. Licht. 1997. *The Comet of 44 B.C. and Caesar's Funeral Games.* Atlanta: Scholars Press.

Richardson, L. 1977. *Propertius: Elegies I–IV.* Norman: University of Oklahoma Press.

Rogers, J. A. 1996. *World's Great Men of Color.* New York: Touchstone.

Rogers, K. 1966. *The Troublesome Helpmate: A History of Misogyny in Literature.* Seattle: University of Washington Press.

Russell, J. 1980. "Julius Caesar's Last Words: A Reinterpretation." In *Vindex Humanitatis: Essays in Honor of John Huntley Bishop,* edited by B. Marshall, 123–28. Armidale, N.S.W., Australia: University Press of New England.

Sadoff, D. 1990. "Black Matrilineage: The Case of Alice Walker and Zora Neale Hurston." In *Black Women in America: Social Science Perspectives,* edited by M. R. Malson, E. Mudimbe-Boyi, J. F. O'Barr, and M. Wyer, 197–219. Chicago: University of Chicago Press.

Saks, E. 1988. "Representing Miscegenation Law." *Raritan* 8:39–69.

Skeat, W. W., ed. 1889. *Chaucer: The Legend of Good Women.* Oxford: Clarendon Press.

Slater, P. 1968. *The Glory of Hera.* Boston: Beacon Press.

Snowden, F. 1970. *Blacks in Antiquity.* Cambridge, Mass.: Harvard University Press.

Syme, R. 1967. *The Roman Revolution.* New York: Oxford University Press.

———. 1978. "Mendacity in Velleius." *American Journal of Philology* 99:45–63.

Teodorsson, S. 1977. *The Phonology of Ptolemaic Koine.* Studia Graeca et Latina Gothoburgensia 36. Lund, Sweden: Berlingska Boktryckeriet.

Terrell, M. C. 1940. *A Colored Woman in a White World.* Washington, D.C.: Ransdell.

Thomas, D. S. 1979. *Swinburne: The Poet in His World.* New York: Oxford University Press.

van Minnen, P. 2000. "An Official Act of Cleopatra (With a Subscription in Her Own Hand)." *Ancient Society* 30:29–34.

Volkmann, H. 1958. *Cleopatra: A Study in Politics and Propaganda.* Translated by T. J. Cadoux. New York: Sagamore Press.

Walker, A. 1983. *In Search of Our Mothers' Gardens.* New York: Harcourt Brace Jovanovich.

———. 1989. *Temple of My Familiar.* New York: Harcourt Brace Jovanovich.

Walker, S., and P. Higgs, eds. 2001. *Cleopatra of Egypt: From History to Myth.* Princeton, N.J.: Princeton University Press.

Weintraub, S. 1987. "Introduction to Shaw." In *George Bernard Shaw,* edited by H. Bloom. New York: Chelsea House Publishers.

Wilder, T. 1948. *The Ides of March.* New York: Harper.

Index

CPSIA information can be obtained
at www.ICGtesting.com
Printed in the USA
BVOW08s0715271017
498779BV00001B/20/P